The First Junk Bond

The First Junk Bond

A Story of Corporate Boom and Bust

Harlan D. Platt

M.E. Sharpe
80 Business Park Drive
Armonk, New York 10504

Library of Congress Cataloging-in-Publication Data

Platt, Harlan D., 1950–
The first junk bond: a story of corporate boom and bust
/ by Harlan D. Platt
p. cm.
Includes bibliographical references and index.
ISBN 1–56324–275–3.—ISBN 1–56324-276–1 (pbk.)
1. Drexel Burnham Lambert Incorporated.
2. Milken, Michael.
3. Securities industry–United States–Corrupt practices.
4. Junk bonds—United States.
I. Title
HG4928.5.P58 1993
332.63′2′0973–dc20
93–17066
CIP

Printed in the United States of America
The paper used in this publication meets the minimum requirements of
American National Standard for Information Sciences—
Permanence of Paper for Printed Library Materials, ANSI Z39.48-1984.

∞

BM 10 9 8 7 6 5 4 3 2 1

To Ron Copeland
for his judgment and guidance,
but most of all
for his friendship.

To Peter Stabell
Someday, Ricky, they may be scarce.

To Jesse,
who is new since the last one.

Contents

PART IV.
FINANCIAL LESSONS

APPENDICES

BIBLIOGRAPHY   223

INDEX   229

ABOUT THE AUTHOR   237

List of Tables and Figures

Tables

Figures

Preface

In 1977, a small domestic oil and gas company managed by an aggressive entrepreneur sought fresh capital to grow. Having exhausted its regular sources of finance (bank loans and private placements), the company relied on Drexel Burnham Lambert (Drexel), then an inconsequential investment banking house, to raise new cash. Drexel and its guiding spirit, Michael Milken, were to pioneer the notion that the capital market could accommodate more than just the largest 500 companies. Milken anticipated the burst of creativity, technological innovation, and jobs creation that would emanate from small companies in the coming decade. His role would be to raise capital for the new entrepreneurs. Texas International was his first issue.

Drexel offered investors a $30 million Texas International, Inc. (TEI), bond issue in April 1977. To attract buyers for the unknown company's debt, the bond paid interest at 11.5 percent, nearly 150 percent of the prevailing prime interest rate. Following a warm investor response, an additional $20 million tranche of the note was sold in July 1978. TEI's 11½ percent subordinated debenture was the first junk bond. Its sale began a beautiful relationship between the company and Drexel that endured for more than a decade and encompassed every aspect of the investment banking function, as Drexel grew into a financial powerhouse and TEI emerged on the international oil scene.

For many years the purchasers of the first junk bond were delighted with their investment, which paid a higher return than they would have earned had they purchased a less risky bond at the same time. However, in April 1988, TEI filed for bankruptcy protection and commenced nearly two years of corporate reorganization. At that time, each bond, which originally had cost $1,000, was worth less than $200. The court-approved plan of reorganization created a new company and gave all of the stock in that company to the owners of TEI's bonds. Today the securities received by the 11½ percent subordinated debenture holders are worth about $990.

Junk bonds are erroneously portrayed in the popular press as a contemporary phenomenon. In fact, forerunners of junk bonds appear throughout history; the distinguished Rothschild family made its fortune buying French government bonds for a penny on the dollar when the marketplace misjudged the tides of war; back home in the early 1800s, U.S. government bonds traded down to fifteen cents on the dollar. In both examples, government bonds were junk bonds.

The name junk bonds is a misnomer. They are really high-yield bonds. A high-yield bond is a security providing the investor an above-market rate of interest to counterbalance its elevated credit risk. Normally, interest-rate changes are the principal determinants of bond prices. Not so with high-yield bonds. Their prices respond more to default potential than to the interest-rate environment.

The company spotlighted in this book issued junk bonds starting in 1977. The sobriquet, the first junk bond, is deserved, since it was the first bond issued by Drexel Burnham Lambert, the company that created the modern junk bond industry in the 1980s. Both Texas International and Drexel Burnham Lambert, its investment banker, went bankrupt. In contrast, most junk bonds thrived; the expectations of bond buyers that they would have significantly higher default rates proved to be prescient.

This book records the unusual events that befell the company that issued the first junk bond: corporate growth and decline, debt exchange offers, bankruptcy, and corporate rebirth. Some readers may find the early chapters' recitation of corporate history less gratifying than the later chapters' discussion of financial wheeling and dealing; they are encouraged to move on quickly. Readers wanting a background on the oil and gas industry should begin with the environmental analysis in the appendices.

Acknowledgments

The motivation for writing this book is not only to describe Drexel's (and TEI's) first bond or that company's bankruptcy. Those subjects are merely points of embarkation and arrival. The company's journey itself is extraordinary, encompassing fascinating people, financial innovations, and successive rounds of high-stakes poker. I hope that as much is learned from the reading as was learned in the writing.

Since writing *Why Companies Fail* in 1985, I have studied the role of bankruptcy and business turnarounds in modern finance. I have learned from many people. Among my colleagues at Northeastern University, Emery Trahan, Jeff Born, Al Alford, and Don Margotta have primed my theoretical consciousness. My associates at Prospect Street High Income Portfolio, Inc., John Frabotta, Richard Omohundro, C. William Carey, John Albanese, Joe Cote, Clemente Tiampo, and Nathan Meyohas have strengthened my understanding of the real world. Former students, notably Barry Evans, Jon Pederson, and Nikesh Arora, have kept me abreast of current developments.

Many ideas presented here evolved from the development of and instruction in my Business Turnarounds class in the M.B.A. program at Northeastern University. The students who have taken that course have contributed to its growth and to mine. I am indebted to them. I would especially like to thank Mario Batista, Olivier Szynkocviak, Rand Askog, Thomas Updike, M. Daniel Stevenson, John Giangrande, Natalie Durand, J.R. Howell, and Howard Bailey. To all these and to others too numerous to mention, I extend my appreciation.

Two Business Turnaround students, Chris Decker and Pierre Poulin, got hooked on the idea of rebirth from bankruptcy. They devoted six months of their graduate studies to research topics for this book. To acknowledge their dedication, I credit them with coauthoring the appendices.

Thanks are due to Lynne Clark and Jeffrey (Jay) Lown for data collection, data entry, and helpful comments. Judy Aguais, a Simmons College M.B.A.

student, worked with me for ten weeks in 1990, during which time she untangled nearly twenty years of financial documents. Without her dedication this book would be numberless.

Discussions and assistance from the following people aided my research: Russ Berget, Helen Hanson, James Kishpaugh, Joe Romano, Jim Gregory, George Lawrence, Judge Paul Glennon, Chris Ryan, James Swanson, Dan Rice, Peter Nevitt, Dave Leggett, Dennis Simon, Ed Altman, David Ferrari, Rick Michels, Dan Cohn, Les Brown, Martin Fridson, Michael Milken, Lorraine Spurge, Andre Danesh, Ken Peak, and James Osten. Special thanks go to copyeditor Jill Mason and to the helpful staff at the Dodge Library at Northeastern University.

The First Junk Bond

1

Introduction

Companies like Wal-Mart and Microsoft are rare and remarkable. This book describes another remarkable company, though the storyline is less dazzling than Microsoft's. Texas International, Inc. (TEI), flourished for a brief luminous moment but then crashed to earth and was consumed. Like the mythical Egyptian bird that rose from the ashes, however, TEI[1] has been reborn with the prophetic name The Phoenix Resource Companies, Inc. This book trails TEI from success to failure and beyond.

TEI was not the first company to succeed merely to succumb subsequently to failure. Traveling that well-worn path alone does not make a company remarkable. TEI's saga is noteworthy because of the company's resilience and ingenuity in coping with the changing environment of the 1980s, its execution of innovative corporate strategies that were widely imitated, and its extraordinary trading history. The company exemplifies the 1980s, having deployed virtually every stratagem espoused in that go–go decade as a paradigm for success. Among the milestones that define the company are the following:

- It issued the first junk bond.
- It achieved the largest percentage gain on the New York Stock Exchange (NYSE) in 1986, but the following year it suffered the largest percentage loss and was delisted.
- It issued one of the first bonds secured by a physical commodity and then later issued one of the first PIK (payment in kind) bonds.
- It was one of the first vulture investors, and later it was itself assaulted by vulture investors.
- It faced an insider trading scandal involving the company president and a well-known college football coach.
- It innovated strip financing to encourage bond holders to empathize with the concerns of stockholders.
- It engaged in several workouts to sell off operations and raise cash to reduce debt.

- It completed three exchange offers that converted debt into equity.
- It owned but sold a major part of Aspen, Colorado.
- It filed for bankruptcy protection and emerged as The Phoenix Resource Companies, Inc.

TEI's chronicle is more than the tale of a meteoric company that stumbled badly and sought protection from creditors by filing a petition in the bankruptcy court. It is also the story of a corporate Don Quixote whose entrepreneurs attempted to convert the smallest U.S. international oil company into a giant. In its quest, TEI became an innovator in both the stable world of petroleum exploration and the mercurial world of modern corporate finance. While some of the strategies yielded beneficial results, others proved disastrous.

It is enlightening to revisit TEI's halcyon days. The time is February 1985. An enormous oil discovery is reported in Egypt, nearly 6,000 barrels of oil per day. Priced at $20 per barrel, this one well represents $40 million per year in revenue, and many other wells can be drilled. Several months before, the company was on the brink of bankruptcy: creditors demanded repayment, new funds could not be raised, and the common stock (on the New York Stock Exchange) had crumbled to less than $1 per share. The Egyptian information means a major turnaround. Soon the stock price hits $6.50 per share. Even better news follows: Conoco, a major oil company, agrees to provide all the capital necessary to exploit the discovery and to repay TEI's initial expenditures in exchange for 50 percent of Egyptian revenues. The future is assured; nothing can go wrong. Forty-two months later TEI is dead, another bankrupt company littering the corporate highway.

This book recounts the singular events of a company's emergence from the catacombs, its ascension of a king's throne, and its plunge into the grave. The story is told in four parts. Part I describes the growth years, the period beginning with formation and ending in 1981. During the last ten years of this period, corporate revenues increased by 1,000 percent. Part II, "The Period of Decline," describes the roller coaster events in the eight years after 1981, during which a running battle was fought with creditors, the mother lode oil field was discovered in Egypt, and finally international economic exigencies strangled the company. Three exchange offers prolonged the agony and will interest contemporary corporations burdened with heavy debts. Part III, "Death and Rebirth," reports the demise of TEI and the birth of The Phoenix Resource Companies. It recounts how the bankruptcy filing affected various stake holders, details the bankruptcy negotiation process, and considers alternative post-bankruptcy financial structures. Part IV, "Financial Lessons," interviews a fund manager and a former stockholder and reviews what we have learned.

Growth, decline, and rebirth are the natural stages in the life cycle of the modern corporation. Familiarity with one company's misfortune may not educate other companies in how to avoid bankruptcy, but it may prepare business people for the hazards ahead. The growth stage has its difficulties but is a company's best moment. Decline is inevitable, but in most cases, it is interrupted before it annihilates the company. Fortunate companies escape decline; some return for another journey through the growth phase. Death is also inevitable but not rebirth. Only about one out of every ten failed businesses is reborn; the rest are liquidated. Rebirth means that the company is reorganized and its prior debts are satisfied somehow.

Today TEI is gone, but its progeny, The Phoenix Resource Companies, Inc. (Phoenix), survives; its stock trades on the American Stock Exchange. Phoenix is committed to the oil and gas business on several continents and may someday rival its parent. Phoenix's future is limited only by its management's talents (also TEI's at the end), which one hopes have been sharpened during the journey.

Note

1. TEI was the New York Stock Exchange stock symbol for Texas International.

Part I
The Growth Years

2

The Beginning

In 1966, George Platt (no relation to the author) was named chief executive officer of Nordon Corporation, Ltd., a small publicly traded oil and gas company. Platt, an Oklahoman with a petroleum engineering background, had lofty ambitions for the fledgling enterprise despite its long history of mediocre performance. (Appendix A at the end of the book overviews oil and gas industry basics for readers unfamiliar with the industry.) Located in Oklahoma City, Nordon held interests in both the production of oil and gas and a separate well-servicing business. The diminutive company owned eight drilling rigs and had gross revenues of $4.4 million in 1967.

Nordon was a model candidate for a business turnaround. At year-end 1967, it had negative working capital, and yet Platt was able to arrange a $5.6 million private sale of equity and warrants, which was augmented in 1969 with an additional sale of $4.3 million in public equity and warrants.[1] These cash infusions reversed the working capital deficit.

Platt pursued an aggressive growth strategy; $17 million worth of Nordon common stock was traded for J.C. Trahan, Inc., a Shreveport, Louisiana, drilling contractor and oil and gas producer. With interests in 900 wells in Louisiana, Texas, Mississippi, and Arkansas,[2] Trahan was another turnaround candidate. Additional working interests were acquired in West Virginia, Kansas, Pennsylvania, Oklahoma, Ohio, Texas, Louisiana, and Mississippi. An auspicious future was envisioned, and the company's name was changed to Texas International Petroleum Company. Oil and gas properties generated 70 percent of corporate revenues. Residual revenues came from oil and gas servicing subsidiaries, including Tracer Surveys (wirelogs), Snyder Tucker (well servicing), and Petroleum Purchasing (mainly equipment rental). When Platt became CEO in 1966, Nordon stock traded in the neighborhood of $3 per share; by the end of the decade it was worth $16 per share.

Growth in the Early 1970s

Success is a delicate stew to brew. It requires company managers with an appetite for success, a well-crafted action plan or blueprint that crystallizes corporate strategy, and, perhaps most important, serendipity. Consider some examples of what happens when serendipity is missing: after achieving success with copiers, Xerox rejected an offer to be the pioneer manufacturer of personal computers; similarly, a number of movie studios turned down George Lucas's *Star Wars* concept as too prosaic. Unable to control serendipity, companies concentrate their aim on choosing the right managers and strategies.

TEI defined and redefined its corporate mission many times as it pursued a winning strategy that would yield consistent profits. With each strategic turn-about, the mix of corporate revenues shifted among oil and gas production, oil field well services, oil field equipment manufacturing, and land development, as described for the period 1969 to 1973 in Table 2.1. In 1969, the company was primarily an oil and gas producer; by 1973 it was an oil field manufacturer. The strategic shift was precipitated by world events (low oil prices) and an endless corporate quest for growth.

Table 2.1

Revenues by Sector: 1969 and 1973

	1969	Percent	1973	Percent
Oil and Gas Sales	$3,329,080	49.46	$7,458,083	28.54
Oil Field Services	$2,186,000	32.48	$7,440,000	28.47
Manufacturing Sales	$892,447	13.26	$8,689,000	33.25
Real Estate	$104,000	1.55	$1,897,000	7.26
Miscellaneous	$218,844	3.25	$651,000	2.49
Total	$6,730,371		$26,135,083	

With four small divisions (energy exploration, well servicing, manufacturing, and real estate) by 1969, TEI appeared to have adopted an Orwellian strategy: "Any growth is good growth." Consider its success: Over a twelve-year period through 1981, the compound *annual* growth in revenues was 25 percent, in net income 21 percent, and in assets 23 percent.[3]

In this interval, companies were regularly bought and sold. Financial statements were revised to reflect acquisitions and divestitures. Reasonably consistent multiyear income statements and balance sheets are presented in Tables 2.2 and 2.3. During the growth years, the company's size steadily increased. Corporate revenues leaped from $6 million to $142 million; reported profits grew from less than $1 million to more than $7 million.

TEI grew but at a cost. Long-term corporate indebtedness rose from $10 million in 1969 to $260 million in 1981. Interest payments grew from less than $1 million in 1969 to $25 million in 1981. During these years, net income was calculated using the "full-cost accounting" method. Full-cost accounting permits most drilling expenses, including dry hole costs and some general and

Table 2.2

TEI Income Statement 1969–1981 (dollars in thousands)

	1969	1970	1971	1972	1973	1974[a]	1975	1976	1977	1978[a]	1979	1980	1981
Operating Revenues	6,512	9,494	13,104	17,868	25,484	24,565	41,716	46,613	64,153	22,748	34,109	78,054	142,238
Other Revenue	219	624	800	708	651	2,472	1,391	279	988	3,860	7,072	6,214	3,833
Total Revenues	6,731	10,118	13,904	18,576	26,135	27,037	43,107	46,892	65,141	26,608	41,181	84,268	146,071
Cost of Goods	3,109	5,057	7,189	10,214	14,542	12,414	24,079	25,628	39,023	7,607	10,456	19,609	41,142
Depreciation, Depletion & Amortization	1,240	1,399	1,685	2,088	3,228	3,484	4,681	5,484	6,526	9,796	10,126	16,711	34,848
General & Administrative	728	1,414	1,982	2,989	3,337	2,771	6,676	9,626	11,866	5,735	11,433	16,100	28,632
Interest	959	1,203	1,092	1,164	1,979	2,587	3,084	3,339	4,871	10,803	7,616	10,880	25,344
Total Expenses	6,036	9,073	11,948	16,455	23,086	21,256	38,520	44,077	62,286	33,941	39,631	63,300	129,966
Operating Income (loss)	695	1,045	1,256	2,031	2,327	5,952	3,554	1,320	3,095	(2,073)	4,280	14,801	10,697
Net Income (loss)	625	1,045	3,667	2,031	2,927	7,193	5,429	4,097	6,661	8,544	(5,437)	15,856	7,247
Unmeasured Costs Exploration[b]	2,544	4,138	5,882	8,357	11,898	10,157	19,701	20,969	31,928	6,224	8,555	16,044	33,662

Source: TEI annual reports, 1969–1981.

[a] Denotes data revised by the company following acquistion or divestiture.

[b] These expenses were calculated by the author; they did not appear in accounting reports due to the choice of accounting methods.

Table 2.3

TEI Balance Sheet 1969–1981 (dollars in thousands)

	1969	1970	1971	1972	1973	1974[a]	1975	1976	1977	1978[a]	1979	1980	1981
Current Assets	5,700	7,932	11,624	15,830	19,436	30,650	40,637	48,728	69,391	95,119	108,883	119,555	138,114
Long-Term Assets	29,944	32,622	40,000	49,109	58,400	76,876	92,107	108,137	195,788	205,974	161,768	217,405	388,184
Total Assets	35,644	40,554	51,624	64,939	77,836	107,526	132,744	156,865	265,179	301,093	270,651	336,960	526,298
Current Liabilities[b]	5,388	7,449	12,053	16,847	15,016	25,731	30,289	31,677	39,712	66,399	96,822	92,423	127,389
Long-Term Debt	10,128	11,297	13,297	17,427	27,302	37,398	44,646	57,827	133,110	110,636	79,594	122,386	260,408
Equity	20,074	21,494	25,322	29,966	34,829	43,350	54,530	62,290	74,742	98,252	76,261	92,567	102,399
Equity + Debt	35,644	40,554	51,624	64,939	77,836	107,526	132,744	156,865	265,179	301,093	270,651	336,960	526,298

Source: TEI annual reports, 1969–1981.

[a]Denotes data revised by the company following acquisition or divestiture.

[b]May include current portion of long-term debt.

administrative costs, to be capitalized (i.e., written off slowly) instead of expensed. Net income and retained earnings would have been lower had the alternative "successful-efforts accounting" method been in place. (Appendix B, "Oil and Gas Accounting," compares the two accounting choices.) The estimated dry hole costs that would have been reported had the company used successful-efforts accounting appear at the bottom of Table 2.2. When profits are recast following the successful-efforts method, instead of earning a profit in twelve of thirteen years, TEI earned a profit in one year, 1978, and lost money in the other years.

The Road to Eden

If the 1970s were the energy decade, 1973 was the oil year. The OPEC oil embargo (see appendix G) began in October of that year and ushered in an eight-year period of rising oil prices. Small oil and gas exploration companies (e.g., Inexco, Barber Oil, and Crystal Oil) benefited from OPEC's actions as their sales, profits, and stock prices escalated. On the other hand, oil service and manufacturing companies lagged far behind. TEI was not blind to the disparity. After 1973, it began to emphasize the oil and gas division. Platt stated in the annual report, "All the stops are being pulled out and the throttle is being moved forward to accelerate Texas International to the forefront in the energy industry." This statement was equivalent to Caesar's famous proclamation on crossing the Rubicon, "Iacta alea est": The die is cast. Success would now come from exploration or would not come at all. Each division is discussed in appendix C. Appendix D discusses industry segments.

The Early Years: 1970–1975

Wildcatting is a speculative business. The risks are high, but so too are the rewards. Standard Oil of Ohio discovered the Alaskan Prudho Bay field in the 1960s; it was the most spectacular North American oil find in decades. The initial discovery well cost over $100 million. The field was estimated to contain five billion barrels of recoverable reserves worth approximately $100 billion, giving a sound profit-to-cost ratio of 1,000 : 1. A discovery on this scale is a company maker.

TEI's domestic exploration objectives were straightforward: it aspired to the big leagues. But its exploration behavior would need to be less conservative. Several changes in 1973 moved TEI in the right direction: it acquired working interests in Alaska, an Alaskan joint venture with Amoco was initiated at Cathedral Bay, and acreage was purchased in the South Cook Inlet of Alaska.[4] Additional drilling was conducted in New Mexico, Pennsylvania, the Delaware Basin, south Louisiana, and Mississippi.

Other ordinary actions bolstered domestic reserves, too. In West Virginia, old wells on 80,788 acres were reworked, adding 4.4 Bcf of natural gas to reserves.

Eloi Bay, Louisiana, was a prime company asset. The company had begun drilling there in 1962 and now had sixty-two wells; the 1976 capital budget included monies for "work overs" in Eloi Bay.

The oil price spike created ideal conditions for oil and gas exploration (see appendix G, "Industry Conditions"). TEI took the bait and in 1975 drilled eleven domestic exploration wells, three of which were successful; four of fourteen wells drilled in 1976 struck commercial quantities of oil. Long-term drilling-success rates are detailed in Table C.1 of appendix C. High prices and initial successes built the company's confidence and led it to eschew its regular source of drilling capital, public drilling partnerships (described in appendix E), in favor of assuming 100 percent of the risk itself. Drilling partnerships provided inexpensive funds but shared discoveries with limited partners. Now the company was going for broke.

The search for oil extended overseas as well. Leases were acquired off the coast of Panama, in Argentina, and in the Saudi Arabian Red Sea; negotiations transpired in Europe, South America, Africa, and the Far East. Although international expansion slowed in the mid-1970s, sizable leases were acquired off Malaysia, in Australia, and in the Sinai Peninsula of Egypt.

The Interim Phase: 1975–1980

A throng of energy regulations were implemented after a public outcry over rising energy prices (see appendix F, "Oil and Gas Regulation"). Legislation to control the escalation in energy prices and to tax away "unearned" profits from energy producers in fact backfired and created shortages by eliminating the producer's incentive. Several "free-market" zones slipped through the bureaucratic net, and it was only here that domestic producers could earn returns commensurate with the risk.

As the second half of the decade began, the domestic energy exploration business was moribund. Federal energy regulations had created an artificial differential between domestic well head oil prices ($7.67) and world spot oil prices ($10.43). The natural gas environment was worse; decades of regulations had priced natural gas at less than one-third its true Btu (i.e., energy) value. For example, Appalachian natural gas was priced below thirty-two cents per Mcf, equivalent to a $2 per barrel oil price. With the profit motive missing, publicly funded venture capital deserted the energy market. TEI was forced to continue self-funding its drilling and had to reduce its budget to $7.4 million from $13 million the previous year.

The Energy Policy and Conservation Act, enacted in 1976, allowed a free market for oil and gas discovered at great depths. In response, both spot oil and gas prices escalated, as shown in Figure 2.1. The act created a two-tier pricing policy that encouraged deep oil and gas finds and enhanced oil recovery, and that restrained prices on existing production. Natural gas prices achieved Btu price

Figure 2.1. **U.S. Natural Gas Prices versus U.S. Oil Prices**

Source: Monthly Energy Review 1973–1988, U.S. Department of Energy/A.P.I. (American Petroleum Institute), *Basic Data Book 1990.*

[a]*Note:* Natural gas is priced at the barrel equivalent oil (BEO) level. BEO is found by multiplying natural gas prices by six.

parity with oil in 1986. From the driller's perspective, oil and gas at shallow depths were uneconomic unless they could be sold in the intrastate market.

TEI's management was not disheartened by the loss of venture capital or governmental interference in its market, and barreled ahead. On the one hand, deep drilling in Eloi Bay was begun in response to the Energy Policy and Conservation Act; on the other hand, shallow intrastate energy became a priority on new acreage in West Virginia and throughout Appalachia. The 1976 annual report stated, "The 1977 budget includes $26 million in domestic exploration and production and $50 million in capital expenditures," a tripling of the budget.

How $76 million would be raised was unclear. Cash flow and earnings were insufficient, and investors were losing interest in the industry. Yet during 1977, TEI raised $177 million of new debt and $9 million of new equity. Existing debt of $94 million was retired (half of the total), leaving $83 million of new money for fresh ventures. Perhaps the most important element of the public portion of the new debt was the lead underwriter: Drexel Burnham Lambert (Drexel), a relatively obscure investment bank. Drexel had discovered an unserved market niche, raising capital for small, growing, mid-sized corporations. A syndicate of fifty-nine investment banks was assembled to place (i.e., sell) the debt. Drexel was so new to the game that by itself it sold only $7.5 million out of the $50 million issue.[5] The firm had yet to establish the energetic legion of buyers and sellers of high-yield bonds that flourished during the 1980s.

Debt instruments sold by Drexel would later be known as high-yield or junk bonds. Two issues were sold in April 1977 ($30 million) and July 1978 ($20 million) bearing interest at 11.5 percent, nearly 150 percent above the prime rate (see Figure 2.2). With the stock and bond offering successfully completed, a $100 million bank line of credit was easily arranged. Having fully charged its batteries, the company was primed to initiate an aggressive search for new reserves. By 1977, 3,500 people were employed in operations throughout the United States and Canada, with products marketed in forty-eight countries.

Figure 2.2. **Prime Rate from 1961 to 1985** (in percent)

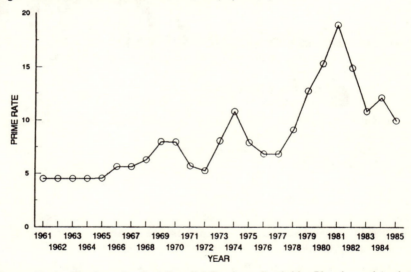

Source: Derived by the author from Datadisk Database, Cambridge Planning and Analytics, Cambridge, MA.

Note: Rate is average per year.

Funds were put to work expeditiously. In 1977, a $66 million capital expenditures program was instituted, including a $30 million expenditure to acquire a 52 percent interest in a company called Phoenix Resources Company.[6] The ownership position was acquired by buying creditors' claims against King Resources Company (King), which was bankrupt and protected by Chapter 10 of the old federal Bankruptcy Act. These claims were converted into stock under terms of King's approved plan of reorganization. Chapter 3 details the acquisition. The King bankruptcy was in the courts for seven years, 1971–1978, and created at least four new energy companies: Phoenix Resources Company, Royal Resources, the forerunner of Petro Lewis, and Global Natural Resources.[7]

The position in Phoenix Resources Company was accumulated to gain corporate control by means of a technique designated as "vulture investing." A vulture investor bides his or her time until a desirable asset either is facing extreme financial distress or has filed for bankruptcy protection. The vulture then swoops down and tries to acquire the asset cheaply. If the target company is still solvent, the vulture may offer to exchange cash for a sizable percentage of the equity; if the quarry is bankrupt, the vulture may acquire senior debt obligations from creditors unwilling to wait out the bankruptcy process and use this position to influence the bankruptcy outcome. In the case of Phoenix Resources Company, TEI acquired senior debt obligations of the bankrupt concern, paying slightly more than par value.

External Threats

Stagnant production and rising costs led to a cash deficiency in 1979. Of greatest concern was a year-end $30 million principal payment due to the First National Bank of Chicago that was collateralized by the Phoenix Resources Company holdings. The nonenergy businesses, except for the real estate division, were put on the blocks.

Compounding management's distress, a December 12, 1979, article in the *Wall Street Journal* identified TEI as the target of an impending bidding war. An unsolicited bid of $22 per share had been received from UNC Resources for 49 percent of TEI's outstanding shares. The stock market discounted the proposal, leaving the equity priced below $20 (see Figure 2.3). The *Journal* article suggested that several white knights lurked in the wings, and a buy-side analyst proclaimed that TEI would keep rising. A group led by James Ling, a founder of LTV, Inc., was said to have prepared a TEI buy-out proposal that never surfaced. UNC announced that even though $22 was its highest offer, "it was not going to walk away."

In response to the combined cash-flow and take-over pressures, in January 1980 the major portion of the energy equipment manufacturing division was sold for $48 million to Amcon Group. A foundry business was sold for $8.8 million. The energy services division had been sold in its entirety to NL Industries for $100 million in December 1978. In April 1979, two cemeteries owned by TEI sold for $6.1 million. By December 31, 1979, the company was down to 1,721 employees, but it had raised nearly $163 million.

Back to Basics

With a much healthier, albeit smaller, company, the corporate philosophy was refocused on oil and gas exploration instead of oil production. Exploration has the potential to radically alter a company's future by gaining access to new capital or through a major discovery; in contrast, production is conservative and yields a

Figure 2.3. **TEI Stock Price** (dollars per share)

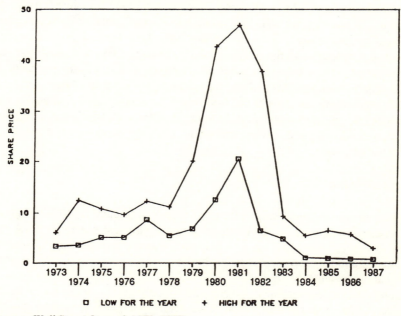

□ LOW FOR THE YEAR   + HIGH FOR THE YEAR

Source: Wall Street Journal, 1973–1987.

steady income stream, and will never bankrupt a company. The exploration strategy was valiant and unambiguous. New acreage was leased in Eloi Bay and Texas, and a search for highly profitable deep natural gas was planned for 1981.

Equities move on the anticipation of news, and Platt had fed the market its favorite foods: strengthening financial statements and prospects for a major discovery. Oil prices were climbing, as was TEI's stock.[8] From a low of $3½ per share in 1979, it reached $21⅜ in 1980 and $47 in 1981. TEI's future looked bright.

The Disaster: 1980–1981

The drilling business is similar to five-card stud poker; the value of each element in the game is uncertain until the final round of play. Consider this scenario: You are playing poker and the first two cards dealt to you are the ten and the jack of spades. Like the other betters at the table, you ante up, but you limit your bets due to the uncertain value of the hand. On your next card you receive the queen of spades. Again you match the bets. When your fourth card is the king of spades, the set of possible outcomes is clear: an ace of spades yields an unbeatable hand, a royal flush; another spade yields a flush; another ace yields a simple straight; if the final card matches one of the cards in your hand you have a pair;

and with any other card you have king high. By noting the cards lying face up on the table, you can refine the estimated probabilities of each outcome. In each round, however, bets are placed before knowing the value of your hand or your opponents' down card.

In oil drilling, the dealer is nature. First, land with geologic potential is leased or purchased. Then a core of people and equipment is assembled on the site. Once drilling commences, mishaps such as broken drill bits or collapsed wells delay and sometimes even end the program. At various depths, "logs" are recorded to document the porosity and composition of sediment; encouraging readings are designated as oil "shows." At the final drilling depth, the last card is dealt, and the well is uncapped and tested for oil or natural gas. Original geologic characteristics and the number and size of oil shows are unimportant at this stage—anything is possible.

The one sure bet in the oil business looked to be deep drilling after President Reagan deregulated oil prices in 1981. The ability of industrial energy users to freely switch between oil and gas gave a free-market upward push to both natural gas and oil prices. Gas prices reached nearly $10 per Mcf on the free market, and oil prices hit $40 per barrel.

At the center of TEI's exploration program was Eloi Bay, offshore Louisiana. A profusion of natural gas in the bay had induced major petrochemical companies to construct onshore facilities. A major discovery in one of the fields caused a commotion, since there was a similar physical structure on TEI's tract except at a greater depth, 18,000 feet underground. Prior to 1980, only one well in the area had been drilled to a depth below 10,000 feet. TEI decided to drill its #1 wildcat well to a depth that stretched technology, 20,000 feet, on State Lease 7,688. At 11,160 feet, a fantastic 186 feet of oil and gas pay was indicated in a 6,000-acre Miocene structure. Seismic information hinted at an additional 12,000-acre structure at a depth of over four miles. Naturally, the company kept drilling. If these big shows were confirmed, the company would enter the world of big oil.

Deep drilling was outrageously expensive, but the well's profit potential was even greater, especially since 90 percent of the well was company owned. TEI's per-foot drilling costs rose from $58 in 1978 to nearly $110 in 1982, as seen in Figure 2.4.

Oil companies report discoveries as reserves after confirming initial results with additional drilling. Four step-out wells were drilled to confirm the initial wildcat well's findings. Technical problems ensued: the first step-out well tested a paltry 6 Mcf of natural gas and 940 barrels of oil per day, and just past the halfway point, the well's casing collapsed, ending the test and damaging the well. Two wells had mechanical problems and flowed only water when tested. The final well was dry. Independent petroleum engineers hired by the company estimated proven undeveloped reserves to be a healthy 1.4 million barrels of oil and 33 Bcf of gas, based on the initial wildcat test results and the partially successful step-out well.[9]

Figure 2.4. **TEI Drilling Costs 1978–1982**

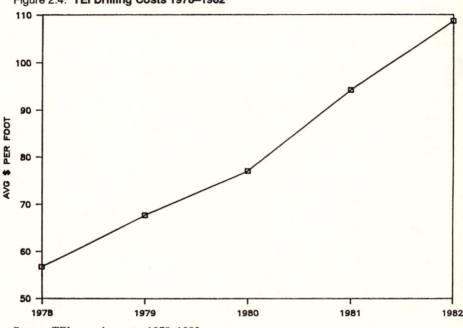

Source: TEI annual reports, 1978–1982.

TEI consumed $90 million in exploration and related activities in 1982, with negligible results. Lease obligations forced two more deep wells to be drilled in the next two years in the adjacent Breton Sound at a cost of $32 million; another deep well was drilled in Texas, but again mechanical difficulties arose.[10] However, independent petroleum engineers obtained sufficient information to estimate proven reserves of 3.1 Bcf deep gas at 16,000 to 17,000 feet. Between 1979 and 1983, TEI spent $532 million on exploration and development; in 1981 alone, over $200 million was expended, as detailed in Table 2.4. These sums were staggering for a company with only $102 million in equity in 1981. Yet Wall Street endorsed the program. The stock price rocketed on the New York Stock Exchange, increasing over 200 percent, from $15.25 in the fourth quarter of 1980 to almost $47 by mid-February 1981. In one day, the stock jumped almost $10 per share.

The gamble on deep drilling had cost approximately $160 million. Each of the deep wells was a dry hole or shut in by mechanical problems. In short order, a profitable mid-sized energy firm with excess cash was transformed into a profitable firm with debts in excess of $387 million. During the next ten years, it struggled to remain in business and to reduce indebtedness. Had fate not smiled on TEI again, the tale would have ended here. Chapter 5 recounts the second honeymoon.

Table 2.4

TEI Costs Incurred (Capitalized or Expensed) in Oil and Gas Activities
(in $ millions)

	1979	1980	1981	1982	1983
Acquisition Costs:					
Unproved Properties	$5.5	$13.0	$39.7	$9.5	$8.0
Proved Properties	$1.6	$0.2	$14.9	$0.8	$0.0
Exploration	$6.5	$26.2	$95.9	$90.1	$64.1
Development	$15.1	$31.1	$54.0	$30.6	$25.6
Totals	$28.7	$70.5	$204.5	$131.0	$97.7

Source: TEI 10-K reports, 1979–1983.
Note: Total costs do not include the acquisition cost of Phoenix Resources.

Paying for the Failure

TEI had an easier time finding investment money than oil or gas. In 1981, supported by Drexel, several innovative methods for raising oil money were pioneered. First, $30 million of a relatively new instrument known as Euro-convertible bonds were sold in the highly liquid and unregulated Eurobond market.[11] Second, with Drexel again as the lead underwriter, a zero-coupon bond was sold. Zero-coupon bonds pay no cash interest: instead, interest accrues and is paid at maturity. The issue was priced to yield 19.25 percent versus a prime rate of about 18 percent. Proceeds were $41 million, but the company was obligated to return $140 million at maturity in 1987. It is not clear that much attention was given to how these monies would be repaid, as the company rode the euphoric wave sweeping the oil and gas industry.[12] Third, commercial bankers increased the revolving credit line to $225 million from $61 million, with Phoenix Resources stock serving as collateral.

Other Facts

The acquisition of Phoenix Resources Company was completed in June 1982 after three years of controversy. TEI exchanged 5.9 million new shares of its stock for all shares of Phoenix Resources not already owned by TEI.[13] Including previously invested cash, the acquisition cost $115 million; $10.1 million more than Phoenix Resources' net book value. James Kishpaugh, formerly the president of Phoenix Resources, became president of TEI.[14] George Platt remained chairman of the board until August 1, 1982, when he resigned. On February 7, 1983, the SEC sued Platt; his son Stephen; Barry Switzer, the head football coach at the University of Oklahoma; and ten others, "alleging that they benefited illegally from insider trading in stock [of Phoenix]."[15] The suit claimed that they bought the stock before the June 10, 1982, public announcement (at approximately $42 a share) and sold their shares after the announcement (at near $69 per share). It alleged that they earned a profit of about $700,000, with the bulk of the profits earned by the others and not the Platts. In February 1984, the SEC reported that the two Platts settled the complaint, paying $16,000 without admitting or denying guilt. The suits against three other defendants were dropped.[16] After Platt's resignation, Bob Gist, a key financial manager and long-time employee, assumed the chairmanship.

A Halt to Deep Drilling

Wildcat drilling in Eloi Bay and Breton Sound continued, with a mounting appetite for drilling pipe and other supplies eroding corporate cash. At the end of the first quarter of 1982, deep-well drilling in Louisiana was discontinued. The gamble had failed: the deep-drilling program had squandered 30 percent of total assets, half of net worth, and had left long-term debt at $260 million, or 49 percent of total assets. Even worse, $220 million of debts were scheduled to be repaid between 1984 and 1986, and no cash was available.

To raise money, asset sales and new financing vehicles were pursued, while Gist sought concessions from the banks. Many banks hesitated, since they had taken a financial beating on their oil and gas portfolios.[17] Yet the bank consortium led by Chemical Bank cooperated and lowered the interest rate on the revolving credit line from the prime rate (about 11.5 percent) to 1.9 percent below prime and increased the credit line by $30 million to $275 million. In exchange for these concessions, the line was collateralized with 90 percent of domestic reserves. This was a critical juncture. Perhaps the company should have filed for bankruptcy then, before the bank line was secured. When all loans are unsecured, banks and other debtors are equals in a bankruptcy and could each have been given "a haircut" (i.e., exchange their indebtedness for equity), possibly leaving more value for common shareholders. News of the purported bank concession caused investor optimism to ebb, and the stock fell from over $37 at the beginning of 1982 to $6 by the end of the first quarter, 1983. On a single day, it fell by $10 per share.

Kishpaugh Assumes Control

Gist resigned and Kishpaugh was appointed chairman of the board while remaining president. Early in 1983, Drexel raised $100 million from the sale of 100,000 units. Each unit consisted of a $1,000 senior-subordinated debenture paying 13.125 percent interest, nineteen shares of common stock, and nine stock warrants exercisable at $8.90 per share. Proceeds reduced bank debt by $25 million and paid $68 million to retire the zero-coupon note issued in 1981. Interest costs on the zeros were too high, and they had sparked negative publicity in the June 6, 1983, issue of *Barrons*.[18] Meanwhile, asset sales continued.

In fall 1983, Drexel sold $50 million in oil-indexed notes paying 9 percent interest for the company. At maturity, bond holders had the option to receive $1,000 or twenty-nine barrels of crude oil. Had all bond holders chosen the twenty-nine barrels option, the company would have been obligated to deliver 1,450,000 barrels of oil, or about 18 percent of its total reserves. Table 2.5 describes the bond's indenture provisions. This was nearly the first commodity-indexed bond ever sold. Drexel had underwritten a Sunshine Mining silver-indexed note in 1980 and a $52 million oil-indexed offering by Petro-Lewis Corp. Total debt now stood at $350 million, with bank debt at $153 million.

Table 2.5

Nine Percent Senior-Subordinated Oil-Indexed Notes Due October 1, 1995

Terms
Par amount—$50 million.
Redemption value—Payable at maturity or earlier (see below) at the greater of:
   1) $1,000 in principal plus accrued interest, or
   2) 29 barrels of oil multiplied by the price of oil.
Call option—If redemption value exceeds $2,000, company may call the note.
Sinking fund—Company must redeem $5 million annually 10/1/86–10/1/94. Early redemption is netted out of sinking fund requirements. Holders may elect to redeem another $5 million each year.
Price of oil—Average price of West Texas Intermediate (sweet) listed by Amoco, Mobil, and Shell.
Maintenance requirement—Reserves must exceed 400% of the note issue.

Evaluation for 12/1983:	
Current oil price	$25.88
Barrels to back note (in millions)	1.932
Total U.S. reserves (in millions)	10.715
Ratio	455%

Ranking—Equal in rank to the $13^1/_8$% senior-subordinated notes issued the same year. Both are senior to all other subordinated debt.

Investors bought the notes as a hedge against inflation; beyond the break-even oil price, the twenty-nine barrels were more valuable than the cash. In exchange, they accepted a lower interest rate. They would receive more by accepting the oil and converting it into dollars. Kenneth Peak, a senior vice-president at TEI, noted that a similar subordinated note without the oil-index feature would have had to pay 16 percent to attract investors. The company had swapped the potential price appreciation on 18 percent of its oil reserves (beyond $35.71 per barrel) for a seven percentage-point reduction in interest costs on $50 million. Given that oil prices fell, it was an excellent transaction. Had oil prices risen, bond holders would have shared the gain. Table 2.6 illustrates that at $90 per barrel with constant production, bond holders ex-

Table 2.6

Profit Distribution in a High-Price Scenario:
Bonds Redeemed at Maximum Value

Production at 1983 Rates[a]	Total ($000)	Per Barrel
Oil Revenue	$59,772	$29.42
Production Costs	$34,467	$16.96
Gross Margin	$25,305	$12.45
Oil Price = $90.00		
Oil Revenue	$182,880	
Production Costs	$34,467	
Gross Margin	$148,413	
1983 Gross Margin	$25,305	
Profit Due to Oil Prices	$123,108	$60.58
Redemption[a]		
Bond Redeemed at	$2,000	
Principal	$100,000	
Accrued Interest	$9,000	
Total Cost to Redeem	$109,000	
Face Amount	$50,000	
Bond Holders' Share of Profit	$59,000	$29.04
Profit Allocation[b]		
Incremental Profit	$123,108	
Bond Holders' Profit	$59,000	
Company Share of Profit	$64,108	$31.55

Notes:
[a]Based on TEI's 1983 production level of 2.032 million barrels of oil.
[b]Profit figure does not account for taxes.

changing their debt consume about 48 percent of TEI's incremental profits *for one year*. Either way, TEI benefited.

Success in raising capital was not matched in the field. Devastating news was rendered by a new team of independent petroleum engineers hired to estimate 1984 reserves. They concluded that proven undeveloped reserves were overstated in two of TEI's primary gas and oil fields, at Eloi Bay and in Canada. Eloi Bay reserves were restated downward by 23 Bcf of deep gas and 0.9 million barrels of oil, 70 percent and 65 percent, respectively. Another 24 Bcf of gas was removed from the Canadian reserves. Kishpaugh explained that the adjustments were "based upon new information and not upon the eyeglasses through which engineering firms are looking at them." Industry observers reasoned that bank lenders were exerting pressure on engineers after suffering losses from inadequate reserve collateral.

The report was unexpected and dismayed shareholders. The next day the stock price plunged from $5.25 to $2.75. Eventually, eight lawsuits were filed, later combined into a single class-action suit, accusing TEI of misleading investors.[19]

Adverse news offers an opportunity to disclose other bad news, in a corporate form of house cleaning. For example, in 1991 Quaker Oats reported that it would spin off to shareholders its Fisher Price subsidiary when it announced that its earnings were below some analysts' forecasts. TEI opted to convert from full-cost to successful-efforts accounting at this time. Although successful-efforts accounting was favored by the Financial Accounting Standards Board and employed by most major oil companies (see appendix B), it was not required or adhered to by many of TEI's smaller competitors. The change resulted in a major financial write-off. Kishpaugh noted, "We think it more accurately reflects ongoing business results."[20]

TEI was no longer a star. It had taken major reserve and financial write-downs and was now a disaster. The write-off reduced assets by $270 million, $100 million being charged to 1983 alone. Liabilities remained unchanged. Net income was restated historically, as seen in Table 2.7. Instead of successive profits, with successful-efforts accounting TEI was profitable once in thirteen years. Stockholders' equity was now *negative* $95 million. Kishpaugh wrote in a report to shareholders:

> This does not mean your company is worth a minus $95 million. Net worth on the balance sheet for oil and gas companies is largely based on historical costs as opposed to the fair market value of the company's oil and gas reserves, land, etc. This can be misleading if you think about the balance sheet net worth as the value of your company—it is not. Stockholders' equity is a summation of historical earnings and the proceeds from the issuance of common stock. Thus, to look at history using Successful Efforts, the company has cumulatively lost money.[21]

On the positive side, the accounting change eliminated from the income statement huge depreciation charges (associated with prior failed efforts). Although dry-hole cost would now be immediately written off, a smaller depreciation charge increased the likelihood of ever reporting a profit. Not only did the company predict positive cash flow from operations for 1984 of $35 million, but it reported that banks would lend it still more money. A $50 million capital-spending program was planned.

Kishpaugh exuded confidence, "We've endured the reserve cuts and change in accounting method without violating any of our loan agreements. We're not in default on any agreement. Our bankers, suppliers, and joint venturers are supportive." His strategy was to replace current production with new reserves from

Table 2.7

TEI Net Income Before and After Accounting Method Change 1969–1981 (dollars in thousands)

	1969	1970	1971	1972	1973	1974[a]	1975	1976	1977	1978[a]	1979	1980	1981
Full-Cost Accounting	625	1,045	3,667	2,031	2,927	7,193	5,429	4,097	6,661	8,544	(5,437)	15,856	7,247
Successful-Efforts Accounting	(1,919)	(3,093)	(2,215)	(6,326)	(8,971)	(2,964)	(14,272)	(16,872)	(25,267)	2,320	(13,992)	(188)	(26,415)

[a]Restated by TEI.

low-risk drilling. His conservative plan limited working interests in wells to 25–50 percent, aimed new exploratory drilling at shallow targets, and restricted deep drilling to one or two wells per year.

The program achieved some success. Secondary production methods were applied to rework Eloi Bay's mature oil and gas fields (over twenty million gross barrels had been produced since 1960), allowing reserves to increase by 11 percent in 1984. With funds short, an arrangement was struck with key suppliers, including Baker Hughes Inc., wherein they would accept common stock for up to half of each invoice. Several suppliers locked in the stock's current price by short selling. Baker Hughes did not short sell and filed a claim years later in bankruptcy court for the loss incurred by the fall in value of the stock between the date it was issued and the date it was sold. Despite the efforts of Christopher J. Ryan, a renowned workout specialist, the claim was disallowed by the court. An article in early 1985 in the *Oil & Gas Journal* glorified the efforts of the rework engineers. The bay now accounted for 47 percent of TEI's total revenues.

Real excitement came out of Egypt. The Khalda Concession was acquired in the merger with Phoenix Resources. In early 1983, TEI discovered oil by reentering a well that had been abandoned by an earlier concessionaire. It flowed at the prodigious rate of 700 barrels per day. A second well in the Khalda field tested at 900 barrels per day in the fall of 1984. In February 1985, the Salam 2x well in the Salam field, a half mile from the Khalda field, tested at 6,000 barrels per day at a depth of just over 9,000 feet. In comparison, a typical American oil well might yield 15–20 barrels per day. Obviously, these discoveries had the potential to revive the company.[22] Chapter 3 is devoted to the merger with the Phoenix Resources Company and chapter 5 to the Egyptian concession.

Oil discovery is the first step on a long road to oil profits. Substantial capital would be required to exploit the discovery. Some production could be trucked to the coast, but to generate sizable revenues a pipeline was required to the Mediterranean Sea over 100 miles away. Pipeline cost would exceed $10 million. A step-out well to confirm the Salam 2x discovery was needed, and the concession had to be renewed with the Egyptian government in April 1985. Egypt had agreed to a two-year renewal in exchange for a $500,000 signing bonus and an $8 million capital drilling commitment. However, one-third of the concession's 250,000 acres would automatically revert to Egypt unless the concession was developed expeditiously. Still more money was needed for drilling planned in Texas and Louisiana.

The financial situation was bleak: by mid-year 1985, net income was negative $18 million, working capital was negative $33 million, and cash had dwindled from $20 million at year-end 1984 to $7.3 million. More portentous, $32 million of debt principal was scheduled for repayment in 1985, and another $140 million was due between 1986 and 1988. Clearly, the Egyptian discovery could not be funded by internally generated funds.

Table 2.8

Bank Credit Line Payment Schedule (in $ millions)

	March 1984 Agreement[a]			March 1985 Agreement[a]	
Time Period	Amortization Payment	Total Commitment Outstanding	Time Period	Amortization Payment	Total Commitment Outstanding
4/1/84	$0.0	$160.0	6/85[b]	$25.0	$116.0
4/1/85	$20.0	$140.0	6/86	$25.0	$91.0
4/1/86	$14.5	$135.5	6/87	$32.0	$59.0
4/1/87	$27.5	$108.0	1/88	$28.7	$30.0
1/1/88	$92.0	$16.0			
Totals	$154.0			$110.7	

Source: TEI 10-K reports, 1984 and 1985.

Notes: Credit lines are secured by TEI's domestic oil and gas properties.

[a] Floating interest rate based on one of the following (TEI's choice): Prime + $1/2$%; London Interbank Offer Rate + 1%; Certificate of Deposit + 1.125%.

[b] Quarterly payments (in $ millions) begin: 6/85 = $8; 9/85 = $8; 12/85 = $9.

Despite the bleak outlook, $13.5 million was raised in an asset sale, and in March 1985 the banks agreed to defer for two months a $20 million revolving credit payment and to accept quarterly payments. Comparing the old and new credit-line amortization schedules in Table 2.8 reveals that the banks agreed to a $44 million reduction in TEI's repayments by January 1988. In exchange, they reduced the size of the credit line.

A "permanent" solution was needed. Drexel, again performing its Sir Galahad role, recommended a debt-exchange offer to revise the contractual terms on all the subordinated debt. Chapter 6 tracks this and two subsequent exchange offers. Kenneth Peak, the chief financial officer, described the 1985 exchange offer in confident terms:

> At the 85 percent acceptance level, the exchange offers would result in additional cash flow of approximately $76 million over the next two and half years. This cash flow would contribute to funding the Company's exploration and development expenses on its Egyptian concession and domestic operations as well as payment of interest and principal obligations on the Company's remaining indebtedness.[23]

The debt exchange enabled TEI to pay interest in either cash or common stock. After several sweetened offers and good news out of Egypt, 88.1 percent of subordinated debt holders agreed to tender their holdings for the new debt, which had higher interest-rate coupons and earlier maturity dates. If the offer had failed, the company would have voluntarily filed a Chapter 11 bankruptcy petition, or its creditors would have involuntarily put it into bankruptcy.

With the debt problem temporarily resolved, how to finance Egypt headed the agenda. The solution was to joint-venture or "farm out" the property to Conoco. Conoco agreed to fund an estimated $150 million development program in return for a 50 percent interest in the concession. Discovered fields would be developed, eight exploration wells would be drilled, and pipelines and processing facilities would be constructed over an eighteen-month period. In addition, Conoco reimbursed TEI for $18 million of previously incurred expenses, creating a liquidity cushion.[24]

Meanwhile in the United States, international oil companies were raising cash by selling off smaller properties. One such property for sale was Phillips Petroleum's working interest in Eloi Bay. Despite TEI's poor credit standing, a New York bank lent $27 million, on a nonrecourse basis, to fund this acquisition. If a nonrecourse loan is not serviced or repaid, the lender can then seize the securing asset—in this case, Phillips' working interests in Eloi Bay—but is denied access to other corporate assets. Reserves in the bay increased by 4.7 million barrels of oil and 2.1 Bcf of gas, worth approximately $90 million in future revenues.

What a year it had been. The debt crisis was lifted, an Egyptian partner was snagged, and a sizable U.S. asset had been acquired on a nonrecourse basis. It is not surprising that TEI was the biggest winner on the NYSE in 1985, rising 411.1 percent in value, ending the year at $5.75, and at one point reaching $6.50 per share.

The stock's rise was short lived, however. Oil prices plunged 50 percent in the first quarter of 1986. TEI's financial report for 1986 was qualified by the accounting firm of Arthur Andersen pending negotiations to refinance the bank debt. A qualified report is the accounting profession's way of saying, "Do not hold us responsible if this company fails." On April 18 the New York Stock Exchange suspended trading in the company's stock for violating the exchange's minimum net worth requirements, which coincidently had not been met for the past three years. The Pacific Stock Exchange listed the stock. Later in 1986, the liability policy protecting officers and directors was dropped due to cost considerations. Two directors resigned, and three new members were elected to the board.

By mid-1986, it became apparent that the $58 million in annual interest payments could not be paid, nor could scheduled principal payments. The banks agreed to exchange the credit line for term debt due January 1, 1988, provided that $15 million was paid down, and contingent on at least 75 percent of the $205 million of publicly traded unsecured debt being restructured by September 30, 1986.[25] This ultimatum served both the bank and the company. Thus began the second exchange offer, which is further discussed in chapter 6.

Newfound Optimism

In June 1987, $4 million was invested to purchase 80 percent of PT Corporation, a recently formed corporation. PT was an investment vehicle that bought a portfolio of high-yield (and high-risk) corporate debt securities. At its inception, PT sold preferred stock and 20 percent of its common stock to a Drexel affiliate for $209.2 million. The preferred stock paid a fixed cumulative dividend that was 85 percent tax exempt for corporations.

The key to PT was its ability to use TEI's tax loss carryforward (arising from prior year losses) to shield income from taxation. Since no income taxes were paid, the 15 percent per annum earned on the high-yield bonds was equivalent to a 30 percent profit margin for a taxable company. TEI received about $4 million per year for contributing its tax loss carryforward.

TEI was set to go again with cash flow under control, the liquidity crisis resolvable in the second exchange offer, and the Egyptian properties a potential gold mine. But world events intervened to upset these dreams.

Notes

1. *Wall Street Transcript,* November 10, 1969.

2. The net ownership of these wells was 183 oil and 105 gas wells on 27,688 net acres of producing lease properties.

3. These figures exclude divisions sold off in 1974 and 1978.

4. While TEI was in bankruptcy in 1989, this property was sold off to Atlantic Richfield for several million dollars. The company retained a 0.5 percent overriding royalty interest in the property because of Kishpaugh's (the company's CEO) belief in the area. In October 1991, Atlantic Richfield reported that the first exploratory well in the area flowed significant quantities of both oil and gas and that the company would expend an additional $60 million drilling offset wells to define the extent of reserves. In April 1992, the company estimated potential reserves at 750 million barrels.

5. See Connie Bruck, *The Preditor's Ball: The Junk Bond Raiders and the Men Who Staked Them,* p. 47.

6. By December 31, 1980, the market value of this investment had grown to $96.95 million.

7. GNR appears again when it tries to acquire a bankrupt TEI.

8. Some analysts predicted $100 per barrel by the end of the century.

9. Years later, in 1991, a settlement was approved from a class-action lawsuit brought by individuals who had purchased the equity from January 22, 1981 to January 27, 1984. A $9.5 million settlement fund provided for the return of up to $27 per share to stock purchasers who had bought stock at allegedly inflated prices due to statements made concerning either potential reserves or proven reserves. Only $100,000 came from TEI. The balance was paid by individual defendants, engineering firms, and insurance companies. Plaintiffs received about $.09 for every dollar claimed.

10. It can be argued that deep drilling is deep drilling. Hence, the company had not created a portfolio of activities to lower its risk.

11. The Eurobond market is an unregulated market that started in the early 1960s. Trading is centered in London, where governments and corporations issue debt denominated in their domestic currency. The market expanded in the 1980s; trading volume soared from $16 billion in 1980 to $63 billion in 1984. U.S. denominated debt in the Eurobond market is not subject to SEC regulations and may be sold only to non-U.S. investors.

12. An article in *Barrons,* June 6, 1983, detailed TEI's zero-coupon bond and argued that the company would have difficulty repaying the matured value.

13. The terms of the transaction required TEI to exchange 1.1 of its shares for every 1 share of Phoenix Resources. The initial offer provided only 1 TEI share for 2 shares of Phoenix. The market value for the 5.9 million TEI shares, based on the closing NYSE price of $9.375, was $55.6 million.

14. Prior to 1978, James Kishpaugh was manager of engineering and planning for TIPCO. He had held various engineering and operations positions at Exxon.

15. *Wall Street Journal,* February 2, 1983, and February 7, 1983.

16. *Wall Street Journal,* February 22, 1984.

17. In July 1982, Penn Square Bank, with $2 billion in assets, and one of the most prosperous banks in Oklahoma, was closed by the FDIC. It had benefited from the rush to drill deep gas in Oklahoma's Anadarko Basin. The ripple effect of this closure was felt across Oklahoma and eventually led to the largest-ever federal bank bailout: Continental Illinois Bank.

18. In fact, *Barrons* later corrected its facts. The original article described the zero as a $100 million issue (actually $50 million), due in 1985 or 1986 (actually 1987), which would have a cost at maturity of $300 million (actually $140 million).

19. *Wall Street Journal,* April 17, 1984.

20. TEI, "Getting the Past Out of Our Future."

21. Ibid.

22. Net revenues to TEI were determined by a complex formula agreed upon by the Egyptian government. Basically, the company's net share of taxes amounted to 10 percent of the total Khalda Concession oil revenues, or an additional $8 million annually at current oil prices, tax free. All natural gas belonged to the Egyptian government.

23. TEI annual report, 1986.

24. TEI was to repay this advance out of future Egyptian operating revenues; if this debt was not repaid by 1991, all of TEI's Egyptian revenues would be transferred to Conoco until the debt was repaid.

25. The outstanding bank balance was $71 million, since funds raised by property sales had been used to pay down debt.

3

The Merger with Phoenix Resources

If TEI had not acquired the Phoenix Resources Company and the Egyptian Khalda Concession it controlled, this tale would have ended years sooner. Creditors may have balked at the 1985 exchange offer, which gave them an earlier maturity date in exchange for higher interest payments payable in cash or stock, if they had not believed that the Egyptian asset had the potential to generate enough cash to meet the maturity schedule. Instead, they would have pushed the company into bankruptcy and sought to liquidate the assets. However, Egypt created the possibility that TEI was worth more alive than dead.

The Khalda Concession agreement (between Egypt and the concessionaire) contained one clause that always troubled investors and creditors. It stated that the concession would automatically revert to Egypt in the event that the concessionaire filed for bankruptcy. However, it was uncertain who Egypt might interpret the concessionaire to be. Was it Phoenix Resources of Egypt, the actual signatory of the document, or TEI, its parent company, or Conoco, the farm-out partner. Some creditors interpreted the provision as a guarantee that TEI would never voluntarily file for bankruptcy. After TEI went bankrupt, these creditors speculated that the Egyptian government had agreed to define the concessionaire as Phoenix Resources of Egypt, which was not a participant in the bankruptcy proceedings.

The merger with Phoenix Resources Company gave TEI a second valuable asset: James Kishpaugh, Phoenix Resources Company's president. Not only was Kishpaugh an experienced oil man, but he was also a brilliant negotiator. During his tenure at TEI, a series of horse trades yielded superb results for the company, and yet his trading partners were convinced that they had bested him. He assembled an impressive team to manage the company, including Ken Peak as chief financial officer, Charles Reimer as senior vice-president responsible for operations, Frank Dickerson, and Joe Romano.

Vulture Investing

Phoenix Resources Company was the reorganized successor to the King Resources Company, named after James King. King was the first seller of drilling deals to the general public. It reorganized in bankruptcy from 1971 to 1978. King's history is laced with notable figures, including Robert Vesco and Bernie Cornfeld, and the Investors Overseas Service (IOS) and the Fund of Funds.[1]

In 1979 Phoenix Resources Company had proven reserves of 162 Bcf of natural gas, oil reserves approaching four million barrels, and promising undeveloped leases in the United States, Canada, Egypt, and the Canadian Arctic. These reserves were worth in excess of $300 million.

Corporate takeovers are not uncommon business events. Both bankrupt and nonbankrupt companies are candidates, though taking over a bankrupt company has more pitfalls. A nonbankrupt company is acquired by gaining control of its board of directors. The board of directors elects the individual who will serve as president and approves major strategies and policies. The direct route to gaining control over the board is to purchase a majority of the common equity; however, a company with diffuse stock ownership may be captured by purchasing just a controlling stake of the equity, which may be as little as 25 percent or 30 percent. On the other hand, companies with staggered boards of directors may be able to hold off a raider even when majority ownership is achieved.[2]

Gaining control over bankrupt companies is more problematic. The reorganization process seeks to resolve old claims in a manner that is fair, equitable, and feasible. New debt or equity may be coined to create something of value with which to induce claimants against the bankrupt estate to drop their original claims. Pre-bankruptcy equity may be wiped out after the company emerges from bankruptcy. Hence, acquiring a controlling interest in the old equity may leave the investor owning 100 percent of nothing. Moreover, there is no accepted formula or established routine that defines a priori how the equity in the reorganized company will be divided between old debt and old equity holders. A review of actual bankruptcy cases reveals an array of ownership outcomes that can be characterized as follows:

(a) Retention: original equity retains ownership.
(b) Compromise: old equity and debt holders split ownership.
(c) Abrogation: old debtors take complete control.
(d) New Value: new investors bring fresh capital.

Retention is unusual and likely to occur only in a bankruptcy in which the value of the company's assets greatly exceeds its liabilities, e.g., Texaco. Abrogation is more likely when the firm's assets are worth less than its combined indebtedness, while compromise is likely if asset and debt values are similar. Several factors may lead to a new-value outcome, including a need for more capital or debt holders unwilling or unable to accept equity. Given the range of outcomes, there is risk in selecting a strategy to acquire a bankrupt company.

An event transpiring early in the King Resources bankruptcy proceeding identified the correct course to engineer a takeover of Phoenix Resources. The U.S. district court in Colorado determined that the common stock of King was worthless; the senior creditors were deemed to be the company's beneficial owners once a plan of reorganization could be approved. TEI gained control of $30.8 million, or approximately 48 percent of debt claims against King Resources, by purchasing claims from creditors who preferred to sell out immediately rather than wait for the bankruptcy proceedings to drag through the courts. Some bankruptcy cases languish in court for ten years; hence, cash up front, even when the seller receives a fraction of its claim's value, may be more advantageous than receiving more several years later. After swallowing its initial stake, in December of 1977 TEI offered to purchase approximately $13 million more publicly held claims. Nearly $4.3 million of claims were tendered in January of 1978, bringing TEI's stake to 52 percent. For accounting purposes, despite being the majority owner, the purchase was shown on TEI's balance sheet at the cost of acquired claims, since no corporate control was exercised.

In March 1978, the SEC filed suit against TEI, charging that it violated the Williams Act by allegedly failing to make required filings disclosing all material facts, and misstating certain material facts in connection with the offering for Phoenix Resources. The company believed the suit lacked merit. Following the SEC's complaint, a class-action suit seeking $1.8 million plus interest and costs was filed by the concerned claim holders. The outcome of the class-action suit would not impact the ownership of the Phoenix Resources shares already purchased.

In early 1978 the King Resources Company bankruptcy was consummated, that is, put into place. The approval spawned several entities, the largest of which was Phoenix Resources Company. TEI was the majority owner of Phoenix Resources Company and filled four of six board of director seats. One of the remaining board seats was occupied by James Kishpaugh, the chairman, president, and CEO of Phoenix. TEI's special insider's knowledge of Phoenix Resources was augmented by an agreement that began in November 1978, whereby Phoenix paid TEI $39,000 per month to perform its accounting and data processing services. Although this agreement was terminated in June of 1979, it provided TEI with an exceptional opportunity to ascertain Phoenix Resources' potential.

In August 1979, the boards of directors of both companies approved a plan whereby TEI would receive an undivided 52 percent interest in all the assets and liabilities of Phoenix in exchange for all of TEI's Phoenix securities. This plan was subject to the approval of Phoenix Resources' other security holders. Before putting the plan to a vote, a tax ruling was required from the Canadian government. TEI preferred waiting, too. "Promising" results from a deep gas well in Breton Sound in 1980 exaggerated internal estimates of available funds and suggested that TEI could buy the whole company. After all, the initial $35 million investment in Phoenix Resources Company was now valued at nearly $100 million.

A disgruntled Phoenix Resources stockholder filed a lawsuit seeking to enjoin the exchange of assets for shares. He also sought damages should this transaction occur. Phoenix Resources' board of directors believed this suit to be without merit. Several other suits were filed concerning the Phoenix reorganization: subordinated debenture holders alleged the plan was unfair to certain creditors, and King Resources Company common stockholders challenged the insolvency argument that "crammed down" their loss of ownership.

In September 1980, following continued delays from the Canadian government, TEI proposed a share-for-share merger of the two companies. This offer was withdrawn in January 1981 because it was not supported by the two unaffiliated directors or the stockholders, and was viewed as unfavorable to minority holders by an investment bank retained by Phoenix.

At a special meeting of Phoenix's board of directors on December 7, 1981, TEI proposed a merger that would exchange one of its shares for two of Phoenix's. The board voted 4–1 to hire Morgan Stanley & Co. to evaluate the merger offer. One of the two outside directors of Phoenix resigned the next day. Following a preliminary review with Morgan Stanley, TEI revised its proposal to provide for the exchange of one and one-tenth shares of TEI for each share of Phoenix. With the modified accord, minority shareholders received more than double the original offer. Phoenix's board then unanimously supported the merger.

Shareholders were told by Morgan Stanley that the price was "fair and equitable from a financial point of view." On June 18, 1982, shareholders of both companies approved the merger.

Notes

1. See Charles Raw, *Do You Sincerely Want to Be Rich? The Full Story of Bernard Cornfeld and IOS.*
2. Staggered boards are elected a few each year. Thus, even after buying up all the stock, an acquirer could have to wait several years to take board control.

Part II
The Period of Decline

4

Reacting to Industry Conditions

After rising continually for eight years, energy prices began to decline in 1981. Crude oil prices in the United States had jumped almost tenfold from $3.54 per barrel in 1973 to $35.14 in February of 1981. Of all the forces that conspired to halt the upward price spiral, the single most important may have been President Reagan's decision to deregulate the energy market. Deregulation impelled Adam Smith's invisible hand to deploy capital (physical and human) into that activity with the highest expected return: exploration for oil and gas reserves. At $35 per barrel, amazing fortunes could be made in oil exploration. Entrepreneurship bloomed in the oil patch accompanied by a number of sizable hydrocarbon discoveries.

Rising energy prices affected the consumer, too. During the eight-year price spiral, the price of a gallon of gasoline rose by 265 percent, residential electricity prices increased by 152 percent, and residential natural gas prices jumped by 252 percent. Higher prices usually elicit a swift cutback in consumption; however, factors peculiar to energy consumption inhibited the consumer response to higher prices. Economists describe energy consumption as a "derived demand," meaning, for example, that no one has a desire for electricity per se; what people really desire are the services provided by electricity (e.g., lighting or cooling). Consumption of a derived-demand commodity can be reduced in two ways: through a cutback in usage or by upgrading the efficiency of the physical unit. Higher prices can lead to immediate usage reductions, since they do not require changes in the existing stock of equipment; alteration in the stock of equipment is a long-run response. Energy conservation in the home, on the road, and in the factory is delayed by the durability and cost of the physical stock of energy-using equipment.

Consider Mr. Average and the new average car he bought in 1973. It weighed in excess of two and a half tons, had eight cylinders, comfortably carried six passengers, got about eight miles to the gallon in city driving, and would take Mr. Average about four years to pay off. When gasoline prices doubled late in 1973 and early in 1974, Mr. Average could only dig deeper into his pocket each time he filled up the car. Not only were there few energy-efficient models available, but the resale value of his behemoth had plunged, and he could not afford to replace it. Whenever he could, he carpooled with a neighbor. Five years later, in 1978, Mr. Average bought a new, more fuel-efficient car, averaging about twelve miles per gallon in city driving, but luck was against him again. Oil prices skyrocketed in 1979, as the Shah of Iran was deposed. Once again, Mr. Average had an average car that he could not afford.

Through a combination of usage reduction and stock modification, consumption habits changed. Although it took nearly a decade, energy demands stopped growing and began to fall. Also, worldwide oil supplies grew, as countries—including the thirteen-nation oil cartel, the Organization of Petroleum Exporting Countries (OPEC)—produced more oil to sell to a thirsty world. Higher supplies coupled with falling demands produced lower prices. As national revenues declined in OPEC nations, intercountry competition emerged for markets and money, leading to still higher production and lower oil prices. Internal squabbling afflicted OPEC and led to countless emergency meetings with agendas designed to support the current oil price level or to develop formulae to apportion total OPEC oil production among the thirteen members. Neither procedure alleviated the intrinsic problem: too much oil.

The irresolvability of OPEC's dilemma is partly explained by variations among the thirteen member nations. The largest producer, with a practically endless reserve, Saudi Arabia, has a minuscule population. Smaller producers such as Algeria and Nigeria, ironically, have burgeoning populations and ambitious development plans. National diversity almost guaranteed catastrophe. Even worse, two OPEC members, Iraq and Iran, began a disastrous eight-year conflict, which propagated antipathies among members and greatly increased those two countries' capital requirements.

Accepting its inherent inability to support a $42 per barrel mandate, OPEC dramatically reduced oil prices to $28 per barrel in 1982. An already wounded TEI began a long descent. Factors that had fostered its growth as prices rose now hastened its decline. The value of the company's oil reserves declined by more than the 34 percent fall in oil price, because the accepted banking industry methodology for reserve calculations compared a field's cost of production to the current market price. Marginal reserves were displaced from the proven-developed category into the proven-undeveloped category by a fall in price. Banks do not lend against undeveloped reserves.

Many lenders were unprepared for the OPEC price-cut announcement. Despite the weakness in oil markets, they had "protected" the value of bank capital by delaying the revaluation of customer reserves used as loan collateral. OPEC's announcement left the banks little choice but to revalue lending–borrowing bases. In certain cases, banks were now exposed to significant loan losses. Companies whose reserves were valued below their loan balance were asked to reduce the loan principal, put up more capital, and halt expenditures, and they were denied further monies. Drilling activity slowed, oil service companies failed, real estate values plunged, and an economic slowdown pervaded the southwestern region of the United States, from which it has yet to recover by 1993. Energy loan defaults contributed to the S&L and commercial bank debacles at the end of the 1980s.

TEI's bankers worried that the bank line could not be serviced. Then OPEC further lowered the world price of oil to $24 per barrel, and again to $18 per barrel; finally, in 1986, as producers scrambled for market share, the bottom dropped out, and prices momentarily fell to $8 per barrel. The era of glory and money in the oil business was over.

The oil and gas industry entered a period of sustained economic decline whose ramifications permeated the economy. For example, in 1986 35 percent of all defaulted bonds in the corporate sector had been issued by oil companies; in 1987 the ratio rose to 52 percent. Over 2,100 oil and gas companies went bankrupt from 1985 to 1988, as seen in Table 4.1. The combined liabilities of these companies exceeded $6 billion.

Table 4.1

Number of Oil and Gas Failures and Their Liabilities (in $ millions)

Year	Number	Liabilities
1985	565	$1,533
1986	731	$3,031
1987	469	$1,493
1988	374	$813

Source: The Dun & Bradstreet Corporation, *Business Failure Record, 1985–1988*.
Note: Corresponding data are unavailable for earlier years, when oil and gas failures were combined with mining failures.

TEI's Troubles

Lower oil prices reduced TEI's revenues, but its expenses, especially interest payments, remained high. (See Tables 4.2 and 4.3 for financial statements during the period of decline. The first two columns in the financial tables are based on full-cost accounting, while the remaining columns, including the two restated years, are derived with successful-efforts accounting.) Interest payments were especially invariant, hovering near $45 million per year from 1982 to 1986. With fixed-rate debt instruments, interest obligations remain high unless principal is reduced. Debts can be repaid with cash flow or new money. Cash

Table 4.2

Income Statement, 1981–1989 (in $ thousands)

	1981	1982	1981ᵃ	1982ᵃ	1983	1984	1985	1986	1987	1988	1989
Operating Revenues	142,238	166,667	142,238	166,667	121,442	126,140	95,619	56,777	16,632	28,723	24,469
Other Revenue	3,833	5,532	4,794	11,977	15,751	14,133	11,231	6,940	19,292	6,599	11,232
Total Revenues	146,071	172,199	147,032	178,644	137,193	140,273	106,850	63,717	35,924	35,322	35,701
Cost of Goods Sold	41,142	44,948	45,821	74,803	47,853	38,000	28,863	20,469	11,267	21,382	15,331
Exploration	33,662	36,776	45,080	51,805	64,982	21,668	11,845	2,156	5,581	6,087	3,151
Depreciation, Depletion, and Amortization	34,848	53,587	26,784	50,360	39,517	37,467	32,881	29,876	2,850	2,332	1,791
General and Administrative	28,632	18,764	36,858	25,378	26,117	20,703	18,563	14,902	10,486	9,663	10,299
Interest	25,344	37,174	29,248	44,076	44,567	43,870	44,515	45,789	26,652	11,130	4,699
Total Expenses	163,628	191,249	183,791	246,422	223,036	161,708	136,667	113,192	56,836	50,594	35,271
Operating Income (loss)	10,697	8,618	(37,096)	(69,169)	(86,430)	(23,274)	(32,306)	(51,607)	(44,737)	(15,272)	430
Net Income (loss)	7,247	4,293˙	(42,849)	(76,556)	(99,680)	(21,959)	(31,881)	(50,798)	(44,222)	(15,272)	430

Source: TEI annual reports, 1981–1989.
ᵃRevised by TEI.

Table 4.3

TEI Balance Sheet (in $ thousands)

	1981	1982	1981[a]	1982[a]	1983	1984	1985	1986	1987	1988	1989
Current Assets	138,114	141,763	138,114	136,860	67,190	55,570	64,275	154,862	21,378	17,676	24,072
Long-Term Assets	388,184	527,623	284,047	337,964	276,056	240,581	196,947	40,837	27,288	19,538	15,388
Total Assets	526,298	669,386	422,161	474,824	343,246	296,151	261,222	195,699	48,666	37,214	39,460
Current Liabilities	127,389	83,002	127,389	83,196	65,151	84,197	49,885	131,963	162,923	191,512	16,318
Long-Term Debt	260,408	388,116	260,408	387,033	350,032	307,242	322,726	193,013	22,745	2,617	32,609
Equity	138,501	198,268	34,364	4,595	(71,937)	(95,288)	(111,389)	(129,277)	(137,002)	(156,915)	(9,467)
Debt + Equity	526,298	669,386	422,161	474,824	343,246	296,151	261,222	195,699	48,666	37,214	39,460

Source: TEI annual reports, 1981–1989.
[a]Revised by TEI.

flow roughly equals the sum of net income plus depreciation, depletion, and amortization. Applying this formula after 1981 in Table 4.2, TEI had negative cash flow except for 1984 and 1985. The option of borrowing new money at lower interest rates was impractical given TEI's impossible financial condition. Yet, in 1984, the Trust Company of the West lent $25 million (face amount) of new money secured by oil properties at nearly a 20 percent effective rate of interest. In the five years 1981–1985, TEI lost more than $273 million on revenues of $710 million. Total expenses peaked at $246 million in 1982, *a year after* oil prices began to decline. Exploration expenditures were trimmed starting in 1984 and again in 1985 and 1986. General and administrative expenses were cut each year, including a $3.6 million cut in 1987, but became a growing percentage of revenues, reaching 23.3 percent in 1986 and 29 percent in 1987, due to diseconomies of scale.

Survival was imperiled. The company embarked on a twofold strategy aimed at reducing debt to a level commensurate with revenues by selling off assets and restructuring the company's indebtedness to reduce cash interest and lengthen maturities. These efforts were moderately successful. Nearly a quarter billion dollars were raised selling assets, including a corporate jet, two cemeteries, an attractive land parcel in California that yielded approximately $26 million, and virtually all U.S. oil and gas assets, which realized approximately $110 million. The restructurings, too, were moderately successful. The company's indebtedness was partially deferred, and more important, the company issued what are now referred to as PIK bonds. A PIK, or "payment in kind," bond allows the issuer to pay interest in cash or by issuing more of the security itself. TEI's PIK allowed the firm to pay interest using common stock. These exchanges are detailed in chapter 6.

5

Egypt and the Khalda Concession

In January 1983, with Kishpaugh now president, the corporation followed a new direction: development activities in the deep Breton Sound were abandoned, investments were written down, and a stricter accounting method was adopted. The company and its industry had both lost their luster. The worst development was that bankers stopped lending and instead sought to have older loans repaid or recollateralized. TEI's common equity fell from $42 per share in 1981 to less than $2 per share at the end of 1984. The proverbial noose was tightening about the company's neck. A bankruptcy prediction model, the Oil Score, forecast an ominous future (see chapter 11). The end was in sight.

Miracles do happen, however. In early 1983, short of cash but desperate for a discovery, Kishpaugh ordered his Egyptian team to drill at an abandoned well site. At a depth of almost 6,000 feet, the well flowed crude oil at a rate of approximately 700 barrels per day. Further testing was necessary, but, potentially, this was a major discovery. Ironically, the discovery well was a reentry of a well that had been drilled about a decade earlier by a team from Phillips. Phillips had abandoned the well at a relatively shallow depth.

The average oil well in the United States produces less than twenty barrels per day. If the Khalda #1 well was more than a fluke, "a coke bottle buried in the desert" in the opinion of one skeptic, the company might be saved. Months later, in the fall of 1984, a confirmation well, the Khalda 2x, drilled about a half mile from Khalda #1, flowed 900 barrels per day at a depth of 9,000 feet. The Khalda field was for real. But what other treasures were hidden beneath the desert sands? Seismic studies indicated that as many as eight fields lay beneath the sands of the Khalda Concession. In February 1985, the Salam 2x well was tested and reported a remarkable flow rate of 6,000 barrels per day. It was truly a major discovery. The price of TEI's stock, which began the year at $1.12, moved up dramatically, reaching $6.50 per share and ending the year at $5.75.[1] TEI's equity was the largest percentage gainer of the year on the New York Stock Exchange. More important, the banking community noted these achievements and lessened pressures on management; similarly, the investment banking community became more agreeable to a workout of loan difficulties. A rumor circulated that British Petroleum was considering buying the company to acquire the concession.

The drilling history of the Khalda Concession is outlined in Table 5.1. The map in Figure 5.1 demarcates the field's location. Until a pipeline was built, drilling was exploratory to uncover new fields. There is no need to drill extra holes on a known discovery until production is possible. Later discoveries had less oil, but some, especially Tarek, were major natural gas producers.

Figure 5.1. **Overview of the Khalda Concession**

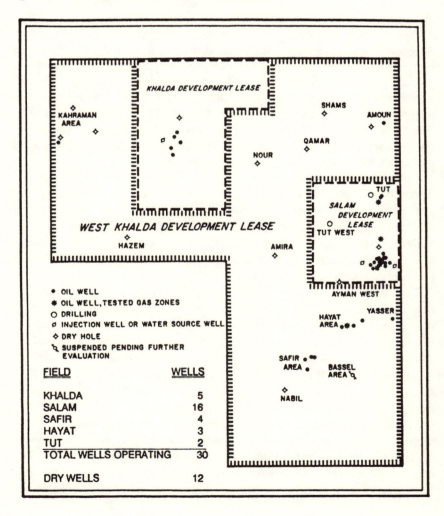

The Khalda Concession

The Khalda Concession was owned by a subsidiary, Phoenix Resources of Egypt. The concession granted exploration rights in the Western Desert of Egypt, about 100 miles east of Libya. Originally the concession included 500,000 acres. Kishpaugh had negotiated the rights to the concession from two private companies, one in the United States and one in Europe, in 1979, while he was chairman of Phoenix Resources.

The Middle East was not unfamiliar turf to TEI. Phoenix had been a participant in a much ballyhooed 40,000-barrels-per-day Israeli oil field in the occupied portion of the Gulf of Suez. Following the Camp David Peace Accord in 1979, the company exchanged this producing property for a one-time payment of $3.3 million, funded by the U.S. government. Nor was TEI alone in the Western Desert. A consulting firm in London had sold a report to many oil and gas producers in late 1982 on the Western Desert's prospects. The report characterized the region as having "major potential as a petroleum province."[2] As a result of TEI's success, a number of major oil companies acquired concessions in Egypt, including Phillips, Conoco, Shell, BP, Petrofina, Amoco, and others. However, it is doubtful that the Phoenix Resources acquisition was instigated to obtain the Khalda Concession. It was an unexpected bonus.

Independent petroleum engineers estimated proven reserves in the Khalda Concession at 882,000 barrels of crude oil at the end of 1984, as seen at the top of Table 5.1. The annual report translated these physical reserves into TEI's discounted future revenue stream ($10.9 million), reflecting the hiatus between discovery and production. Further drilling enhanced the total. Khalda's potential was promising, but a major investment was required to clarify the size of the deposit, to develop a production system, and to bring the product to market.

Kishpaugh's predicament was critical: on the one hand, Egypt was a possible savior; on the other hand, the till was empty. His employment at Phoenix Resources had overlapped the King Resource Company bankruptcy. Undoubtedly, he hoped to avoid those treacherous waters again. Yet somehow he needed to raise about $100 million. The equity market was out of the question: oil prices were at decade lows, and investors had lost interest in oil and gas companies. Management and existing stockholders, too, were reluctant to sell stock at a price 95 percent below its recent $42 high.

Another possibility was to sell the company to a healthy producer with the necessary resources to develop the discovery. In 1985, the book value of total assets equalled $261 million, while total liabilities were $373 million. If the company were sold for 150 percent of book value, $391 million, debt holders would appropriate nearly all the proceeds. Shareholders would receive about $.50 per share. By contrast, if the Khalda Concession were developed and the value of the company increased, shareholders might receive considerable value.[3]

A leveraged buyout (LBO), the current financial fad, also made no sense. In an

Table 5.1

Drilling History of the Khalda Concession

Discovery Well	Field	Date of Discovery	Discovery Flow Rate Oil (barrels/day)	Gas (MMcf/day)	Estimated Proven Reserves Oil (000's B/D)	Gas (MMcf/day)	Estimated Future Net Revenues ($000) (discounted at 10%)	Average Price of Oil/Gas
Abandoned Wepco Well	Khalda	Early 1983	700					
2x Khalda	Khalda	Fall 1984	900					
Total Proven Reserves as of 1984[a]					882	0	$10,888	N/A
Salam 2x	Salam	February 1985	6,000					
Salam 3x	Salam	July 1985	15,000	35				
Total Proven Reserves as of 1985[a]					2,455[b]	0	$32,029	N/A
Hayat #1	Hayat	April 1986	5,000					
N/A	Safir	Late 1986	2,000					
Salam Tut	Tut	Late 1986	1,100	0.2				
Salam North	N. Salam	Late 1986						
North Safir	Safir	Late 1986						
2 Wells	S. Kahraman	Late 1986	<1,000					
Total Proven Reserves as of 1986[a]					8,227	0	$56,266	N/A
Amoun	Amoun	June 1987	4,200	12.5				
Yasser #1	Yasser	June 1987	9,000	13.6				
Tarek #1	Tarek	June 1987	3,000	33.1				

Total Proven Reserves as of 1987[a]	9,638[c]		0	$51,100	$16.26
Various Discoveries, Extensions and Revisions	344[f]	10,642[g]			
Total Proven Reserves as of 1988[a]	8,312[d]		10,642	$30,232	$13.11
Various Discoveries, Extensions and Revisions	120[f]	(1,164)[g]			
Total Proven Reserves as of 1989[a]	5,401[e]		7,350[h]	$37,835	$17.86

Source: TEI 10-K reports, 1983–1988.

[a] For the Khalda Concession as a whole.
[b] Based on production during year of 6,861,000 barrels.
[c] Based on production during year of 1,006,000 barrels.
[d] Based on production during year of 1,670,000 barrels.
[e] Based on production during year of 3,029,000 barrels oil and 2.128 billion CP gas.
[f] Total reserves in thousands of barrels of oil.
[g] Total reserves in millions of CF gas.
[h] After sale of 20% interest to Samsung.

LBO, a small amount of equity is combined with a large level of debt to buy a company. An LBO might revitalize a poorly managed company that had relatively low debt, but TEI was the opposite. Kishpaugh was a good manager in a debt-laden company: long-term debt equalled 123 percent of total capitalization. There was no room for additional leverage and few nonstrategic assets left to sell.

The final option was to participate in a joint venture. In the oil business, when one partner contributes an oil field and the other partner(s) provides money, the transaction is described as a "farm-out." Farm-outs enable companies to minimize exploration and development funds by sharing costs. High-quality projects such as the Khalda Concession are not usually offered to competitors on a farm-out basis. Why would a company share its winners? Kishpaugh had a tricky marketing job. If the potential partner inferred TEI's level of desperation, then the partner would demand an excessive share of total profits. On the other hand, if the concession's potential were not accurately represented so that it appeared to be a typical farm-out, the prospective partner would not be prepared to provide adequate support to develop the concession.

The farm-out concept was broached with other producers in Egypt. (The corporations involved in Egypt's oil production history are discussed in appendix H, "Egyptian Oil and Gas Production History.") Perhaps the strongest selling point was the fact that the Salam 2x well was the first discovery outside of Saudi Arabia to have produced oil from the geologic Jurassic region. Most Middle Eastern structures, including the Khalda field, produce oil from the Cretaceous region, which is closer to the surface than the Jurassic strata, which coincides with the time of dinosaurs and flying reptiles. The Jurassic connection created the prospect that TEI had discovered the next Saudi Arabia. Rumors of a one-billion-barrel field resonated across the Western Desert, through Cairo, and on to Wall Street. Not surprisingly, the possibility of farming out the new Saudi find attracted the attention of every major oil company. Most interested was Conoco, a top-twenty oil major with worldwide interests, and its subsidiary, Conoco Egypt. Conoco was itself owned by E.I. DuPont de Nemours and Company.

A Conoco affiliate, Sahara Petroleum, had explored in the Western Desert between 1954 and 1958 in a region close to the Libyan border; Libya, in fact, was Conoco's dominant international oil interest. Conoco Egypt also held more concession drilling rights in Egypt than any other firm. (Amoco Egypt produced 75 percent of Egypt's total current production at that time.) Conoco had pursued exploration in the Nile Delta, the Sinai Desert, the Gulf of Suez, and southern Egypt. Table 5.2 shows Conoco's Egyptian interests prior to 1982. The Khalda discoveries provided the critical mass to enable Conoco Egypt to be a 50 percent participant in a 110-mile oil pipeline to be built from the Mediterranean seaport of El Alamein to an adjacent concession, Meleiha. The pipeline, with initial capacity of 90,000 barrels per day and the potential to expand to 140,000 barrels per day, was scheduled for construction in early 1986.

Table 5.2

Conoco Egypt's Original Egyptian Interests

Rights Agreement	Estimated Year of Agreement	Acreage/Sq. Miles	Partners	Conoco % Ownership
Northern Region of Nile Delta	1974	3.5 million acres	Agip (Italian)	N/A
Southern Region of Nile Delta	1974	2 million acres	None	100
Southern/Central Region of Egypt	1976	80 million acres	N/A	33
Southern Portion of Nile Delta	1977	126,000 sq. miles	Marathon Agip	25
Sinai Desert Region	1977	890,000 acres	Marathon Hudson's Baya Oil & Gas	53
Southern Egypt—Below W. Desert	1977	N/A	Marathon Shell Winning	33
North of Southern Egypt Concession	1977	22.2 million acres	Marathon Shell Winning	33
Sinai Desert Region	1978	214,000 acres	N/A	N/A
Southern Sinai Desert Peninsula	1980[b]	371,000 acres	None	100
Northern Gulf of Suez	1980	296,500 acres	None	100
Gulf of Suez	1980	12,400 acres	None	100
Mid Gulf of Suez	1981[c]	300,000 acres	N/A	39
Onshore—Gulf of Suez	1981	11,800 acres	N/A	39

Source: International Petroleum Encyclopedia, 1974–1989.

Notes: The Egyptian Petroleum Corporation participates in all ventures.

[a]Hudson Bay Oil & Gas was 53% owned by Conoco.

[b]Egypt represented 15% of Conoco's total net undeveloped acreage, or the largest holding of any one country.

[c]Conoco was forced by concession agreements to relinquish 2.2 million acres, leaving approximately 10 million net undeveloped acres.

TEI was desperate for cash. It sold assets throughout 1984 and into 1985. Confounding the problem was the fact that U.S. oil prices were averaging $4 less than Middle East spot prices and seemed to be trending downward. These financial imperatives should have destroyed TEI's bargaining position in negotiations with Conoco; however, Conoco either overlooked the news or feared losing the prospect to another bidder. In June 1986 the U.S. government inadvertently improved TEI's hand when U.S. foreign policy considerations forced Conoco to drop its lucrative joint venture in Libya. Conoco's one-third ownership of 49 percent of the Oasis oil venture in Libya had occurred subsequent to Colonel Qadaffi's nationalization of foreign oil interests in the late 1960s. Oasis possessed an estimated 305 million barrels of proven reserves, or approximately 33 percent of Conoco's total proven reserves.

Meanwhile, good news continued to pour out of Egypt. Days after TEI's first debt-exchange offer began in June 1985, another well hit big in the Salam field. The Salam 3x well tested at 15,000 barrels per day, or the net equivalent of $9 million annually after adjusting for the Egyptian General Petroleum Corporation's (EGPC) share of production revenues. Most important, it was another find from a Jurassic sandstone structure. The debt-exchange offer was completed in July and August of 1985. At this point, Conoco capitulated and agreed to a farm-out of the Khalda Concession on terms most favorable to TEI.

The terms of the farm-out agreement met virtually all of TEI's critical needs and more. Phoenix of Egypt would take no further risks; Conoco Egypt was now the risk taker. In exchange for a capital funding commitment of at least $150 million, Phoenix Resources gave up half of its interest in the concession. Conoco Egypt was committed to pay all costs attributed to pipelines, airports, roads, employee facilities, and development. Moreover, TEI was reimbursed $18 million for prior expenses by Conoco Egypt, which would collect these funds, without interest, in the future. If additional fields were discovered, other than Khalda or Salam, Conoco Egypt would pay 85 percent and Phoenix Resources 15 percent of exploration and development costs. However, if Phoenix decided that a field was uninteresting after the first wildcat was completed and tested, it had the option to discontinue paying costs and forego future interest in the field. Phoenix would also receive an increasing proportion of oil revenues from the Salam field; after thirty million barrels of cumulative production, Phoenix Resources' share would rise from 50 percent until it reached 75 percent of the contractor's production revenue at seventy million cumulative barrels. In addition, Phoenix Resources received a 10 percent free-carried interest on new concessions that Conoco might receive in Egypt (that is, Conoco was responsible for paying all the bills).

Conoco based its bid on the Khalda Concession's vast potential. Conoco's annual profit share would amount to $33 million if production reached 50,000 barrels per day with oil prices at $20 per barrel, and $115 million per year with production at 100,000 barrels per day at a price of $35 per barrel. In either case, the purchase price would easily be recouped. (Appendix I, "The Khalda Concession Financial Model," uses a computer-based model to simulate Conoco's decision-making process.)

The Concession Agreement

The most common form of concession agreement between international oil and gas companies and host-country governments is the joint venture. The Khalda Petroleum Company was the joint-venture holding company that took responsibility for exploration, development, and production activities in the Khalda Concession. Original participants were the EGPC and Phoenix Resources of Egypt; after the farm-out, Phoenix's shares were split with Conoco. Phoenix Resources of Egypt and Conoco Egypt were known as the contractors or the concessionaires.

Concessions are awarded to enable countries to develop their resources. Concession terms vary depending on risk and greed. If the host country is too greedy, the contractor will not participate; the contractor must be able to recover its investment and earn a profit. Nigeria is perhaps the most generous country, allowing concessionaires up to 40 percent of revenues; on the low side, countries with totally nationalized oil industries like Saudi Arabia permit foreign companies to earn pennies per barrel produced. Nationalization is a risk to the contractor. In the 1960s, Libya, and subsequently other OPEC producers, nationalized its petroleum industries and took a majority share of oil and gas production revenues. A majority of revenues from the Khalda Concession belongs to the Egyptian government.

Provisions in the Khalda Concession for recovering investment dollars were standard: contractors recover exploration, operating, and capital costs out of a "cost-recovery" oil pool. Cost-recovery oil is the first 40 percent of production revenues. Companies are at risk if production is economically too low to recover costs, though under-recovery in one year may be collected out of the next year's cost-recovery oil. After cost recovery, profits are split between the EGPC and the contractors. The EGPC's standard participation was 80 percent of profit oil versus 20 percent for the concessionaires; however, the EGPC agreed to a 75–25 percent split on the Khalda Concession.[4] Egypt agreed to the split because the Western Desert had not been explored for over ten years.

Host governments usually receive a signing bonus when the concession is allocated to an oil company. Governments also receive production bonuses when certain daily production levels are reached. Again, the contractors negotiated a more favorable deal as compared with most of the other Egyptian agreements shown in Table 5.3. For one thing, no production bonus was required; however, similar to BP's Gulf of Suez deal, the share of profit oil would adjust upward by 2.5 percent to a maximum of 85 percent in favor of the EGPC as production escalated. (Appendix J, "Original Khalda Concession Terms," more fully outlines the production sharing agreement.)

Table 5.3

Other Egyptian Production Sharing Agreements

Agreement	Year of Agreement	Private Partners[a]	Acreage (AC) or Sq. Miles (SM)	Total Capital Commitment (Includes Signing Bonus)	Average Cost Per Sq. Mile or Acre	No of Years of Commitment	Production Revenue Split	Production Bonuses
Nile Delta	1974	Mobil	2,355 SM	$13	$5,520	4	80%–20%	N/A
Gulf of Suez	1974	Deminex (W. German)	772 SM	$13	$16,839	8	80%–20%	$9 million total
Gulf of Suez	1980	British Petroleum	700 SM	$9	$12,857	3	80%–20% 83%–17% 85%–15%	80,000–100,000 b/d 100,000–200,000 200,000 or more
Western Desert	1980	Shell	N/A	$23.5	N/A	8	N/A	N/A
Sinai Desert	1977	Conoco, Marathon, Hudson's Bay Oil & Gas	890,000 AC	$27	$30 AC	3	80%–20%	N/A
Western Desert	1984	Shell	2,500 SM	$38	$15,200	8	N/A	$2 / 50,000 b/d $2.5 / 100,000 b/d $5 / 150,000 b/d
Gulf of Suez	1984	Getty, British Petroleum	135 SM	$78	$577,778	7	N/A	N/A
Gulf of Suez	1984	Occidental, Elf Aquitaine (French)	97 SM	$78	$808,290	7	N/A	$4 / 50,000 b/d $6 / 100,000 b/d $8 / 150,000 b/d
Gulf of Suez	1984	Deminex (W. German)	44 SM	$22	$500,000	5	N/A	$4 / 25,000 b/d $6 / 50,000 b/d $8 / 75,000 b/d

Source: International Petroleum Encyclopedia, 1974–1989.
[a]It is assumed that the Egyptian Petroleum Corporation is a partner in all ventures.

During 1986 and 1987, continued drilling successes were reported in the Khalda Concession. At least four more oil fields were discovered. A June 1989 report from the Khalda Petroleum Corporation estimated that the concession contained 79.1 million barrels of proven ultimate oil reserves, 117.8 million barrels in the more generous proven and probable category, with an additional 8.4 and 20.6 million barrels of oil condensates either proven or proven and probable. TEI's share, if all these reserves were produced, would exceed 20 million barrels.

In general, Phoenix Resources of Egypt's share of total revenue was 10 percent free and clear of costs and Egyptian taxes; however, the share would vary depending on oil prices, lifting costs, and flow rates. A computer simulation established an expected range for this share of between 9 percent and 15 percent. With oil at $18 per barrel and production of 20,000 barrels per day, the company would generate approximately $36,000 per day in free cash flow.

The Khalda farm-out yielded further benefits to TEI when the EGPC awarded five new concession rights in the Western Desert to a group led by Conoco in the spring of 1988. Conoco was to operate the concessions for affiliates of two foreign producers, Norsk Hydro of Norway and Oranje Nassau. As specified in the farm-out agreement, Conoco bestowed a free-carried interest in these concessions on Phoenix Resources of Egypt: 6.5 percent in four concessions and 10 percent in a fifth concession. As shown in Figure 5.2, the concessions are large and spread out across the Western Desert. Conoco paid Phoenix's share of the signing bonuses and exploration costs and would recover those costs through cost-recovery oil and gas. TEI now had interests in over 3.3 million gross acres in the Western Desert.

Long-term prospects did little to ameliorate TEI's immediate troubles. Following the sale of Eloi Bay in March 1987, the Khalda Concession represented 85 percent of TEI's proven reserves and was virtually its only source of revenues. Egyptian production expanded in three years from a trickle (at first, trucks carried oil to the coast) to a respectable level of 20,000 barrels per day worth $15 million per year to TEI. Despite hopes that Egyptian production would continue to grow, it stagnated at that level. When oil prices weakened, TEI's cash position became precarious.

The downturn hit Egypt hard, too. Egyptian oil production peaked at 930,000 barrels per day in 1986, as seen in Figure 5.3. Thus, each 1 percent decline in world oil prices reduced Egyptian oil export revenues by a similar amount. Oil revenues help deflect the feeling of desperation arising from abject poverty and an inequitable income distribution, which creates political instability in Egypt. Hence, falling oil export revenues are tantamount to a national crisis. In 1987, Egypt kindled a fresh strategy to increase oil exports. The plan was simple but astute: substitute domestic gas production, which was then being flared (burned) in the atmosphere, for crude oil burned in domestic consumption. The concessionaires were ordered to desist from additional flaring of natural gas. According

Figure 5.2. **Areas of Egyptian Interests**

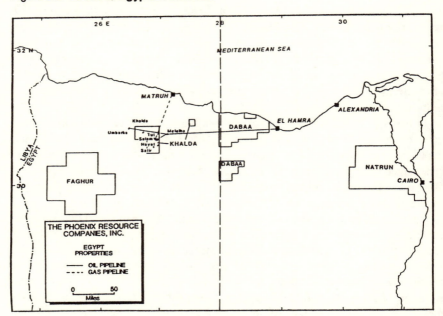

to the concession agreement, all natural gas belonged to Egypt. Although the concession did not require the contractors to gather natural gas, it similarly did not authorize them to waste natural gas. The cost of developing a natural gas infrastructure at Khalda was not inconsequential, and naturally the concession-aires balked at bearing these costs without compensation. Meanwhile, since the oil and gas reserves were contiguous, oil production could not be increased. TEI was caught between the wood (Egypt) and the bark (Conoco), and watched helplessly as its lifeblood drained away.

The Egyptian strategy treated natural gas flaring as an economic waste, since gas flared one day would be unavailable to promote Egyptian development the next. When Conoco did not buckle, the EGPC turned up the pressure and ordered the concessionaires to: (a) stop producing oil from wells with significant gas flows, (b) halt production from existing viable wells, and (c) discontinue further exploratory testing. Most of the exciting prospects in the deeper Jurassic region were prone to gas and were put on hold.

Bilateral negotiations began in late 1987. One tentative plan was for the concessionaires to build a $17 million, fifty-mile pipeline and processing facility (gas separation and distribution) for separating gas from oil. On Egypt's part, it would build a natural-gas–fueled electricity-generating plant in Matruh (see Figure 5.2) and guarantee purchase of the gas. More important, a natural gas agreement, called the Gas Clause, would be appended to the concession agreement.

Figure 5.3. **Egyptian Oil, Production, and Proven Reserves Growth**

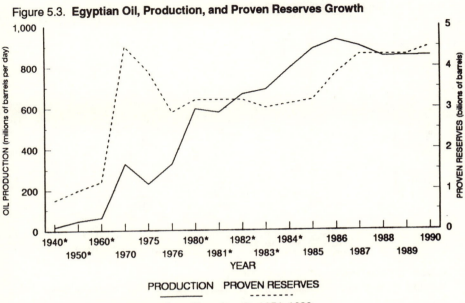

Source: *International Petroleum Encyclopedia* 1974–1989.

* Estimates for proven reserves.

Concessionaires would realize a percentage of natural gas revenues that was comparable with the oil split, and natural gas would be priced at a 15 percent discount from oil on a Btu basis.

Conoco's decision to extend the gas clause negotiations for nearly one and a half years probably was economically justified, but certain Wall Street analysts argued that Conoco was punishing TEI for outmaneuvering it at the negotiating table. Others wondered if Conoco planned to acquire TEI after forcing it into bankruptcy. Like the Russian proverb, it was said, "If you sit down to eat with a bear, some day you will be dinner."

Negotiations with the EGPC to amend the concession agreement with a gas clause took eighteen months. Meanwhile, production remained at 20,000 barrels per day. Cash flows from these restricted operations were insufficient to cover debt service requirements. TEI filed for bankruptcy on April 26, 1988. Its subsidiary, Phoenix Resources of Egypt, did not file for bankruptcy protection, as such a filing might have returned the concession to Egypt.

Conoco's Perspective on the Deal

Hydrocarbon reserves in the United States were plummeting. Conoco was in worse shape than other major oil companies. In the two decades since 1969, as seen in Figure 5.4, Conoco's oil reserves fell from more than three billion barrels

Figure 5.4. **Conoco's Declining Oil Reserves**

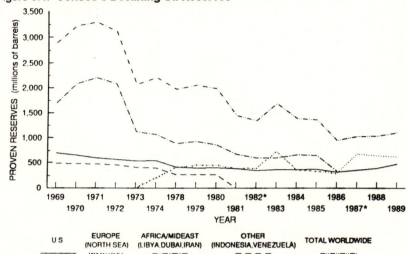

Source: Conoco 10-K reports for years listed.

*In 1982 "Other" was incorporated into "Africa/Mideast"; in 1987 "Africa/Mideast" and Europe became "non-U.S."

Figure 5.5. **Conoco's Declining Natural Gas Reserves**

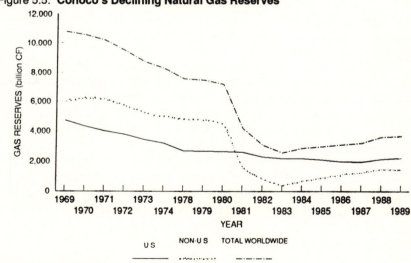

Source: Conoco 10-K reports for years listed.

to less than one billion barrels, and its natural gas reserves went from 11,000 Bcf to 4,000 Bcf, as seen in Figure 5.5. With its declining production and reserves (see Figure 5.6), Conoco was a dinosaur.

Figure 5.6. **Conoco's Declining Oil Production**

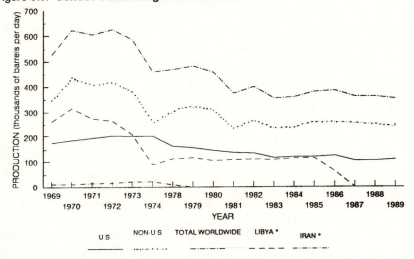

Source: Conoco 10-K reports for years listed.

*From 1974 through 1978, Conoco purchased approximately 50% of its Libyan production and purchased from Iran 100% of its production.

Figure 5.7. **Replacement Ratios for Conoco, Majors, TEI, and Independents**

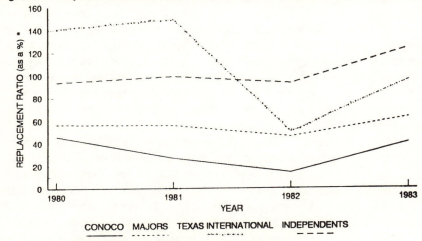

Source: Arthur Andersen Co., *Oil & Gas Reserve Disclosures.*

*Replacement ratio = additions divided by production

The last major international oil discovery, the English sector of the North Sea, occurred in the early 1970s.[5] Conoco, like the other majors, struggled to find enough new reserves to replace production.[6] The majors experienced a ratio of new reserve discovery to production (known as the replacement ratio) in 1977 equal to 67 percent; in 1978 it equalled 43 percent; and in 1980 it equalled only 30 percent. Figure 5.7 contains replacement ratios for Conoco, TEI, the majors, and the independents. When the replacement ratio is less than one, a company is being liquidated, since production exceeds reserve acquisition. Conoco's ratio averaged about 35 percent. One consulting firm estimated Conoco's proven reserves' depletion life at a low 6.7 years.[7] Oil and gas operations accounted for nearly 80 percent of Conoco's profits in 1980.

The cheapest way to acquire oil reserves was to buy another oil company on Wall Street. Reserves bought this way cost $4 to $8 per barrel of oil. In contrast, reserves bought from companies selling proven fields commanded up to $12 per barrel. Wall Street acquisition costs were economical compared with the cost of finding new oil. The cost of procuring pristine acreage, exploring, and developing new reserves averaged $11 and $15 per barrel of oil equivalent for foreign and U.S. discoveries, respectively.[8]

Several major oil companies were acquired on Wall Street, including Gulf Oil and Conoco. The Conoco acquisition occurred in August 1981 and involved E.I. DuPont de Nemours and Co., one of the largest chemical companies in the world. DuPont paid $7.8 billion in a hard-fought take-over battle. The conflict kicked off in May 1981 when a large Canadian oil producer, Dome Petroleum, tendered for 20 percent of Conoco at $65 per share, which was a 33 percent premium to the stock price prior to the offer. Spurred by new Canadian government policies for subsidizing domestic companies' exploration costs, Dome intended to swap the Conoco shares for Conoco's 51 percent ownership of another Canadian independent oil company, Hudson Bay Oil and Gas Company (which coincidentally was exploring in the Western Desert of Egypt). Dome's offer was so generous that 50 percent of Conoco shareholders tendered their shares.

The offer put Conoco "in play" and precipitated a secret proposal for a 20 percent ownership by Seagram, another Canadian firm, which had recently disposed of its U.S. oil interests for approximately $2 billion. Conoco, over a month later, publicly disclosed the Seagram offer and further divulged that it had been negotiating a merger with another large major oil firm, Cities Service. Combined, the firms would be the seventh largest U.S. oil firm. Negotiations with Cities Service dissolved; Conoco sued Seagram to inhibit its offer; and then DuPont joined the bidding war as a "white knight." Texaco also expressed a mild interest in Conoco. DuPont's winning bid of $98 per share, comprising both cash and DuPont shares, was eclipsed by a bid from Mobil that began at just over $100 per share and finally reached $120. Mobil's bid was unsuccessful, however, because investors feared an antitrust lawsuit, because of mistrust of Mobil's intentions for Conoco, and because of possible misunderstanding by investment bankers.

Seagram ended up a 25 percent owner of DuPont because of the large number of Conoco shares it owned and then tendered to DuPont. Seagram's owners, the

Bronfman family, negotiated an agreement with DuPont by which it would seat three Seagram officers on the DuPont board. Since 1981, Seagram's earnings have included DuPont dividends; in 1988, they accounted for 70 percent of earnings. The Bronfmans, however, have agreed to limit their DuPont ownership to less than 25 percent and to remain uninvolved in day-to-day operations of DuPont.

An oil company acquisition had strategic value for DuPont, since it provided a hedge against future volatility in oil and gas pricing and would ensure a reliable supply of feed stock for its chemical production. Hydrocarbons are a key input in fabricating chemicals. DuPont had earlier participated in two gas exploration joint ventures with Conoco. Despite the stratospheric purchase price, the payment translated into a price of only $6 per barrel of oil equivalent cost. However, DuPont's long-term debt increased sixfold to $6.4 billion, and annual interest costs increased fivefold to over $500 million. Wall Street expected DuPont to relieve this heavy debt burden by selling off major Conoco oil fields; yet by late 1982, only 15 percent and 7 percent of Conoco's U.S. oil and gas production, respectively, were divested.

Conoco's hydrocarbon reserves continued to shrink. As seen in Figure 5.8, over the period 1980–1983, Conoco's reserves declined in both 1982 and 1983, TEI's reserves *grew* until the asset sale in 1983, major oil companies had reserve growth of about 5 percent, and the independents held steady. Yet the interest expense resulting from the acquisition of Conoco caused a financial burden at DuPont. How to contain the exploration budget and production costs became critical management issues at Conoco. Fields with high exploration costs, such as

Figure 5.8. **Proven Oil Reserves for Conoco, Majors, TEI, and Independents**

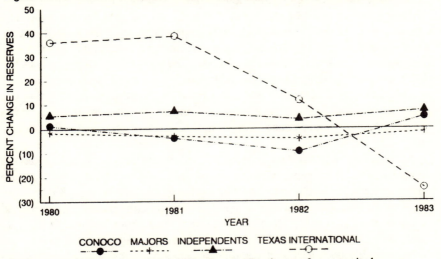

Source: Arthur Andersen Co., *Oil & Gas Reserve Disclosures* for years cited.

the North Sea, could be economically justified only if geologic data indicated the strong likelihood of a major oil discovery. As 1984 began, the president of petroleum operations at Conoco, Constantine S. Nicandros, spoke of his orientation toward frontier search, deep-water exploration, and broader international operations.[9] He stated that Conoco would be looking for new plays, so that it could diversify the areas in which it operates.[10] Egypt's Western Desert gained strategic importance in this diversification plan.

Exploration Strategy

Historically, in the search for new reserves, drilling has been the economic choice, as compared with purchasing reserves. However, these relative positions reversed during the 1980s. Companies worked to control their exploration costs. Conoco cut its finding costs from $17 per barrel of oil equivalent (BOE) in 1980 to $7 BOE in 1983; by 1986, cost had climbed back to $10 BOE. Median acquisition costs for purchased reserves ranged from $6 to $7 BOE in 1985.[11]

Oil companies budget the risk they will tolerate in exploration and development activities. Conoco's conservative management usually minimized risk exposure by participating in joint ventures. Joint ventures spread a company's drilling funds across a portfolio of opportunities and increase the probability of achieving some success. Joint ventures also enable firms to expeditiously gain entry into top exploration regions and facilitate the acquisitions of strategic geological information. While a prudent policy (given that a single exploratory well in the North Sea might have capital investment costs in excess of $100 million), it inhibited Conoco's search for new reserves, since copartners had to be persuaded to invest or to allow Conoco into the partnership.

Joint ventures reduce country risk. Country risk includes escalating production and profit-sharing allocations to host governments and total nationalization. Most countries except the United States treat onshore, in-terra mineral rights as government property. Private firms, under government guidance, operate oil fields and participate in the profits. Drilling in foreign lands, as demonstrated by the majors' experience with OPEC, can backfire. As soon as OPEC countries achieved technological independence from the majors, the majors were compelled to become junior concession partners (at best) or to abandon the concession.

Nationalization is not a major risk in Egypt; foreign expertise and capital are needed, since oil revenues nurture the entire economy. Oil exports compose approximately 25–30 percent of foreign exchange income and 10–15 percent of government revenue.[12] In addition, Egypt's burgeoning population is forecasted to cause energy consumption to grow by 3 percent annually through the year 2000. Without the capital of foreign oil producers, Egyptian oil production would possibly decline. Egypt instituted an open-door policy to attract foreign exploration firms and to lift the odds of discovering new oil and gas reserves.

Figure 5.9 **Active Drilling Rigs in Egypt**

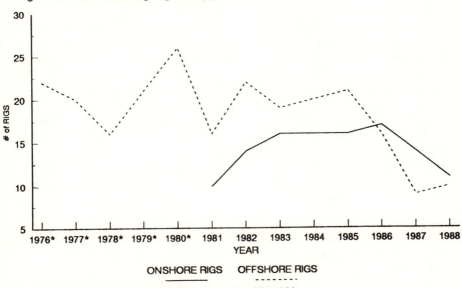

Source: *International Petroleum Encyclopedia* 1974-1989.
*Majority of drilling is off shore.

The Khalda Concession

The initial reaction to the Conoco/TEI transaction was favorable. After reviewing the Salam field's geology and reported flow rates, industry analysts concluded that the field would eventually yield 500–800 million barrels in proven reserves.[13] Conoco's net-of-cost revenue potential was $4.7 billion, using unescalated oil prices. Wall Street percolated with rumors that adjacent concessions (operated by Conoco, Amoco, and Phillips Petroleum) would cooperate to build a 300,000-barrel-per-day pipeline that would suggest combined reserves of 3 billion barrels or more. Conoco probably expected to have 35,000–40,000 barrels per day of production by 1988 and in anticipation boosted drilling capacity on the concession to six rigs.[14] In all of Egypt, fourteen onshore drilling rigs were working in 1988. As seen in Figure 5.9, drilling in Egypt had historically favored offshore sites. The Khalda Concession changed that relationship.

DuPont's 1986 and 1987 annual reports both mention the Khalda Concession as one of Conoco's key exploration options. A further sign of Conoco's confidence in the concession was its agreement permitting TEI to borrow $20 million from an affiliate of the World Bank (the International Finance Corporation or IFC), secured by Phoenix's interests in the Khalda Concession. The loan covenants required Phoenix to commit 20 percent of Khalda's cash flow to repayment. If the cash flow was insufficient, the IFC could readjust the cash-flow percentage. Furthermore, if TEI or Phoenix of Egypt went bankrupt or was liquidated, the loan was immediately due in full.

Optimistic revenue estimates implied a robust return on Conoco's $150 million capital investment in Khalda Petroleum. This sanguine outlook and oil prices both faded in 1987. Low oil prices retarded Conoco's worldwide operating margin (see Table 5.4), which strained its ability to cover costs. A second and more critical problem arose when the EGPC restricted the amount of gas that could be flared from the concession. The EGPC wanted Conoco to build a natural gas pipeline to help Egypt substitute natural gas for oil. EGPC escalated the pressure, for a time, when it failed to renew the lifting agreement that authorized Conoco to export oil on outbound ships. In other words, the concessionaires could produce oil in Egypt, but they could not ship it out. It was inconceivable to many that Conoco, an international oil company with significant worldwide experience, had failed to anticipate this catch–22 predicament.

Table 5.4

Conoco's Operating Margins for Oil Exploration and Production
(in $ millions)

	1986	1987	1988	1989
Revenue	2,828	2,829	2,564	2,936
Operating Profit (before taxes)	389	111	29	178
Operating Margin	13.8%	3.9%	1.1%	6.1%

Source: Conoco 10-K reports, 1986–1989.

It is possible that Conoco was aware of the EGPC's desperation but was willing to sacrifice oil production because it grasped that Khalda was a gas field more than an oil field. As concession operator, Conoco had a unique vantage point to assess the true characteristics of the Khalda's probable and proven reserves. Moreover, Conoco should have been aware of the EGPC's stated position on gas production. In December 1984 the Egyptian oil minister, Abdel Hadi Kandil, publicly disclosed that negotiations to change the current gas rules were taking place. At the time, both Shell Winning (a subsidiary of Royal Dutch/ Shell) and GUPCO (a joint venture between Amoco and the EGPC) had discovered large, mostly gas deposits in two wells in the Western Desert and were busily negotiating new gas clauses.

Conoco was the largest holder of concession rights in Egypt and more than any other company should have understood the concession's terms. It may have assumed that it possessed more leverage with the oil ministry or the Egyptian parliament than in fact was true. Evidence existed to the contrary, however: Khalda Concession crude is "sweet," which makes it more valuable in the refining process and on world markets; yet Egypt had agreed to pay only a few cents more than the rate paid on inferior Gulf of Suez crude.

A final possibility was that Conoco hoped to force TEI out of the concession by delaying the gas negotiations. Conoco would then gain Phoenix Resources' ownership share through default. Perhaps Conoco hoped to persuade the EGPC to force Phoenix to give up the concession because of financial insolvency. TEI did file for bankruptcy, but its subsidiary Phoenix of Egypt did not.

Regardless of Conoco's intentions, the realization that Khalda was mostly a natural gas find and not an immense oil field must have come as a terrible shock. Approximately 10 percent of its 1984 annual $1 billion worldwide exploration budget (see Figure 5.10) had been expended to discover natural gas owned by someone else. Moreover, gas was cheaper than oil on a Btu basis and always had been. It was alleged that the Conoco executive who had negotiated the Khalda deal lost his job.

Figure 5.10. **Conoco's Worldwide Exploration Expenditures**

Source: Conoco 10-K reports.

Conoco's parent corporation, DuPont, was distressed. It was earning about 10 percent annually after tax on its initial $7.8 billion investment in Conoco. Its own return on equity was hovering near 15 percent. DuPont's shares traded below the industry average price-earnings multiple. Industry analysts argued that shareholder value could be increased if DuPont sold off Conoco, or sold off Conoco assets, or spun off Conoco to shareholders as a separately traded company. Unfortunately, industry conditions were not conducive to selling oil assets. DuPont placed intense pressure on Conoco's management to amplify investment returns.[15]

In 1990 Conoco gave up: it sold its interest in the Khalda Concession to Repsol, a Spanish oil company whose principal owner is the government of

Table 5.5

Capital Investment Analysis for Conoco—The Khalda Concession
(in $ millions)

		Future Value of Cash Flows		
	Unadjusted Cash Flow	Conservative Return at 15%	DuPont's Desired Return at 20%	High-Risk Return at 25%
1986				
Profit Oil	0	0	0	0
Cost-Recovery Oil[a]	0	0	0	0
Capital Investment	(107,000)	(215,215)	(266,250)	(326,538)
1987[b]				
Profit Oil	7,690	13,450	15,946	18,774
Cost-Recovery Oil	23,901	41,803	49,561	58,352
Capital Investment	(75,000)	(131,175)	(155,520)	(183,105)
1988				
Profit Oil	6,866	10,442	11,864	13,410
Cost-Recovery Oil	44,854	68,217	77,508	87,605
Capital Investment	(15,000)	(22,813)	(25,920)	(29,297)
1989				
Profit Oil	9,019	11,928	12,987	14,092
Cost-Recovery Oil	54,586	72,190	78,604	85,291
Capital Investment	(42,000)	(55,545)	(60,480)	(65,625)
1990				
Profit Oil	13,324	15,323	15,989	16,655
Cost-Recovery Oil	73,788	84,856	88,546	92,235
Capital Investment	(40,000)	(46,000)	(48,000)	(50,000)
Total Profit Oil	36,899	51,142	56,787	62,932
Total Cost-Recovery Oil	197,129	267,067	294,218	323,483
Total Capital Investment	(279,000)	(470,749)	(556,170)	(654,565)
1991				
Sale of Concession Interest to Repsol, a Spanish Company[c]	150,000	150,000	150,000	150,000
Net Cash Flows	105,028	(2,540)	(55,165)	(118,151)

Notes: This analysis is an estimate of how Conoco's management might have analyzed the investment in the concession. All cash-flow future values are as of the end of each year, except for Repsol sale. All data is based on the Khalda Concession finance model in appendix I.

[a] Cost recovery oil is equivalent to return of capital for Conoco.

[b] 1987 is only for two quarters of production.

[c] The sale is based on a Wall Street analyst's estimate.

Spain. In the final analysis, the Khalda Concession was probably not a good investment for Conoco. Repsol purchased the Khalda interests and Conoco's other Western Desert interests for $180 million; one knowledgeable industry analyst estimated that of the total, $150 million was allotted to the purchase of Khalda. Using this figure, it is possible to calculate that on an undiscounted cash-flow basis Conoco more than recovered its initial investment, as seen in Table 5.5. If future cash flows are discounted at a 15 percent rate, Conoco breaks even; thus, its internal rate of return was about 15 percent. Again, Kishpaugh's skills at the negotiating table proved to be critical in the final analysis.

Conoco, however, remained desperate for oil and gas reserves to feed its refineries and DuPont's petrochemical plants. It expanded exploration in the Dutch sector of the North Sea and, in early 1990, discovered a potentially large field in Indonesia. The discovery well flowed 12,300 barrels and 61.6 million cubic feet per day, or an average of six times the accepted standard for a major offshore field.[16] This discovery may have finalized Conoco's decision to divest its interests in the Khalda.

Notes

1. Nothing having to do with TEI could occur without some degree of controversy. Years later the SEC accused two individuals who were employed by the drilling company hired by TEI, Schlumberge, of trading on insider information: data they obtained at the well site. Their alleged insider profit amounted to less than $15,000.

2. David Buckman, "Egypt: Western Desert Leads Oil Search," p. 443.

3. This point is made in a recent journal article that describes equity holders' tendency to over-invest when they have little to lose. See Robert Gertner and David Scharfstein, "A Theory of Workouts and the Effects of Reorganization Law.

4. Med-Corp Petroleum S.A., incorporated in London, and Anta Corp, a private U.S. company, agreed to pass the concession on to Phoenix in exchange for a 3 percent overriding interest in any oil profits made by the contractors. Phoenix also had to pay several hundred thousand dollars of back costs.

5. The Dutch began to produce natural gas out of the North Sea in the late 1950s.

6. New reserves include additions and revisions to old fields, additions based on new field discoveries and net purchases.

7. Charles J. Ella, "Major Oil Stocks Seen Losing Sheen Yielding Only Average Market Gains Over Next 2 Years," p. 47.

8. Arthur Andersen & Co., *Oil & Gas Reserve Disclosures: Survey of 375 Public Companies 1980–1983*, pp. 26–27.

9. On December 3, 1991, Nicandros was named one of two DuPont vice-chairmen.

10. Marcia A. Parker, "Nicandros: Industry's Changes Spawn Need for New Approach," p. 140.

11. *Oil & Gas Journal*, "Prices for Reserve Purchases on the Upswing," p. 46.

12. Nazli Choucri, Christopher Heye, and Michael Lynch, "Analyzing Oil Production in Developing Countries: A Case Study of Egypt (using dynamic computer simulation, Egyptian Petroleum Model)," pp. 91–115.

13. A report provided in confidence to the author by an investment banker specializing in U.S. petroleum companies.

14. Conoco drilled only sixteen gross wells on international properties that year.

15. Roger Lowenstein, "Close Watchers of DuPont Prefer a Spinoff of Disappointing Conoco to Selling Its Assets," p. C–2.

16. James Tanner, "DuPont's Conoco Discovers Oil, Gas off of Indonesia," p. A–13.

Part III
Death and Rebirth

6

Three Exchange Offers

Background

As 1985 began, TEI was in a precarious position. An unsuccessful exploration program had squandered several hundred million dollars of borrowed money, and the obligation of meeting interest and principal repayment was retarded by a dwindling supply of free cash flow. In the previous three years, TEI had lost $198 million, $138 million of the loss resulting from dry-hole costs. The retained earnings deficit of $240 million meant that, since its inception, the company had cumulatively lost more money than it had earned. Table 6.1 presents an income statement and a balance sheet for the period 1981–1987.

Few firms can afford interest payments equivalent to 35 percent of their revenues, in TEI's case a whopping $43 million in 1984. By comparison, interest expense was only 26 percent and 14 percent of revenues, two and four years earlier, respectively. The interest burden paralleled the extraordinary growth in leverage. Long-term debt grew from $79 million in 1979 to $387 million in 1982. As if the interest burden was not enough, a disheartening reserve report issued at the end of 1983 by independent petroleum engineers had forced a downward adjustment in natural gas reserves attributed to two major natural gas fields: the Connorsville field in Canada and the deep Eloi Bay field in Louisiana. Nearly $190 million of corporate value vanished. Wall Street was bewildered, and TEI's stock plummeted nearly 50 percent in 1983 and a further 60 percent during the first quarter of 1984. Moreover, the revenue outlook for 1985 was dismal.[1]

Falling oil prices and production precipitated a 24 percent decline in revenues from 1982 to 1984, and it was unlikely that either factor would ameliorate soon. The variance report in Table 6.2 breaks out the sources of the revenue shortfall.[2] The two principal negative variance components were the volume of natural gas sales and oil prices, with the former accounting for $25 million in lost revenue compared with 1982. Natural gas prices had a positive variance, indicating that the company received a higher price for gas in 1984 than in 1982.

Table 6.1

TEI Income Statement and Balance Sheet (in $ thousands)

	1981[a]	1982[a]	1983	1984	1985	1986	1987
TEI Income Statement							
Operating Revenue	142,238	166,667	121,442	126,140	95,619	56,777	16,632
Other Revenue	4,794	11,977	15,751	14,133	11,231	6,940	19,292
Total Revenues	147,032	178,644	137,193	140,273	106,850	63,717	35,924
Cost of Goods Sold	45,821	74,803	47,853	38,000	28,863	20,469	11,267
Exploration	45,080	51,805	64,982	21,668	11,845	2,156	5,581
Depreciation, Depletion, and Amortization	26,784	50,360	39,517	37,467	32,881	29,876	2,850
General and Administrative	36,858	25,378	26,117	20,703	18,563	14,902	10,486
Interest	29,248	44,076	44,567	43,870	44,515	45,789	26,652
Total Expenses	183,791	246,422	223,036	161,708	136,667	113,192	56,836
Operating Income (loss)	(37,096)	(69,169)	(86,430)	(23,274)	(32,306)	(51,607)	(44,737)
Net Income (loss)	(42,840)	(76,556)	(99,680)	(21,959)	(31,881)	(50,798)	(44,222)
TEI Balance Sheet							
Current Assets	138,114	136,860	67,190	55,570	64,275	154,862	21,378
Long-Term Assets	284,047	337,964	276,056	240,581	196,947	40,837	27,288
Total Assets	422,161	474,824	343,246	296,151	261,222	195,699	48,666
Current Liabilities	127,389	83,196	65,151	84,197	49,885	131,963	162,923
Long-Term Debt	260,408	387,033	350,032	307,242	322,726	193,013	22,745
Equity	31,145	(6,810)	(95,389)	(119,097)	(114,725)	(132,561)	(143,172)

Source: TEI annual reports, 1981–1987.

[a]Restated by company to reflect change in accounting method.

Table 6.2

Variance in 1984 Revenues
(in $ thousands; decreases in 1984 shown in parentheses)

	1984–1983	1984–1982
Crude Oil and Condensate		
Prices	(1,593)	(7,562)
Sales Volume	17,275	(659)
Natural Gas		
Prices	0	2,574
Sales Volume	(6,525)	(25,128)
FERC Order No. 94	547	547
Plant Product Revenues	(398)	(1,469)
Net Trading Revenues	(2,365)	(4,367)
Other Operating Revenues	(2,243)	(4,463)
Total Operating Reveneus	4,698	(40,527)

Source: TEI annual reports, 1982–1984.

Another complication was the large amount of bank debt, in excess of $250 million. Banks have a poor record of discriminating between good and bad credits, for example, third world loans, real estate loans, and energy loans. On the other hand, banks excel at forcing creditors to secure their indebtedness with their assets. Secured lenders are better protected in bankruptcy provided that the value of the assets at least equals the indebtedness. TEI's bankers imposed additional covenants restricting management prerogatives. Moreover, whenever assets were sold, the proceeds were appropriated by the banks.

At every opportunity, long-term debt was substituted for bank debt. The bankers objected to this strategy in July 1983, arguing that the high implicit interest paid on the zero-coupon senior-subordinated notes weakened the firm and threatened their loan. Kishpaugh was told that the banks "looked at the zero as a cash payment coming in front of us." He was told, "Fix the zero or we call the loans." Paying a $12.5 million premium, the zeros were repurchased. A *Barrons* article that erroneously faulted TEI because the zero-coupon notes paid compound interest on unpaid implicit interest was another catalyst for the repurchase. Regardless of the rationale, the transaction's timing was ill-fated, since irreplaceable cash (the company had raised $150 million in 1983 by issuing the 13⅛ percent senior-subordinated notes and the 9 percent oil-indexed notes) was depleted, and, more detrimentally, the action converted a *noncash* interest obligation into a *cash* interest obligation.

Much needed cash was raised by selling off assets in 1984 and 1985. The principal sale included all U.S. oil and gas assets for $110 million to Total Petroleum. The sale succeeded at a time when oil properties were white elephants on the market. Additionally, a "supplier-equity" financing program with companies like Baker Hughes enabled Kishpaugh to issue equity in a market that would not accept equity. With these supplies, production was tripled in the Eloi Bay. The program provided double benefits of issuing equity and dressing up assets for sale to reduce debts.

The reserve reduction and anxiety about the company's ability to meet required interest and principal payments made 1985 a bellwether year. TEI was restricted from the capital markets. A plan was needed that would clarify how its debts would be repaid. Some of the debt would have to be exchanged for equity, or survival would be impossible.

Section 3(A)9 of the 1933 Securities Act permits companies to exchange new securities for old securities without subjecting the new instruments to an SEC registration. Registration is costly and time consuming and particularly valuable to new investors. But exchange offers are not directed at new investors. The drawback of a section 3(A)9 exchange is that it is conducted by the firm without the assistance of an underwriting firm.

The 1985 Exchange

Overview

Oil prices had fallen for several years, but at $26 per barrel a profit could be earned producing oil virtually anywhere in the world.[3] Kishpaugh had ample material to craft an exchange offer. He prepared a plan to salvage the company based on *expected* output and cash flows.

Discussion

The problem was unambiguous: too much indebtedness requiring too much interest.[4] Unhappily, debt is easier to originate than to terminate. Some of TEI's debts were the worst kind: bank debt with strict covenants secured by *all* of the company's assets. These assets were worth more than the bank loan. Thus, the bank had no incentive to cooperate with management and insisted on full repayment.

In stage one of crisis management, companies raise cash by selling off nonessential assets. Two jet planes, the cemeteries, oil and gas manufacturing enterprises, and numerous parcels of real estate were sold. Monies raised mostly went to the bank, but not enough was raised.

In stage two of wrestling with a crisis, corporations at last confront the real problem: in this case, the debt level. A common remedy to an unmanageable debt level is to seek protection from creditors in the bankruptcy court. However, in the best TEI tradition, a road less traveled was taken: the existing debt would be restructured. In a debt restructuring, new securities are exchanged for older securities. By the 1990s, debt restructurings had become a panacea for troubled enterprises, but in 1985 they were unusual if not unknown. The top of Table 6.3 delineates TEI's indebtedness. The $192.5 million of junk bonds outstanding had face (par) values of $205.6 million; the other notes either had not been issued or had been redeemed. Bank debt was down to $110 million (senior secured debt less current long-term debt), paying 15 percent interest.

The 11½ percent subordinated debentures were the first junk bonds. These were widely held and publicly traded on the New York Bond Exchange. The 8¼ percent convertibles, also called the Euro-converts, had originally been issued as a $30 million tranche, but most had been redeemed due to an expensive "put" provision. The 9 percent and 13⅛ percent senior notes were institutionally held.

The Trust Indenture Act of 1939 precludes companies from adjusting the principal, interest, or maturity of debt without unanimous consent of debt holders. However, debt that has been sold to the public may have hundreds if not thousands of owners, making unanimous consent a near impossibility. For that reason, troubled companies must exchange new debt instruments rather than attempt to induce an entire class of holders to voluntarily agree to a change in terms.

The key to a debt restructuring is to perceive the needs of bond owners. Investors, especially the large institutions that held the majority of TEI's securities, are focused on several common bond characteristics: risk, return, seniority, and maturity. In crafting a restructuring plan, it is necessary to compare the old and new bonds along this four-dimensional array, since a restructuring is a voluntary and not a mandatory act. If the new security is more desirable than the old security, holders may agree to the exchange. The desirability of a bond might be enhanced by upgrading all of its characteristics or just a subset, depending on the needs of bond holders.

Bond safety, defined as the risk of default, might be the foremost concern of investors. Ratings agencies such as Standard and Poors and Moodys assign risk gradients to assist investors in comparing various companies. Across the set of bonds issued by a single company, default risk is equal, but secured bonds have lower price risk than unsecured bonds, since they are guaranteed by a specific physical asset. The agencies classified all of TEI's debt securities as junk bonds. Hence, investors understood that the securities had a relatively high default risk.

A second bond characteristic is income or percentage return on investment. TEI's bonds always paid significantly higher interest levels to investors in order to compensate them for the higher default risk. Another concern is a bond's seniority, which clarifies its relative position versus other bonds in case of a bankruptcy or liquidation. A final concern is maturity date, which specifies when a bond will be redeemed.

To avoid bankruptcy, TEI needed relief from the cash interest paid to bond holders. The $192.5 million of outstanding junk bonds required $23.9 million of annual cash interest. Interest of $20 million was due to the banks and the Trust Company of the West. Bond holders accept lower interest on safer bonds, but, decidedly, a less risky TEI could not be fabricated at this stage. Instead, management conceived of a new type of subordinated bond, which paid interest in cash or shares of common stock. If cash was sparse, interest would be paid in stock;

otherwise, cash would be paid to avoid diluting (i.e., changing the ownership of) the common stock.[5] Acceptance of the new type of bond was encouraged by these additional characteristics:

(a) earlier maturity dates,
(b) higher stated interest levels,
(c) seniority relative to nonexchanged notes, and
(d) ownership of several shares of common stock.

Bond holders accepting the exchange received a new security that would return their investment dollars sooner, pay more interest, and be senior to older securities. The proffered shares of common stock were sweeteners intended to assure acceptance. The equity was trading for about $2 per share. With the 13⅛ percent notes, for example, the bonus stock was equivalent to receiving almost six months' cash interest. Presumably, all the stock received by exchanging bond holders was immediately sold.

Some securities have contractual provisions inhibiting the issuance of new securities with higher seniority. This clause protects the bond holder's investment against devaluation in a liquidation or bankruptcy. Junk bonds, which are the junior-most security anyway, lack this protection. Hence, the company was not constrained from endowing the new securities with seniority above the older securities.

It was announced that a precondition for completion of the exchange offer was that at least 85 percent of the public debt be tendered. Bankruptcy was the unspoken alternative. (Institutional investors prefer out-of-court workouts to bankruptcy, because professionals such as lawyers or accountants engaged on a bankruptcy case may earn fees equal to 10 percent of the value of the company.) There were several reasons for imposing an 85 percent acceptance level. First, the company needed to substantially reduce its interest and principal payments. At less than 85 percent participation, the firm would remain in financial peril. Second, at an 85 percent participation rate, no major holder could act as a "free rider." A free rider refuses to tender but still benefits from a successful exchange, since the company is strengthened.

Consider the case of the 9 percent oil-indexed notes. Like the Euro-converts, their indenture required that a "sinking fund" be established. A sinking fund is a corporate escrow account earmarked for redemption of a bond issue. In addition, they contained a provision that forbade the company from subordinating the issue to new securities without agreement from a majority of holders of the 9 percent oil notes. It would have been impossible to achieve 85 percent compliance on the exchange without participation by the 9 percent oil notes, since they represented more than 25 percent of total debt. However, holders were disinclined to tender due to the impending (1986) inaugural sinking fund payment.

The exchange deadline was periodically extended throughout June, July, and August while negotiations continued. A missed interest payment due on July 15 to the 13⅛ percent bonds put TEI into technical default. The bond's indenture allowed the trustee to force early principal repayment in the event of a missed interest payment. Cross-default provisions in other public debt instruments would accelerate repayment of the entire debt. Bank creditors had temporarily waived a similar default covenant.

On July 11, 1985, the step-out well in the Salam field, the 3x well, reported flow rates of 15,000 barrels of oil and 35 Mcf of gas per day. Equity holders rejoiced, and the stock moved up 67 percent in one month, ending July at $27⁄16. Yet only 50 percent of the debt holders had tendered. In early August, the exchange offer was sweetened. Twenty-five warrants expiring in December 1985 to buy common stock were included for every $1,000 face amount of debt except for the 8¼ percent Euro-convertibles. Still, too few holders agreed to accept the exchange. The offer was extended six more times. On August 19, the company announced that a majority of the oils had consented to amend the oil's indenture to subordinate the issue to all the new issues being offered in the exchange. This signified that a majority of holders had agreed to swap. The announcement pressured stragglers to join the majority and agree to swap. Ultimately, the exchange was completed on August 23, 1985, with 85 percent of the oils and 88 percent of all public issues being tendered.

The August 19 news release also disclosed that TEI's Phoenix Resources of Egypt subsidiary was in discussions with a company interested in farming out up to one-half of the Khalda Concession. This fact plus the recent news of two commercial discoveries in Egypt assisted the exchange agreement. These discoveries in the Salam field had tested oil flows at 6,000 and over 15,000 barrels per day along with 35 million cubic feet of natural gas. Moreover, Mike Milken, who had originally sold the bonds, may have indirectly urged holders to accept the swap.

The top four issues at the bottom of Table 6.3 were issued to note holders accepting the exchange. The four rows in the table line up and show which bonds received which notes, e.g., $50.0 million of the 9 percent oil-indexed notes accepted the second senior-subordinated notes. The next four securities at the bottom of Table 6.3 are the original issue securities. Of these older notes, $23.8 million survived the exchange offer. The new bonds received four million shares of common stock and four million warrants to buy stock at $3 per share, representing an aggregate 20 percent of common stock or 30 percent of pre-1985 shares.

Seniority changed radically after the exchange. In a bankruptcy, senior issues are expected to be paid in full before junior issues are paid. Table 6.4 shows seniority rankings before and after the 1985 exchange offer. The original issue notes were junior to the newly issued securities. For example, the 8¼ percent Euro-converts became the lowest-ranked notes, while their offspring, the 18 percent notes, were the highest-ranked instruments. Security is discussed further under "Analyzing Exchange Offers," page 90.

Table 6.3

1985 Exchange Offer (in $ millions)

Old Debt Description	Par Amount	Outstanding Principal	Coupon Rate	Annual Interest[a]	Maturity
9% Senior-Subordinated Oil-Indexed Notes	$50	$50.0	9.0%	$4.5	10/95
13 1/8 Senior-Subordinated Notes	$100	$87.4	13.125%	$13.1	7/93
8 1/4 Convertible Subordinated Debentures	$6	$6.3	8.25%	$0.5	1996
11 1/2 Subordinated Debentures[b]	$50	$48.8	11.5%	$5.8	1997
Senior Secured Debt	$137	$136.8	14.7%	$20.1	
Less Current Portion of Long-Term Debt		($26.5)			
Total Long-Term Debt		$302.8		$43.9	
Outstanding Debt to Be Exchanged		$192.5			

New Debt Description	Par Amount	Outstanding Principal	Coupon Rate	Maturity	Annual Interest[a]	Shares per Bond	Sweeteners[c] Common Stock	Warrants[d]
12 7/8 Second Senior-Subordinated Notes	$42.7	$41.5	12.875%	11/91	$5.5	13	554,515	1,037,500
14 1/8 Third Senior-Subordinated Notes	$94.3	$81.7	14.125%	12/91	$13.3	27	2,546,100	2,042,500
18% First Sr. Sub. Notes	$4.7	$4.3	18.0%	3/89	$0.8	65	305,500	0
12% Fourth Senior-Subordinated Notes	$39.5	$37.1	12.0%	2/94	$4.7	16	631,200	927,500
Senior-Subordinated Oil-Indexed Notes	$7.3	$7.3	9.0%	10/95	$0.7			
Senior-Subordinated Notes	$5.7	$5.1	13.125%	7/93	$0.7			
Convertible Subordinated Debentures	$0.9	$0.9	8.25%	1996	$0.1			
Subordinated Debentures	$10.5	$10.5	11.5%	1997	$1.2			
Senior Secured Debt	$122.3	$122.3	14.7%		$18.0			
Total Long-Term Debt		$298.7			$45.1		4,037,315	4,007,500[e]
Old Debt to be Exchanged that Was Not Exchanged		$23.8						
Percentage Exchanged		88%						

Sources: TEI Prospectus for 1986 Exchange Offer and TEI Prospectus for 1987 Exchange Offer.
Notes: [a]Interest is payable in stock or cash at company's discretion. [b]This was the first non-investment grade bond Drexel Burnham Lambert issued. [c]After almost two months TEI experienced a low rate of exchange and was forced to sweeten its offer to all debt holders except the holders of the Euro-converts. [d]Warrants are exercisable for one share of common at an exercise price of $3; the warrants expire on 12/16/85. [e]Common stock and warrants equal approximately 20 percent of total outstanding common stock after the exchange offer is complete or dilutes pre-1985 common by 30 percent.

Table 6.4

Seniority Rankings

Original Notes	Ranking Pre-1985	Ranking 1985
13^1/$_8$%	1	6
9% oils	2	5
11^1/$_2$%	3	7
8^1/$_4$%	4	8
New Issues		
14^1/$_8$%	—	3
12^7/$_8$%	—	2
12%	—	4
18%	—	1

A recent decision in the LTV bankruptcy case may impact the ability of other distressed companies to conduct exchange offers. Judge Burton Lifland in the New York bankruptcy court in 1990 ruled that bonds exchanged prior to bankruptcy may not as usual stake a bankruptcy claim at the bonds' par value, normally $1,000, but must instead claim an amount equal to the fair market value of the bonds *at the time of the exchange*, possibly $500 or less. This ruling will inhibit distressed companies from issuing low-interest notes, PIK bonds, zero-coupon notes, or other securities that greatly reduce their interest obligations but initially trade below par value.

Summary

After the exchange, the total interest owed actually increased. However, the current portion of long-term debt decreased, maturity dates were accelerated, and most of the interest was payable in stock.

New security holders were never sure whether the company would pay interest in cash or stock. Kishpaugh was playing poker with them. He had to keep them guessing; otherwise, they would have short-sold the stock before it was issued to lock in a known price. Their actions would have pushed down the price of the stock and necessitated the payment of even more shares. If they short-sold and the company paid cash on the interest, the stock would rise and short-sellers would lose.

The 1986 Exchange

Overview

Between the 1985 and 1986 exchanges, oil prices collapsed from the mid-$20 range to the low teens. The common stock declined in step with oil prices, as investors lowered their cash-flow estimates. When the stock moved from $3 to $1.50 per share, twice as many common shares would have to be issued to pay interest.

The financial concepts in the 1985 exchange were invalidated by the decline in oil prices and equity value. Once again, Kishpaugh sat down and devised an exchange offer that would allow the company to survive.

Discussion

OPEC adopted a market share strategy in 1986 in place of its former revenue focus (see appendix F). From $24.09 per barrel in 1985, oil fell to $12.60 in 1986, a 48 percent decline. Domestic energy producers could not survive at the new price gradient: bankruptcies destroyed 565, 731, 469, and 374 oil and gas firms in the years between 1985 and 1988, respectively. Their combined liabilities exceeded $7 billion.

The 1985 debt exchange might have sufficed if oil prices had not collapsed. With the disintegration of oil prices, the first restructuring plan actually bred the need for the second restructuring. The 1985 restructuring had traded off earlier maturity dates for the ability to pay interest in cash or stock. But now, most of TEI's existing debt, combining monies owed to banks and to subordinated debt holders, was scheduled for redemption in the next few years. Table 6.5 presents the amount of debt due within five years for each year from 1983 to 1986. As of 1986, over $65 million was due within a year and $107 million within two years, more than twice the amount that had been owed the year before. Without access to the capital markets, new money could not be raised.

Table 6.5

Debt Repayment Schedule: Including Bonds and Bank Debt
(in $ thousands)

Years Until Money Due	December 31			
	1983	1984	1985	1986
<1	$5,108	$26,547	$20,935	$65,652
<2	$3,055	$43,828	$47,692	$42,506
<3	$33,939	$47,873	$47,006	$40,919
<4	$46,581	$46,138	$22,782	$12,521

Source: TEI annual reports, 1983–1988.

Table 6.5 shows that 1983 was the last debt repayment window with less than $10 million owed to creditors within two years. The company seized the opportunity in November 1983 to repurchase $21.7 million of the 8¼ percent convertible subordinated debentures due in 1996, at a loss of approximately $1 million. Despite their 1996 maturity date, the 8¼ percents had an indenture provision that required the company to redeem the notes at 120 percent of par (i.e., $1,200 for every $1,000 bond) as early as 1988 at the discretion of the holder. It was logical to presume that holders would demand redemption given the low interest coupon (8¼ percent) and the high premium (20 percent).[6] Sadly, bank debt (short-term credit due within a year) financed the purchase. The debt repayment schedule, as depicted in Table 6.5, worsened radically in 1984; over $115 million was due within three years.

As of June 1986, forty-four million shares of common stock were outstanding. Scarcely more than thirty million shares had been issued prior to the 1985 exchange. Four million shares and a like amount of warrants sweetened that exchange. The incremental six million shares had gone to holders of the new securities in lieu of cash interest. Stockholders had authorized 100 million common shares. Unissued shares (fifty-six million), called treasury stock, were available for corporate purposes and demonstrate that the current crisis was not an interest payment problem (since it could be paid in stock) but was instead a debt maturity problem.

Again, TEI's management and its adviser, Drexel, opted for a debt restructuring. This time the company offered to exchange outstanding debt securities for a new package of obligations that would delay maturity dates and reduce cash outlays. Table 6.6 outlines terms of the exchange.

Holders of the second, third, and fourth senior-subordinated notes issued in the 1985 exchange, due in 1990, 1991, and 1993, respectively, were offered new issues, the first, second, and third *delayed* convertible senior-subordinated debentures. The new securities delayed maturity by roughly two years. In addition, compared with existing securities, they had lower par value, lower interest coupons, and maintained the option of cash or stock interest payments. Cash interest was out of the question with the old and new bonds until oil prices rebounded.

To enhance the success of the offering, each second, third, and fourth senior-subordinated note tendered received an equity kicker of fifteen, nine, or two shares of common stock, respectively. More important, a portion of the notes was convertible on a quarterly basis into common stock at the holder's discretion. The conversion ratio traded stock at a discount: between 75 percent and 95 percent of the stock's average selling price for ten consecutive trading days prior to the conversion period. Theoretically, this mechanism allowed a holder to "cash-out" of the notes at par value. Bonds not exchanged could only be cashed-out on the New York Bond Exchange at a steep discount. Table 6.7 details how the company had the ability to avoid this dilution by buying in the bonds early.

The other existing debt securities were offered common stock in exchange for their notes. The 18 percent first senior-subordinated notes, 9 percent oil-indexed notes, 13⅛ percent subordinated notes, and 11½ percent subordinated deben-

Table 6.6

1986 Exchange Offer (in $ millions)

Old Debt Description	Par Amount	Outstanding Principal	Coupon Rate	Annual Interest[a]	Maturity
Second Senior-Subordinated Notes	42.7	$41.7	12.875%	$5.5	11/90
Third Senior-Subordinated Notes	94.3	$82.6	14.125%	$13.3	12/91
Fourth Senior-Subordinated Notes	39.5	$37.3	12.0%	$4.7	2/93
Equity Only Exchanges					
First Senior Subordinated Notes	4.7	$4.4	18.0%	$0.8	3/89
Senior-Subordinated Oil-Indexed Notes	5.9	$5.9	9.0%	$0.5	10/95
Senior-Subordinated Notes	5.7	$5.1	13.125%	$0.7	7/93
Subordinated Debentures	10.5	$10.5	11.5%	$1.2	1997
No Equity					
Convertible Subordinated Debentures	0.7	$0.7	8.25%	$0.1	1996
Senior Secured Debt	67.9	$88.4	15.0%	$10.2	
Less Current Portion of Long-Term Debt		($22.5)			
Total Long-Term Debt		$254.1		$37.1	
Outstanding Debt to Be Exchanged		$187.5			

New Debt Description	Par Amount	Outstanding Principal	Coupon Rate	Annual Interest[a]	Maturity	Shares per Bond	Common Stock
First Delayed Convertible Senior-Subordinated Notes	37.2	$36.9	10.0%	$3.7	12/92	15	558,000
Second Delayed Convertible Senior-Subordinated Notes	77.3	$70.4	10.0%	$7.7	12/93	9	695,700
Third Delayed Convertible Senior-Subordinated Notes	30.4	$29.0	10.0%	$3.0	12/94	2	60,800
Second Senior-Subordinated Notes	0.1	$0.1	12.875%	$0.0	11/90		
Third Senior-Subordinated Notes	17	$15.2	14.125%	$2.4	12/91		
Fourth Senior-Subordinated Notes	5.6	$5.3	12.0%	$0.7	2/94		
Equity Only Exchanges							
First Senior-Subordinated Notes	4.7	$4.4	18.0%	$0.8	3/89	400	0
Senior-Subordinated Oil-Indexed Notes	5.3	$5.3	9.0%	$0.5	10/95	330	198,000
Senior-Subordinated Notes	5.5	$5.0	13.125%	$0.7	7/93	285	57,000
Subordinated Debentures	9.9	$9.8	11.5%	$1.1	1997	260	156,000
No Equity							
Convertible Subordinated Debentures	0.7	$0.7	8.25%	$0.1	1996		
Senior Secured Debt	15.4	$15.4	10.0%	$1.5			
Less Current Portion of Long-Term Debt		($18.8)					
Total Long-Term Debt		$178.7		$22.4			
Old Debt to Be Exchanged that Was Not Exchanged		$45.1					1,725,500
Percentage Exchanged		76%					

Source: TEI 10-K reports and Prospectus for 1986 Exchange Offer and TEI Prospectus for 1987 Exchange Offer.
[a]Interest is payable in stock or cash at company's discretion.

Table 6.7

Additional Terms 1986 Exchange Offer

Convertibility Option

Debt holders may convert a portion of their securities into equity, on a quarterly basis as follows:

Security	From	Until*	Conversion
First Delayed CV. SR. Sub. Notes	10/86	7/88	12.5%
Second Delayed CV. SR. Sub. Notes	6/87	3/91	6.25%
Third Delayed CV. SR. Sub. Notes	8/87	5/91	6.25%

Blocking Note Conversion

The company can block any conversion if it buys back notes equivalent to the debt eligible for conversion. However, a junior note conversion cannot be blocked unless all senior note conversions have also been blocked.

Source: TEI Prospectus for 1986 Exchange Offer.
*After until date, notes stop accruing interest.

tures would receive 410, 330, 285, and 260 shares of common stock per $1,000 face value of debt, respectively. With the stock trading at less than $2 per share, the equity offer discounted the bonds by 20 percent to 45 percent depending on seniority; of course, the notes were trading at similar discounts on the bond market. The company announced that without 75 percent acceptance of the offer, it would cancel the exchange.

The initial offer expired on August 13, 1986. Few holders tendered. The offer was extended to August 29, with some issues getting sweetened terms. Par value was increased to $1,000 for the three issues receiving new debt. Shares offered to the first senior-subordinated notes (bearing an 18 percent rate) increased to 615 from 410, but the other issues were left unchanged. The sweetening induced 56 percent of the notes to tender, still not enough. Again the offers were extended, to September 12, with the exception of the oil-indexed notes (the bearer bonds), whose exchange offer was allowed to expire. The acceptance rate neared 75 percent by September 12, but holders of the debt to receive all equity were very reluctant, and the offer was extended a final time to September 26. On September 15 TEI announced that approximately $156 million, or 76.4 percent had been tendered, and the exchange was successful. In total, $42.6 million first delayed, $77.3 million second delayed, and $15.6 million third delayed convertible senior-subordinated notes were issued.

The exchange met its objectives: $24.5 million of debt was exchanged for equity; $107.3 million of debt agreed to a two-year maturity delay; $27 million agreed to a one-year maturity delay; and interest obligations were reduced on an annual basis from $37 million to $22 million.

Summary

The exchange met its goal at a reasonable cost. Bond holders received 3.7 percent of the equity, mostly in the debt for stock exchange. As before, the three new securities received the highest seniority status, just below the 18 percent notes, which had seniority protection. More is said on this issue below.

This second exchange reduced repayment pressures from bond holders, but did nothing to placate the banks that had converted their credit lines into a term loan with strict covenants. Since the banks were secured lenders, their demands were paramount.

Dealing with the Banks

In 1985, the domestic oil and gas subsidiary was listed for sale. No acceptable bids were received through 1986, due to the decline in oil prices, and then the banks turned up the pressure. It became imperative to find a buyer.

Kishpaugh's bargaining skills were put to the test. In February 1987, a unit of Total Cie Française des Petroles agreed to pay $120 million ($110 million after adjustments) for the properties. Kishpaugh described these in the 1986 annual report "as at the right stage to sell . . . , and the proceeds were instrumental in reducing debt and adding financial flexibility." The bank debt was entirely paid off with approximately $100 million of the proceeds. TEI continued to be a troubled company but with a capital structure distinct from most other troubled companies: *it had no senior secured debt*. Bank loans normally have tougher credit terms and impose more restrictions on management than does subordinated debt. Thus, while long-term debt was more than two and a half times greater than assets, management held an unanticipated level of power relative to creditors.

The 1987 Exchange

Overview

The oil price and production scenario underpinning the 1986 exchange was invalidated by a continued decline in oil prices. Company revenues were below expectations. Kishpaugh had to run the company like a man with $200 in the bank who owes four creditors $75 apiece.[7] He had to keep them guessing. His tactics included paying some interest in cash and some in stock, and even buying back some debt. For example, $15.1 million of the first delayed convertible 10 percent notes were bought back in March 1987 to avoid their conversion into common stock. This unexpected move caused the equity to rally to $3 per share. Naturally, fewer shares would now cover the same interest obligation. Common stock outstanding exceeded fifty-nine million shares.

Operating losses mounted. The 1986 loss, released in March 1987, surpassed $50 million. However, cash flow was nearly break-even, since noncash charges included $30 million of depreciation, depletion, and amortization, and $18 million of reported interest had been paid in stock.

In May 1987, with $188 million in outstanding indebtedness and oil prices remaining low, it became clear that there was still too much debt. Debt of $120 million was scheduled to be redeemed by conversion into common stock through 1990. Only 40 million shares remained in the treasury; the success of this conversion was unsure. The company planned a third restructuring.

Discussion

In July 1987, an additional $10.6 million principal amount of the 10 percent first delayed convertible subordinated notes due in December 1992 were eligible to be converted into common stock. The conversion price would be determined by the stock's closing price for the prior fifteen days. While bond holders might choose not to convert, at the depressed stock price, they could acquire approximately 7.5 percent of the company for the $10.6 million debt. A March conversion had been averted with a bond buyback, but there was insufficient cash to duplicate that transaction. Moreover, each time stock was dispensed to pay interest or principal, it brought the number of authorized common shares closer to the current 100 million share limit. A third restructuring was proposed.

Three new securities were offered. Table 6.8 outlines the plan: a delayed convertible senior-subordinated note and second and third dual convertible senior-subordinated notes would replace the first, second, and third delayed convertible subordinated notes created by the 1986 exchange, respectively.

There would now be thirteen different TEI bonds. Figure 6.1 presents a genealogical table depicting the grandparents, parents, children, and grandchildren bonds. The grandparents were the original notes issued prior to the exchange offers; the parents were created in the 1985 exchange, the children in the 1986 exchange, and the grandchildren in the 1987 exchange.

The delayed convertible senior notes had a 14 percent coupon; the second and third notes had 9 percent coupons. In fact, the delayed notes actually paid 18 percent interest for three months, 16 percent interest for the next three months, and then stopped accruing interest altogether, but by then all the notes should have been converted (see Table 6.9). Interest was again payable in cash or stock at the company's discretion, and the notes were redeemable by the company at prices between $3.50 and $4.625 per share. Holders of the new notes could convert into common stock at their discretion beginning in November 1987 for the delayed notes and April and May 1990 for the second and third duals, respectively. The maturity date of the delayed notes was unchanged, but the second and third senior notes delayed maturity by two and five years, respectively. Table 6.9 lists special provisions associated with each new note.

Figure 6.1. **The Exchange Offers**

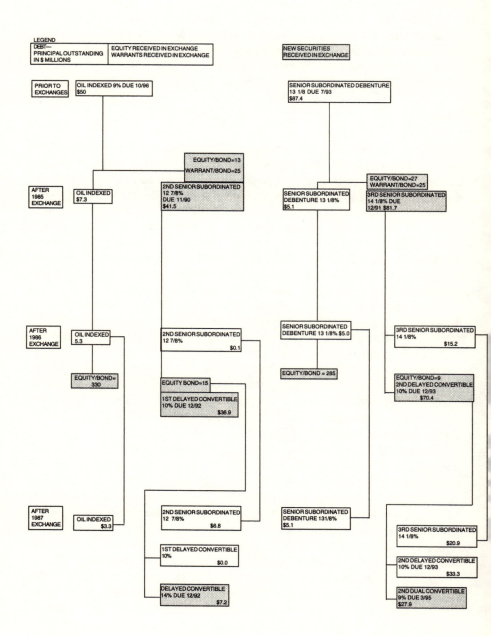

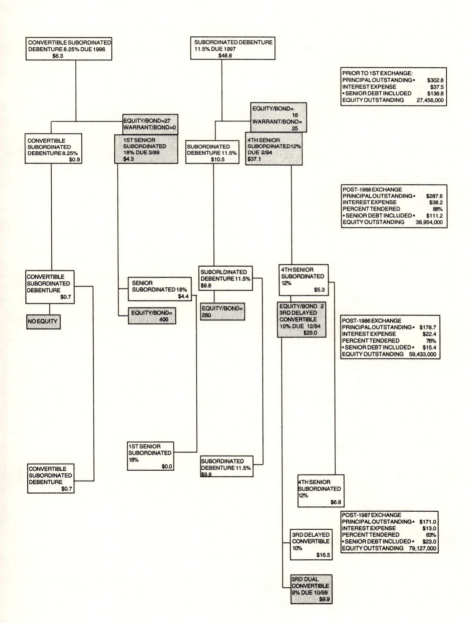

CONVERTIBLE SUBORDINATED
DEBENTURE 8.25% DUE 1996
$6.3

SUBORDINATED DEBENTURE
11.5% DUE 1997
$48.8

PRIOR TO 1ST EXCHANGE:
PRINCIPAL OUTSTANDING • $302.8
INTEREST EXPENSE $37.5
• SENIOR DEBT INCLUDED $136.8
EQUITY OUTSTANDING 27,456,000

EQUITY/BOND=27
WARRANT/BOND=0

EQUITY/BOND=
16
WARRANT/BOND=
25

CONVERTIBLE
SUBORDINATED
DEBENTURE 8.25%
$0.9

1ST SENIOR
SUBORDINATED
18% DUE 3/89
$4.3

SUBORDINATED
DEBENTURE 11.5%
$10.5

4TH SENIOR
SUBORDINATED 12%
DUE 2/94
$37.1

POST-1986 EXCHANGE
PRINCIPAL OUTSTANDING • $287.6
INTEREST EXPENSE $38.2
PERCENT TENDERED 88%
• SENIOR DEBT INCLUDED • $111.2
EQUITY OUTSTANDING 38,954,000

CONVERTIBLE
SUBORDINATED
DEBENTURE
$0.7

SENIOR
SUBORDINATED 18%
$4.4

SUBORLDINATED
DEBENTURE 11.5%
$9.8

4TH SENIOR
SUBORDINATED
12%
$5.3

NO EQUITY

EQUITY/BOND=
400

EQUITY/BOND=
260

EQUITY/BOND 2
3RD DELAYED
CONVERTIBLE
10% DUE 12/94
$29.0

POST-1986 EXCHANGE
PRINCIPAL OUTSTANDING • $178.7
INTEREST EXPENSE $22.4
PERCENT TENDERED 76%
• SENIOR DEBT INCLUDED • $15.4
EQUITY OUTSTANDING 59,433,000

1ST SENIOR
SUBORDINATED
18%
$0.0

SUBORDINATED
DEBENTURE 11.5%
$9.8

CONVERTIBLE
SUBORDINATED
DEBENTURE
$0.7

4TH SENIOR
SUBORDINATED
12%
$6.8

POST-1987 EXCHANGE
PRINCIPAL OUTSTANDING • $171.0
INTEREST EXPENSE $13.0
PERCENT TENDERED 63%
• SENIOR DEBT INCLUDED • $23.0
EQUITY OUTSTANDING 79,127,000

3RD DELAYED
CONVERTIBLE
10%
$16.5

3RD DUAL
CONVERTIBLE
9% DUE 10/99
$9.9

Table 6.8

1987 Exchange Offer (in $ millions)

Old Debt Description	Par Amount	Outstanding Principal	Coupon Rate	Annual Interest[a]	Maturity
First Delayed Convertible Senior-Subordinated Notes	37.2	$36.9	10.0%	$3.7	12/92
Second Delayed Convertible Senior-Subordinated Notes	77.3	$70.4	10.0%	$7.7	12/93
Third Delayed Convertible Senior-Subordinated Notes	30.4	$29	10.0%	$3.0	12/94
Second Senior Subordinated Notes	0.1	$0.1	12.875%	$0.0	11/91
Third Senior Subordinated Notes	17	$15.2	14.125%	$2.4	6/92
Fourth Senior Subordinated Notes	5.6	$5.3	12.0%	$0.7	2/94
First Senior Subordinated Notes	0	$0.0	18.0%	$0.0	3/89
Senior-Subordinated Oil-Indexed Notes	5.3	$5.3	9.0%	$0.5	11/91
Senior-Subordinated Notes	5.5	$5.0	14.125%	$0.8	6/92
Convertible Subordinated Debenture	0.7	$0.7	8.250%	$0.1	1996
Subordinated Debentures	9.9	$9.8	11.50%	$1.1	2/94
Senior Secured Debt	15	$15.0	10.0%	$1.5	
Less Current Portion of Long-Term debt		($18.8)			
Total Long-Term Debt		$173.9		$21.5	
Outstanding Debt to Be Exchanged		$136.3			

New Debt Description[b]	Par Amount	Outstanding Principal	Coupon Rate	Annual Interest[a]	Maturity
Delayed Convertible Senior-Subordinated Notes	7.2	$7.2	14.0%	$1.0	12/92
Second Dual Convertible Senior-Subordinated Notes	29.6	$27.9	9.0%	$2.7	3/95
Third Dual Convertible Senior-Subordinated Notes	10.1	$9.9	9.0%	$0.9	10/99
First Delayed Convertible Senior-Subordinated Notes	0	$0.0	10.0%	$0.0	12/92
Second Delayed Convertible Senior-Subordinated Notes	34.8	$33.3	10.0%	$3.5	12/93
Third Delayed Convertible Senior-Subordinated Notes	16.9	$16.5	10.0%	$1.7	12/94
Second Senior Subordinated Notes[b]	0.1	$6.8	12.875%	$0.0	11/91
Third Senior Subordinated Notes[b]	17	$20.9	14.125%	$2.4	6/92
Fourth Senior Subordinated Notes[b]	5.6	$6.8	12.0%	$0.7	2/94
First Senior Subordinated Notes	0	$0.0	18.0%	$0.0	3/89
Senior-Subordinated Oil-Indexed Notes	5.3	$3.3	9.0%	$0.5	11/91
Senior-Subordinated Notes	5.5	$5.1	14.125%	$0.8	6/92
Convertible Subordinated Debentures	0.7	$0.7	8.250%	$0.1	1996
Subordinated Debentures	9.9	$9.8	11.50%	$1.1	2/94
Senior Secured Debt	23	$23.0	10.0%	$2.3	
Less Current Portion of Long-Term debt		($0.2)			
Total Long-Term Debt		$171.0		$13.0	
Old Debt to Be Exchanged that Was Not Exchanged		$49.8			
Percentage Exchanged		63%			

Sources: TEI 10-K reports and Prospectus for 1986 Exchange Offer, and Prospectus for 1987 Exchange Offer.
[a]Interest is payable in cash or stock at company's discretion.
[b]Portion of debt was classified as current debt in 1986.

Table 6.9

Additional Terms 1987 Exchange Offer

Convertibility Option

Debt holders may convert a portion of their securities into equity, on a quarterly basis, as follows:

Security	From	Until	Conversion
Delayed CV. SR. Sub. Notes[1,2]	11/87	1/88	33.33%
Second Dual CV. SR. Sub. Notes[3,4]	4/90	3/95	6.25%
Third Dual CV. SR. Sub. Notes[5,6]	5/90	10/99	6.25%

1. Interest accrues at 18% from 1/88 to 3/88 and then accrues until 12/88 at 16%. Interest not accrued after 12/88.
2. Converts each month from first date unless stock exceeds $4.50.
3. Second notes convert at a fixed $3.50 per share.
4. Callable at par plus accrued interest provided stock does not exceed $4.50 per share prior to 7/89.
5. Third notes convert at a fixed $3.75 per share.
6. Callable at par plus accrued interest provided stock does not exceed $4.63 per share prior to 7/89.

Blocking Note Conversion

The company can block any conversion if it buys back notes equivalent to the debt eligible for conversion. However, a junior note conversion cannot be blocked unless all senior note conversions have also been blocked.

Source: TEI Prospectus for 1987 Exchange Offer.

Unlike the first two exchanges, no minimum acceptance level was mandated. The company was desperate and knew that bond holders were weary of the financial footwork. The exchange was completed successfully in July 1987 with nearly 20 percent of the first delayed notes, 40 percent of the second delayed notes, and 34 percent of the third delayed notes, or $45 million in all, accepting the offer. A final capital structure is depicted in Table 6.10, with the obligations ranked according to seniority. The company owed $171 million. The World Bank and the real estate mortgage debt were secured obligations. All other notes were unsecured.

Summary

Common stock continued to hemorrhage, as seen in Table 6.11. Over 79 million shares were outstanding by the end of 1987 out of an authorized 100 million shares. In 1987 alone nearly 20 million shares (25 percent of the company) were paid out in lieu of cash interest. The good news was that annual cash interest

Table 6.10

Debt Structure after the 1987 Exchange Offer (as of 12/87)

Debt (in ranking of seniority)	Coupon	Maturity	Amount (in $ millions)
World Bank Note (Secured by Phoenix Properties)	Variable	1989–1994	$20.0
Real Estate Mortgage Notes (Secured)	11.25%	1988–1993	$2.7
Delayed Convertible Senior-Subordinated Notes	14.0%	1992	$7.2
First Delayed Convertible Senior-Subordinated Notes	10.0%	1992	$0.0
Second Dual Convertible Senior-Subordinated Notes	9.0%	1995	$27.9
Third Dual Convertible Senior-Subordinated Notes	9.0%	1999	$9.9
Second Delayed Convertible Senior-Subordinated Notes	10.0%	1993	$33.3
Third Delayed Convertible Senior-Subordinated Notes	10.0%	1994	$16.5
Second Senior-Subordinated Notes[a]	12.875%	1990	$6.8
Third Senior-Subordinated Notes[a]	14.125%	1991	$20.9
Fourth Senior-Subordinated Notes[a]	12.0%	1993	$6.8
Senior-Subordinated Oil Indexed Notes	9.0%	1988–1995	$3.3
Senior-Subordinated Notes	13.125%	1993	$5.1
Subordinated Debentures	11.5%	1997	$9.8
Convertible Subordinated Debentures	8.25%	1996	$0.7
Other Notes Payable	n/a	n/a	$0.1
Less Current Portion of Long Term Debt			$0.2
Total Long-Term Debt			$171.2

Source: TEI 10-K reports.
Note: [a]Portion of debt was classified as current debt in 1986.

payments were reduced to under $4 million, with most issues scheduled to stop paying interest at various dates in the near future.

Prospects for TEI to survive were good. Its debt was finally under control, and its main asset, the Khalda Concession in Egypt, was moving forward.

Analyzing Exchange Offers

Negotiations between management and bond holders are the key ingredient leading to a successful exchange offer. Management pursues the least-cost new debt instrument able to induce a sufficient number of holders to swap existing securities for new securities. Bond holders want a guarantee that their funds will be repaid, higher interest, and nearer maturity. Participants must confront the free-rider syndrome. Presumably, a company considering an exchange offer has low bond values (perhaps thirty cents on the dollar), since the company is in financial difficulties. If sufficient numbers of holders agree to swap, bond holders retaining the original security experience increased value, since the company's default

Table 6.11

Growth of Common Stock Outstanding

Year	Shares (thousands)
1981	
Beginning Balance	19,697
Acquisition of Phoenix Resources	5,816
Other	54
Ending Balance	25,567
1982	
Beginning Balance	25,567
Issued with 13.125% Senior Subordinated Notes	1,889
Ending Balance	27,456
1983	
Beginning Balance	27,456
Ending Balance	27,456
1984	
Beginning Balance	27,456
Ending Balance	27,456
1985	
Beginning Balance	27,456
Issued in Exchange	4,037
Warrants Exercised	4,393
Interest & Supplier Debt Payments	2,868
Other	200
Ending Balance	38,954
1986	
Beginning Balance	38,954
Issued in Exchange	1,749
Debt Converted/Interest & Supplier Payments	18,698
Other	32
Ending Balance	59,433
1987	
Beginning Balance	59,433
Issued in Exchange	0
Debt Converted/Interest & Supplier Payments	19,694
Other	0
Ending Balance	79,127

Source: TEI 10-K reports.

risk declines and some debt may be forgiven. Architects of an exchange offer must avert the free-rider problem; otherwise, the offer will fail, since all investors will attempt to be the free rider.[8]

The next section describes choices presented to public debt holders during the three exchange offers and investigates their propensity to accept an offer. Special attention is given to financial returns.

The Initial Public Debt

Four issues of publicly traded debt were outstanding in 1985 as the need for a debt restructuring became apparent. The oldest issue, the 11½ percent subordinated debentures due in 1997, was the first high-yield or junk bonds issued by Drexel. At the time of issuance these risky securities yielded approximately 150 percent of the prevailing prime rate. Two allotments of bonds were issued: $30 million in 1977 and then, following a warm investor response, an additional tranche of $20 million in 1978. However, weakness in the high-yield market in 1978 forced the company to include ten shares of common stock with each bond to complete the underwriting.

The $30 million 8¼ percent convertible subordinated debentures due in 1996 were issued in March of 1981 and were traded on the Luxembourg Stock Exchange. They were designated as the Euro-converts. Unlike ordinary bonds, the Euro-converts were unregistered securities or bearer bonds that received interest due when the owner submitted a coupon for payment; however, during the exchange offers the company had no way to contact or cajole the holders. The notes were convertible into common stock at $32 per share. The convertibility feature together with a "put" provision that allowed holders to put the notes back to the company at 120 percent of par after March 1, 1986, facilitated the sale of the relatively low coupon bonds. The common stock traded as high as $46.85 during 1981. Proceeds from this offering had paid down bank debt.

Both the 13⅛ percent senior-subordinated notes ($100 million due in 1997) and the 9 percent oil-indexed notes ($50 million due in 1995) were issued in 1983. Of the acquired funds, $68 million retired a previously issued 18 percent zero-coupon bond, and $73 million reduced bank debt. The oil-indexed notes were an inventive security convertible into twenty-nine barrels of crude oil at the holder's discretion. With oil priced at $26 per barrel, this note was backed by $754 of crude oil. If oil prices increased by more than 33 percent, bond holders would earn additional returns through the appreciation of oil. With the price of oil apparently headed for the stratosphere, the conversion feature made the bonds attractive and enabled them to be issued at a below-market rate of interest. Another quality of the oil-indexed notes that investors welcomed was a sinking-fund provision, which compelled TEI to redeem a minimum of $5 million of the notes per year beginning in 1986, and up to $10 million per year if holders desired. The 13⅛ percent notes were sold in a package consisting of one note, nineteen shares of stock, and nine warrants to purchase stock at $8.91. The units were sold at a price close to par, but with the added stock and warrants, the actual yield to investors exceeded 16 percent. A sinking fund of $20 million per year was scheduled to begin in 1989.

Seniority of Original Issues

Securities whose original-issue indenture provisions lack seniority protection risk seniority atrophy. Atrophy occurs when new securities are accorded a superior ranking relative to older issues. As a result of birth order (they were the first notes issued), the 11½ percent notes began as the highest-ranking notes and remained first when the 8¼ percent notes were sold in 1981. However, they were supplanted first by the 9 percent oil-indexed notes in early 1983 and later by the 13⅛ percent notes, which became the senior-most original security.

The importance of seniority arises in bankruptcy or liquidations. In a liquidation, company assets are sold, and the proceeds are applied to repay debts. Debts are repaid in order of seniority; that is, if the asset value is less than the value of total debts, some bond holders may be fully repaid, while others may receive nothing. Similarly, in bankruptcy, a more senior bond is likely to obtain a greater payoff, although the all-or-nothing scenario described for a liquidation is less likely. A low seniority bond with potent indenture provisions, like the 8¼ percent notes, may be more valuable than a more senior bond until a company is bankrupt.

The problem is how to get investors to agree to swap securities for new inferior debt instruments. Among the levers at a company's disposal are: (a) the threat of bankruptcy, (b) seniority atrophy, and (c) the issuance of equity in the form of stock or warrants. Each of these chess pieces was moved by TEI.

The threat of bankruptcy is an effective weapon for several reasons. First, the outcome of bankruptcy is unknown; in fact, it is never clear how long a firm will remain in bankruptcy. Even with "prepackaged bankruptcy plans," which, it is asserted, can expeditiously move a firm through bankruptcy, there is a risk that dissident creditors will delay the proceedings. Firms have spent upward of ten years in bankruptcy court. Second, the payment of interest to unsecured debt is interrupted once a bankruptcy petition is filed. Secured debt, such as bank loans, either receives interest or the interest accrues.[9] Third, companies under the protection of the bankruptcy court dissipate between 3 percent and 5 percent of corporate assets on average in fees to professionals such as lawyers, accountants, and investment bankers. Costs are proportionately greater for smaller firms. Neither the creditor nor the debtor benefits directly from these fees.

Seniority is especially critical when a company files a Chapter 11 bankruptcy petition and prepares to either liquidate or reorganize. The absolute priority rule, a vestige from the older Chandler Bankruptcy Act, requires debtors to be repaid from the bankrupt estate in the order of their seniority. In that case, a junior note would receive nothing unless all senior securities had been fully paid off. Strict application of the absolute priority rule was abandoned in the Bankruptcy Act of 1978 except regarding liquidations; the fairness criteria in reorganizations is judged in reference to the absolute priority rule. Nevertheless, notes whose covenants require priority repayment are generally repaid more than lower seniority issues.

Seniority atrophy, the second tactic, occurs when "musical chairs" is played.

Bond holders who had held good seats but refused to play along with the restructuring are left without any seat when the music stops. By conferring a higher seniority ranking on new securities, companies create a powerful incentive to accept a swap.

The final tactical device is the distribution of equity to swapping debt holders. There are several reasons for giving away equity. First, by converting debt holders into equity holders, the interests of the two classes of creditors are united. In future exchanges, it may be easier to extract concessions from debt holders. Second, equity may be the only thing left with any value that the company can deliver. Both purposes are served if debt holders consent to a package containing restricted stock, i.e., equity that they cannot trade.

In the 1985 exchange, TEI was ineffectual in securing a swap by exploiting seniority rankings alone; hence, the offer was sweetened with the addition of common stock and warrants. Following the 1985 exchange, the comparative seniority was altered. Table 6.12 shows how seniority shifted across the three exchange offers and as bankruptcy approached. Consider the 8¼ percent notes, which had been last in seniority but were well protected by the put provision. The company was anxious to avoid the put and thus offered a new 18 percent debenture, which ranked first in seniority among eight (four old and four new) issues. Only $6.3 million of the 8¼ percent were outstanding prior to 1985; less than $1 million rejected the offer. Dollar amounts for all notes are found in Figure 6.1. Remaining 8¼ percent notes were retired in 1986 when they were put to the company. The 18 percent notes themselves were redeemed for cash in 1987, since: (a) holders unanimously refused to participate in further exchange offers (for stock); (b) the issue's top seniority ranking was fixed by indenture; (c) the issue paid cash interest at an 18 percent annual rate; and (d) the issue was small.

The 9 percent oil-indexed notes adhered to a similar blueprint. Prior to the 1985 exchange, these notes (nearly $50 million worth) were assuaged by a commodity exchange privilege (twenty-nine barrels of oil) and by an inflexible sinking fund. If these note holders were to be induced to accept the exchange, they would have to be offered a better deal. On the positive side, the company offered a higher-yielding (12⅞ percent) note with stronger seniority (second seniority rank); on the negative side, nonexchanging oil-indexed notes would rank below all newly issued securities in seniority, though not below issues currently ranked junior to them. In bankruptcy, a free rider would have $135 million of previously junior debt superseding it due to seniority atrophy. The campaign worked. Approximately 80 percent of the $50 million of oil-indexed notes acquiesced to the 1985 offer. In the 1986 exchange, by reusing the seniority ploy, virtually all of the 12⅞ percent holders again agreed to exchange.

Both the 13⅛ percent notes ($87.4 million) and the 11½ percent notes retained their relative seniority positions, provided that they agreed to successive exchanges. Nonexchanging notes fared poorly. The 13⅛ percent notes, though

Table 6.12

Impact of the Exchange Offers on Seniority

Original Issue	Progeny	1984	1985	1986	1987	1988
$13\frac{1}{8}$%		1	6	9	12	10
	$14\frac{1}{8}$%		3	6	9	7
	10% 2nds			3	6	4
	9% 2nds				4	2
9% Oil Indexed		2	5	8	11	9
	$12\frac{7}{8}$%		2	5	8	6
	10% 1st			2	3	n/a
	14%				2	1
$11\frac{1}{2}$%		3	7	10	13	11
	12% 4th		3	6	9	7
	10% 3rds			3	6	4
	9% 3rds				4	2
$8\frac{1}{4}$%		4	8	11	14	12
	18% 1st		1	1	1	n/a

n/a = No longer outstanding.

always senior to the 11½ percent notes, became junior to the many issues exchanged by holders of the 8¼ percent and 9 percent oil-indexed notes. Hence, a majority of the holders of these two issues regularly accepted the exchanges. Had they not agreed to take the exchange, they would have fallen to the bottom of the seniority pile, with the exception of the original 8¼ percent notes.

Seniority atrophy would be less effective as an exchange-offer tactic at a company that was inhibited from going bankrupt; for example, an electric utility, a family business, or a firm with undeveloped patents. In that case, equity issuance may prove more effective.

Returns to Investors

Investors studying exchange offers are most concerned with the returns to bond holders who accepted or refused the three exchange offers. The analysis is complicated by the fact that the price of the securities varied depending on when they were purchased. It should be noted that these exchange offers are but a single example of debt swaps, and they should not be treated as guides for accepting other exchange offers. However, they do provide a complete picture of one set of exchange offers. They may reveal where to find anomalies that could improve the returns of investors.

The analysis makes several simplifying assumptions to facilitate a comparative review of various strategies. First, it was assumed that investors purchased bonds on the last day of December 1983, 1984, 1985, 1986, or 1987. Second, it was assumed that investors sold their bonds either at the time of the Chapter 11 filing—April 1988—or one year after the bankruptcy case was consummated—April 1991.[10] Third, it was assumed that stock or warrants received by investors before the bankruptcy filing were sold immediately. Several institutional investors queried on this matter admitted to this strategy. Stock dispensed in the bankruptcy plan of reorganization was assumed to be retained. Finally, it was assumed that in-the-money warrants were exercised.

Performance is measured by total annual return in comparison with acquisition cost. Total return includes cash interest, interest paid in stock, additional stock received, and terminal bond value. Acquisition cost is based on average bond prices for the month of purchase. For several infrequently traded bonds, a matrix pricing algorithm estimated bond values.

Tables 6.13 and 6.14 present estimated total annual returns to investors who purchased bonds on each of five possible dates and sold them at each of two concluding dates. The tables are too extensive to discuss each value. Consider an overview instead. Table 6.13 reports returns for bonds that were sold in 1988. *Every single return is negative*; that is, anyone who bought TEI's bonds between 1983 and 1987 and sold them in 1988 lost money. The later the bond was bought, the larger the percentage annual loss, since fewer interest payments were received. Across the family of bonds, the better instruments (determined by maturity, seniority, and coupon interest) suffered the largest annual percentage loss, since they had the highest purchase price. The loss was neither tempered nor accelerated by accepting the exchange offers. The results agree with the notion that one cannot profit by buying bonds early and selling them after a company files for bankruptcy.

Table 6.14 describes annual percentage total returns for bonds sold in 1991. By this time, appreciation in the new equity had given value to warrants provided to bond holders in the bankruptcy proceedings (see chapter 7). Virtually all of the annual returns are positive; that is, bond holders recouped their losses through 1988 and made additional gains, giving them positive total returns. The negative values reported for the 18 percent notes are deceptive, since they accepted all stock in 1987 and therefore could not have been sold in 1991.

Consider a purchaser of a 9 percent oil-indexed note who sold out in 1991. Total return depended on when the original note was bought. The highest annual return, 11.5 percent, was earned by note holders who purchased at the end of 1987.

There is no systematic variation in yields across purchase dates. More important than date of purchase is purchase price. The highest returns were earned by the 14 percent notes that were number one in seniority. The correlation between returns and seniority results from the top-ranked bonds receiving the best deal in the bankruptcy. As James Swanson, an experienced fund manager, recounts in chapter 9, bond holders effectively become shareholders in a bankruptcy. That is how they stand to gain the most.

What about investors with a buy-and-hold strategy? In an analysis similar to

Table 6.13

Total Return to Various Bonds with Alternate Buy Dates

Selling December 1988

Buying Date	Original Issues			
	9% Oil Indexed	13 1/8% Subordinated	11 1/2% Subordinated	8 1/4% Euro-Convertible
12/31/83	−17.3%	−5.2%	−2.5%	−19.1%
12/31/84	−15.0%	−14.8%	−16.5%	−18.1%
12/31/85	−31.2%	−22.5%	−21.5%	−20.0%
12/31/86	−38.2%	−27.6%	−13.1%	−12.9%
12/31/87	−68.4%	−62.9%	−49.5%	−50.0%

Buying Date	Issues Created in the 1985 Exchange			
	12 7/8% Note	14 1/8% Note	12% Note	18% Note
12/31/83	−10.2%	−3.5%	−3.9%	−27.8%
12/31/84	−21.7%	−22.6%	−26.7%	−28.5%
12/31/85	−20.1%	−20.1%	−20.8%	−56.3%
12/31/86	−27.9%	−27.9%	−29.1%	−62.2%
12/31/87	−63.1%	−63.2%	−64.6%	−85.7%

Buying Date	Issues Created in the 1986 Exchange		
	First Delayed	10% 2nd Delay	10% 3rd Delay
12/31/83	−17.3%	−5.2%	−2.5%
12/31/84	−14.3%	−9.2%	−6.4%
12/31/85	−29.2%	−27.5%	−32.5%
12/31/86	−27.4%	−27.9%	−35.2%
12/31/87	−63.2%	−63.2%	−69.4%

Buying Date	Issues Created in the 1987 Exchange		
	14% Note	9% 2nd Delay	9% Dual
12/31/83	−10.3%	−10.3%	−7.5%
12/31/84	−14.1%	−16.6%	−19.5%
12/31/85	−19.8%	−31.9%	−27.3%
12/31/86	−14.5%	−31.6%	−38.4%
12/31/87	−48.5%	−66.8%	−72.3%

Source: Derived by the author with the assistance of Pierre Poulin and Chris Decker.

that described above, a hypothetical purchase in 1983 and sale in 1991 were evaluated for the four original issues. Figure 6.2 presents the results. At the center of the diagram (in the four rectangles) are the original issue notes. The numbers beside each are the *annual* percentage total returns earned from 1983 to

Table 6.14

Total Return to Various Bonds with Alternate Buy Dates

Selling December 1991

Buying Date	Original Issues			
	9% Oil Indexed	13¹/₈% Subordinated	11¹/₂% Subordinated	8¹/₄% Euro-Convertible
12/31/83	1.8%	6.1%	9.1%	0.3%
12/31/84	8.0%	6.4%	16.5%	10.5%
12/31/85	3.1%	3.5%	6.6%	11.9%
12/31/86	10.0%	7.7%	18.6%	26.4%
12/31/87	11.5%	3.6%	15.3%	25.3%

Buying Date	Issues Created in the 1985 Exchange			
	12⁷/₈% Note	14¹/₈% Note	12% Note	18% Note
12/31/83	10.3%	5.6%	7.4%	−13.1%
12/31/84	17.72%	5.8%	16.2%	−6.4%
12/31/85	9.1%	4.5%	6.2%	−18.8%
12/31/86	18.9%	3.9%	7.5%	−18.6%
12/31/87	23.0%	−1.1%	3.5%	−22.7%

Buying Date	Issues Created in the 1986 Exchange		
	First Delayed	10% 2nd Delay	10% 3rd Delay
12/31/83	All	3.7%	6.9%
12/31/84	Retired	3.3%	−15.3%
12/31/85	in	1.5%	5.6%
12/31/86	1987	9.5%	6.7%
12/31/87	Exchange	6.1%	3.6%

Buying Date	Issues Created in the 1987 Exchange		
	14% Note	9% 2nd Delay	9% Dual
12/31/83	5.8%	7.6%	10.8%
12/31/84	13.4%	8.2%	17.4%
12/31/85	9.8%	6.6%	7.6%
12/31/86	21.9%	17.8%	9.9%
12/31/87	20.8%	17.1%	7.9%

Source: Derived by the author with the assistance of Pierre Poulin and Chris Decker.

1991. Each ring in the bull's-eye represents an exchange offer, and each number is the annual percentage total return earned from 1983 to 1991 by a holder accepting a particular swap. Securities in the outer ring were created in the last exchange offer; their lineage can be traced backward along the arrows. *The highest returns were generally earned by investors accepting the exchange of-fers.* Original issue notes generally earned lower returns than did their offspring. For example, following the buy-and-hold strategy, the 11½ percent notes earned 3.04 percent per annum; the 12 percent forth senior-subordinated note created from the 11½ percent notes in the 1985 exchange earned 3.27 percent per annum; the 10 percent third dual convertible notes created from the 12 percent notes in 1986 earned 2.78 percent per annum; and the 9 percent third dual convertible notes created in the 1987 exchange offer earned 9.27 percent per annum.

Figure 6.2. **Return from Buying Issues December 1983 and Selling Them July 1991** (annual percentage return)

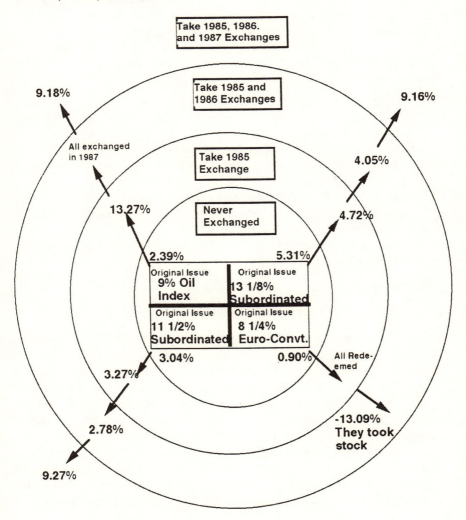

Gaining Control through Debt Exchanges

Another rationale for debt holders to participate in an exchange offer is the opportunity to obtain equity. If enough equity is acquired, control of the company may pass to bond holders. In precise terms, control refers to a company's board of directors; less strictly, control includes the accumulation of a substantial share of a company's equity. By accepting and retaining equity in TEI whenever it was delivered (as a sweetener, in lieu of cash interest, and from conversion of debt into equity) bond holders acquired 65 percent of the equity. However, not all bond holders wanted equity in this company, and some had contractual restrictions forbidding equity to be held. In both cases, their shares were sold to other investors. In addition, after the bankruptcy a new company emerged. Control of that company passed to the owners of the *right* TEI bonds. The bankruptcy control issue is addressed in the next chapter.

Several simplifying assumptions either clarified "facts" that could not be independently confirmed or established a standard of comparison. The assumptions are as follows:

- Original-issue bonds always received cash interest.
- Bonds acquired in exchange offers received stock in lieu of cash interest commencing in June 1985.
- The share conversion price for interest paid in stock adhered to the indenture: a 15 percent discount to market. Stock was dispensed at an average of $2, $1.50, and $1.60 in 1985, 1986, and 1987, respectively.
- Nine hundred thousand warrants distributed in 1983 were assumed not to have converted, since the conversion price, $8.91, exceeded all future equity values.
- Warrants issued in 1985 with a $3.50 conversion price were assumed to have been converted.

Each original security is discussed serially.

The 8¼ Percent Euro-Converts

Prior to the initiation of the three exchange offers, fewer than $7 million of these debentures were outstanding. The company had bought them in, often at a premium-to-par value, to avoid having the owners put back to the company at 120 percent of par. Because they were bearer bonds, the company was unable to locate the owners. In fact, as of April 1993, some of those bonds were still unaccounted for. With so few of the notes remaining, their potential effect on corporate control was minimal.

Approximately $5.6 million of the Euro-converts were exchanged for the 18 percent first senior notes in the 1985 exchange. When funds were available, the company repurchased those notes on the open market to reduce principal and debt service. Subsequently, nearly $1 million of the 18 percent first notes were retired.

In the 1986 exchange, $.5 million of the 18 percent first note holders opted for the all-stock offer: 615 shares per note, or in total 307,000 shares. These shares combined with stock paid as interest to the 18 percent notes aggregated to almost a million shares, or an equity ownership position of just over 1 percent. The remaining 18 percent notes had the potential to be exceptionally dilutive, since the number of shares received in interest rose proportionately with the decline in equity price. Hence, the company retired the issue in 1987.

The 9 Percent Oil-Indexed Notes

The oil-indexed notes were a poor investment. The collateral, twenty-nine barrels of oil exchangeable for the bond, never had a value greater than 75 percent of par. Moreover, the 9 percent rate of interest paid on the bonds was a below-market rate, owing to the bond's collateralization.

Nearly $42 million of the oils swapped for the 12⅞ percent second senior-subordinated notes in 1985; virtually none of these agreed to the all-stock trade offered in the 1986 exchange, though 90 percent accepted the 10 percent first delayed convertible debentures. By 1987, declining enthusiasm for exchanges resulted in only 20 percent of the first delayed converts accepting the first delayed senior converts.

In terms of acquiring shares, over $24 million of the 10 percent first delayed converts were redeemed for stock. With the additional interest received in stock, almost 17.5 million shares, or 22 percent of the stock outstanding prior to reorganization, went to this bond category. A bond holder who converts into equity must believe that the company is going to survive and avoid bankruptcy, or else plans on selling immediately. Not only were the 10 percent first delayed converts wrong in this dream, but they were further disappointed when the reorganization plan provided these old equity holders with no stock in the new company, only warrants to purchase about 3 percent of the equity.

The $7.2 million worth of the 10 percent first delayed converts not taking stock swapped for the 14 percent delayed convertible senior-subordinated notes in the 1987 exchange. They received few shares in TEI. Being the senior notes (see Table 6.12), they instead prospered in the reorganization plan, where they received for each $1,000 bond a note with a face value of $1,057, 30 of the new Class A warrants, and 129 of the Class C warrants.

The 13⅛ Percent Senior-Subordinated Debentures

The 13⅛ percent senior-subordinated debentures arose in 1983 as part of a $100 million unit consisting of a $1,000 par amount note, nineteen shares of common stock, and nine warrants to purchase stock at $8.91.[11] This class received nearly 1.9 million shares when the company had fewer than twenty-five million outstanding shares. Today the units would be described as "strip" securities, meaning that they could be subdivided into several separate securities. A critical feature of strip bonds is how they unify the interests of debt and equity holders. This unity, it is contended, simplifies the crafting of exchange offers. However, in the case of the 13⅛ percent notes, there were no selling restrictions; as a result, it is probable that the shares were promptly sold.

All but $5 million of the issue accepted the 14⅛ percent third senior-subordinated notes offered in 1985. In addition, each bond received twenty-seven shares of equity and twenty-five warrants exercisable at $3.50. These shares together with the interest paid as stock aggregated to five million shares, or 6 percent of the company.

In 1986, $70 million or 82 percent of the 14⅛ percent holders accepted the 10 percent second delayed convertible notes and nine shares of common stock. Over time, with the stock paid as interest and the sweetener stock, they accumulated 12.8 million shares, or 16 percent, of the common stock prior to reorganization (178 shares per bond). Twenty-eight million dollars worth of the 10 percent second delayed convertibles accepted the 9 percent second dual convertible notes in 1987. They accumulated 234 shares per bond in lieu of cash interest payments amounting to 8 percent, or 6.5 million shares of the original common stock.

Few of the remaining 14⅛ percent notes accepted an all-stock exchange (285 shares) in the 1986 or the 1987 exchange offer, leaving $21 million worth of the 14⅛ percent notes. They accumulated a total of 4.6 million shares, or 5.8 percent of the common stock, 218 shares per bond.

In total, the original 13⅛ percent notes and their progeny acquired 30.8 million shares of TEI (including the 1.9 million shares issued originally as part of the unit), nearly 39 percent of the company. Most of these shares, 26.6 million, were acquired in lieu of cash interest. Overall, this class acquired 6 percent of TEI as a reward for accepting the exchange offers; an additional 33 percent was acquired as payment for interest due. Since stock awarded for interest due was converted at a 15 percent discount to the market, nearly 11 percent (6 percent in sweeteners and 5 percent from the 15 percent discount taken on the 33 percent) of the company was given to this class in excess of money actually due. Without largess such as this, most exchange offers would fail.

The 11½ Percent Subordinated Debentures

Approximately $37 million of the original-issue 11½ percent notes acquiesced to the 1985 exchange offer of 12 percent fourth senior-subordinated notes. Of the remaining $10.5 million in securities, $9.8 million accepted no other offers, continued to receive cash interest until the end, and became a claim in bankruptcy. Bonds assenting to the 12 percent note offer received in addition 16 shares of TEI and 25 warrants to buy shares at $3.50, or 1.5 million shares in total.

In 1986 about $.5 million of the 11½ percent notes consented to a 260-share all-stock exchange (130,000 shares); an additional $29 million of the 12 percent fourth notes accepted the 10 percent third delayed convertibles and two shares of stock in the 1987 exchange. In total, these bonds accumulated 156 shares of common stock per bond, for a total of 1.1 million shares.

Of the original notes, $10 million accepted every exchange offer and ended up with the 9 percent third dual convertible notes. These holders accumulated 145 shares per bond, or 1.4 million shares of TEI previous to bankruptcy. In total, this class of debt holders acquired 4.2 million shares, or nearly 5 percent of the company.

Overview

Table 6.15 organizes the amount of stock obtained by each bond across the three exchange offers. For their size, the 10 percent first delayed converts acquired the largest percentage of stock. This issue and the 14 percent delayed converts, which had the top seniority ranking, both arose from the 9 percent oil-indexed notes. That is, one progeny of the 9 percent oil-indexed notes was able to capture control of TEI in the exchange offers, and another descendant was in the best position to capture the successor company created in the bankruptcy court.

Table 6.15

Shares of TEI Stock Obtained by Debt Instruments in the Three Exchange Offers (millions of dollars and shares in millions)

Issue	Issue Size	Shares Obtained	Shares/ Bond
18% Bond	$4.3	0.9	210
10% 1st Delayed Bond	$36.9	17.5	470
14$^1/_8$% 3rd Bond	$81.7	9.6	120
10% 2nd Delayed Bond	$70.4	12.8	180
9% 2nd Dual Bond	$27.9	6.5	230
12% 4th Bond	$37.1	1.5	40
10% 3rd Delayed Bond	$29.0	1.1	40
9% 3rd Dual Bond	$9.9	1.4	140
11$^1/_2$% Bond	$48.8	0.1	4

The 11½ percent notes acquired the fewest shares, and, as original-issue notes, they never received stock for interest and only acquired stock in a straight debt-for-equity exchange. Few holders accepted this offer.

Who Profits from Exchange Offers

Should investors accept exchange offers? This is not a simple question: exchange offers are multidimensional propositions, and our archetype, TEI, had a complex resolution (continued exchange offers, PIK bonds, and bankruptcy), which frustrates sound analysis. Consider the simplest dimension: the amount of cash received. On the one hand, refusing to exchange is best, since the original bonds were cash-pay instruments, while the new issues, at least for some time, paid interest in stock. On the other hand, there was no compunction against selling stock received, and since the stock came at a 15 percent discount to the market (though possibly not a discount by the time the stock was sold), it should have been possible to receive as much from stock distributions as from cash payments.[12]

The control issue is even more ambiguous since it is unclear what is to be controlled. Will TEI survive? Original-issue debt holders could take control of TEI by judicious selection of proffered exchange-offer debt. Negotiations between management and note holders crafted replacement securities to meet their needs. What if TEI were to fail? By concentrating on seniority of bond issues, other note holders would take control of the post-bankruptcy company.

Perhaps the total returns earned by accepting or declining exchange offers is the most important topic. This comparison can be made from a variety of perspectives: each year, until the bankruptcy, through confirmation of the reorganization plan, or when the plan was consummated. From an intellectual perspective, the most satisfying measure of total return is from beginning to end, that is, from date of purchase through the termination of the Chapter 11 proceedings. *On this basis, it appears that seniority is the critical factor.* That is, bond holders who accepted exchange offers that gave them top seniority earned the highest total returns. More is said on this issue in the next chapter as we unravel the bankruptcy.

Conclusion

TEI engaged in three exchange offers. The 1985 exchange gave the company the right to pay interest in stock; the 1986 offer delayed maturity dates; and the 1987 offer did both. Each exchange was progressively more costly to the company.

Several conclusions emerge from the review of TEI's exchange offers. First, exchange offers are complex instruments that are difficult to decipher primarily because the future is uncertain, but also because the alternatives usually involve trade-offs. Second, the free rider may actually be disappointed relative to those accepting offers, because of the importance of seniority. However, had TEI survived, a hold-out strategy might have been best. Similarly, holding out may be a good strategy in a bankruptcy even when there are sufficient assets to settle all debts. Third, smaller issues may have a disproportionate clout in the pre-exchange negotiations, since the outcome of their challenge is less likely to invoke a bankruptcy filing. Smaller issues adhering to the "squeaky wheel" doctrine may conceivably cause a big enough headache to coerce management into redeeming their entire issue.

Good reasons exist not to accept exchange offers despite the loss of seniority position. For example, issues with indenture provisions providing for collateralization, mandatory redemptions, or put options may not need seniority. Moreover, covenants such as these may force companies to offer more in an exchange offer than they otherwise might. The 8¼ percent Euro-converts and the 9 percent oil-indexed notes, which both traded at lower yields (higher prices) than other TEI issues as a result of their covenants, are good examples of this phenomenon.

The four categories of original-issue debt obtained approximately 65 percent of the common equity in TEI via the exchange offers and the payment of interest in stock, demonstrating that it is conceivable to gain control by cooperating with an exchange offer. More control can be acquired if one can dominate the negotiations and thereby adapt offered terms to one's own objectives. Is it a good idea to obtain control? In this case, no, because TEI failed; however, as discussed in the next chapter, the bankruptcy was almost averted, and then control might have been beneficial.

Notes

1. In fact, interest payments would represent over 46 percent of 1985 revenues.
2. A variance report compares values in one year to values in specific prior years.
3. Production costs range from $1 per barrel in Saudi Arabia (costs in Egypt were about $2) to $50 per barrel in the Arctic.
4. Equivalently, the problem was too little cash flow.
5. Bonds that paid interest with more bonds, referred to as payment-in-kind (PIK) bonds, gained acceptance in the late 1980s as financing vehicles for leverage buyouts.
6. However, over $300,000 of these notes are still unaccounted for even in 1993. The Euro-converts were bearer bonds that were unregistered, so that ownership is impossible to trace.
7. In fact, some of TEI's bonds were held by only four institutions.
8. See Robert Gertner and David Scharfstein, "A Theory of Workouts and the Effects of Reorganization Law," 1189–1223.
9. Provided that the asset securing the loan has a value equal to or greater than the loan itself.
10. April 1990, when the Phoenix Resources Companies emerged from the bankruptcy proceedings, was also analyzed. Since those results were similar to 1988's, except regarding the senior-most securities, they were not separately presented.
11. Only $96 million worth of the units were sold. In 1985, $87.4 million were outstanding.
12. This problem can be avoided by shorting the stock before receiving it, thereby guaranteeing a price. In the bankruptcy, one creditor who had agreed to accept stock as payment for supplies reported that it had been unable to sell the stock quickly enough to recoup all the monies that it believed it was owed.

7

Bankruptcy

In July 1987, when the third exchange offer was accepted, it appeared that the company would have the financial wherewithal to repay its obligations. But then new disasters struck. The debt trap eventually proved to have no escape route, and the end came quickly.

The debt burden was the prima facie cause of the bankruptcy. Almost $50 million in principal and cash interest payments were due before 1990 (see Figure 7.1). TEI had gone to the well once too often; creditors were disinclined to accept further restructurings. The real catalyst precipitating the showdown with creditors was an unexpected restriction against selling Egyptian oil production, which completely obliterated cash flow. Even Kishpaugh's mood perceptibly changed, as he conveyed his concerns to shareholders in the third-quarter 1987 report, "We are not dismissing these challenges as insignificant."

When cash flow is low, some companies try to "chase expenses with revenues." They attempt to grow. But corporate growth requires new capital. TEI took the right path and sought to reduce its expenses. However, the cash-flow deficit was too great.

Bankruptcy was another option. It would allow TEI to work out its problems with creditors while its operations continued; however, management would sacrifice its exclusive authority. Bankruptcy establishes a new set of rules. But perhaps a new set of rules was needed, since for many investors TEI had stopped being a long-term oil play and had become a long-term problem. While a bankruptcy filing drapes a short-term focus over events (battles would now be waged in court and on trading-room floors), in the long run, the company could again concentrate on its optimal future course.

Events Leading Up to the Filing

Cash flows were diminished by falling oil prices, the loss of the Egyptian lifting agreement, and continued spending. Oil prices and Egyptian politics were out of

Figure 7.1. **Principal and Interest Scheduled to Be Paid by TEI**

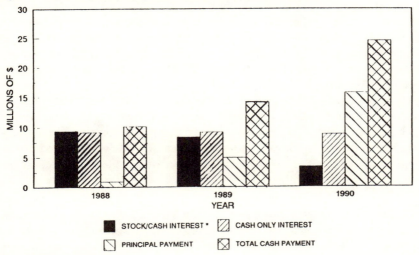

Source: TEI 10-K reports.

*TEI has option to pay in stock, cash, or both.

management's control, but spending was not. A number of cutbacks were made in the home office and in the field, yet the company seemed unable to take control of its expenses. Despite a 43 percent reduction from 1985 through 1987, general and administrative (G&A) expenses remained a high percentage of sales.[1] The annual salaries of the five top executives exceeded a cumulative $1 million.

The company tried to drill its way out of trouble. Seven million dollars was gambled in Malaysia and Ecuador, the latest oil hot spots. In the end, these ventures yielded no new proven reserves or additional cash flows. On the positive side, the partner in the Ecuador venture, Enron Corp., later joined with TEI in bidding on and winning a separate Egyptian concession. Monies were also spent offshore Texas in a partnership with Cliff Drilling that led to a natural gas discovery, the Vermillion field. Later, the bankruptcy court approved additional expenditures to commercialize this find.

The beginning of the end dates from the October 1987 stock market crash. All hopes that creditors might agree to another restructuring were dashed in the collapse of the market—the Dow Jones thirty industrials fell from 2630 to 1900. In February 1988, TEI defaulted on all principal and interest payments. A renewed decline in oil prices broke the camel's back. Oil prices had rebounded in 1987 to $15.42 per barrel from $12.60 in 1986 (a 50 percent reduction from 1985), but they averaged $12.55 per barrel in 1988, and at one point they were poised to break $10 per barrel, a commanding psychological barrier.

The default triggered debt covenants that automatically reclassified all long-term debt as current debt. The company negotiated with creditors, but the talks soon broke down. Creditors were aware of the adverse industry economics and the unfavorable production news from the Khalda Concession; moreover, they could not perceive a solution to the crisis. Some creditors argued that Kishpaugh and his management team were bleeding the company (see chapter 9).[2] In this climate of mistrust and suspicion, TEI filed on April 26, 1988, a voluntary petition for reorganization under Chapter 11 of the United States Bankruptcy Code in the Western District of Oklahoma.

Wall Street had not expected the bankruptcy; the stock was trading near $1 per share. Warning signs were present, however. For one thing, the company had developed a cash horde well beyond its needs. Companies planning a bankruptcy filing accumulate as much cash as possible because of delays expected until a new bank line of credit can be negotiated and approved by the bankruptcy court.

Bankruptcy Basics

A Chapter 11 bankruptcy filing provides a number of benefits to a distressed company. Most important, the company's assets are protected from seizure by creditors owed either interest or principal. The theory behind this sanctuary is that it allows a company to operate while it devises a plan for repaying creditors. Without continued operations, many businesses would expire; their customers would find other vendors to meet their needs.

Management responsibilities continue with the company's officers unless the bankruptcy court suspects that current management is incompetent or has engaged in malfeasance, in which case, the United States trustee working out of the bankruptcy court may appoint a trustee to manage the firm. In bankruptcy the company becomes known as the debtor and its management as the debtor in possession. An example of the appointment of a trustee can be found in the case of Eastern Airlines in which the bankruptcy judge established that the parent firm, Texas Air, and its chairman, Frank Lorenzo, were not managing the airline in the best interests of Eastern or its creditors. Of course, trustees are not infallible; some have argued that Eastern's trustee was misguided and precipitated the airline's forced liquidation.

Kishpaugh continued to run TEI without a trustee. However, an examiner was appointed: Charles E. Ramsey, Jr., of Dean Witter Reynolds, Inc. The first thing Ramsey examined was management; he gave it a clean and favorable bill of health. Among the chief responsibilities of an examiner are to ensure that committees are formed to represent disparate financial interests, as prescribed by the Bankruptcy Code, and to ensure that the committees have access to adequate and accurate information.

An initial step in the bankruptcy process occurs when the office of the United States trustee instigates the formation of committees by the twenty largest creditors. The number of committees established depends on the association and similarity among the types of debt. One factor considered in determining the appropriate number of committees is the absolute priority rule, which had been a cornerstone of the prior bankruptcy code, the Chandler Act. Generally, secured debt holders, unsecured debt holders, trade creditors, and equity holders will each have a committee to represent their interests. However, equity committees will not be established if there are too few assets. For example, the Pan American Airlines bankruptcy had no equity committee.[3] With fewer committees, each has more leverage, and fewer dollars will be spent on professional services. Moreover, with fewer committees, more issues are resolved outside the courtroom, by the committees. Conceivably, with less dissension or suspicion among committees, the reorganization process may be expedited. Yet in the LTV case, an attempt to pile disparate creditors onto the same committee backfired, and it was eventually broken into four separate groups.[4]

Creditors and potential creditors have ninety days after the filing of a bankruptcy petition to assert a claim in court. The debtor must make a good faith effort to inform known creditors of its bankrupt status. Claims not filed within the grace period are extinct and not eligible for any payout from the bankrupt estate. TEI's indebtedness included payables owed to suppliers, vendors, the Internal Revenue Service (IRS), publicly traded unsecured notes, and equity holders; these are listed on the left-hand side of Table 7.1 in order of seniority. At the top are administrative expenses incurred in the bankruptcy, followed by tax claims. Equity holders come last.

The Bankruptcy Code endows the debtor with certain rights, which support the pursuit of a fair and equitable plan of reorganization. For example, the debtor is given an exclusive right to file a plan of reorganization during the first 120 days. Some courts extend the exclusivity period nearly endlessly. Eventually the court will remove the exclusive right and permit others including creditors or outsiders to submit alternate plans of reorganization. In addition, the debtor can arrange superpriority status in the bankruptcy hierarchy for banks extending *new* credit, which enables the firm to maintain normal operations.

The objective of the Bankruptcy Code is to provide a legal framework to enable interested parties (the debtor, creditors, and equity holders) to mutually pursue diverse goals. The debtor's objective in Chapter 11 is to construct a new capital structure (i.e., a blend of debt and equity) and a viable operating environment to enable the company to reemerge as a healthy nonbankrupt company. Trade creditors seek repayment and the continuation of a healthy business relationship with a customer. Other creditors pursue the return of loaned funds; often, when cash money is unavailable, they agree to accept equity in the new company in exchange for forgiveness of old debts. Finally, equity holders, who are at the bottom of the payment hierarchy, attempt to maintain ownership of the emerging company.

The Bankruptcy Code requires certain features to be common to all reorganization plans. Table 7.2 lists these items. Item 7 may be the most important, because it describes how the former debts are to be resolved. The disclosure statement is similar to a prospectus issued by a healthy company when it seeks to

Table 7.1

Final Distribution to TEI Creditors and Old Stockholders upon TEI Emerging from Bankruptcy
(all $ figures in millions and shares/warrants in thousands)

Debt (in ranking of seniority)	Amount of Claims		Estimated Cash Distributions	Distribution of Stock & Warrants						Dilution Analysis—% of Common Stock Outstanding after Warrants Exercised			
	Estimated Amount Filed to Recover Claim	Estimated Allowed Claim		New Senior Notes	New Common Stock	"C" New Senior Noteholders	"B" Other Creditors	"A" Old Stockholders	Total Stocks & Warrants	If No Exercise	If A's	If A's & B's	If All Warrants
Administrative Claims[a]	$6.4	$6.3	$5.6										
Tax Claims	$2.0	$1.6	$1.6										
Trade Claims	$0.2	$0.1	$0.1										
Note Claims[b]	$1.3	$0.7		$0.7		96.1			96.1				0.2%
14% Delayed Convertible Senior Subordinated	$7.2	$7.6		$7.8		971.2			971.2				1.9%
9% Second Dual Convertible Senior Subordinated	$30.5	$28.8		$28.8		3,699.0			3,699.0				7.4%
9% Third Dual Convertible Senior Subordinated	$10.4	$10.1		$10.1		1,301.5			1,301.5				2.6%
10% Second Delayed Converted Senior Subordinated	$36.2	$35.1		$2.7	6,112.3	346.8	4,151.9		10,611.0	30.6%	20.4%	23.5%	21.2%
10% Third Delayed Conv. Senior Sub.	$17.3	$17.0			3,210.2	2,180.5			5,390.6	16.1%	10.7%	12.4%	10.8%

Claim									
$12\frac{7}{8}\%$ Second Senior Subordinated	$7.8	$7.3	1,385.1	940.8	2,326.0	6.9%	4.6%	5.3%	4.7%
$14\frac{1}{8}\%$ Third Senior Subordinated	$24.0	$22.2	4,191.3	2,846.8	7,038.1	21.0%	14.0%	16.1%	14.1%
12% Fourth Senior Subordinated	$7.2	$7.0	1,320.5	896.9	2,217.5	6.6%	4.4%	5.1%	4.4%
9% Senior Subordinated Oil	$3.5	$3.5	659.0	447.8	1,106.7	3.3%	2.2%	2.5%	2.2%
$13\frac{1}{8}\%$ Senior Subordinated Indexed	$5.2	$5.3	1,004.5	682.3	1,686.8	5.0%	3.3%	3.9%	3.4%
$11\frac{1}{2}\%$ Subordinated Debentures	$10.5	$10.5	1,978.1	1,343.6	3,321.6	9.9%	6.6%	7.6%	6.6%
$8\frac{1}{4}\%$ Convertible Subordinated Debentures									
Other Bond Claims[c]	$0.7	$0.7	137.3	93.3	230.6	0.7%	0.46%	0.53%	0.5%
	$0.002	$0.002	0.4	0.3	0.7	0.002%	0.001%	0.002%	0.001%
Old Common Stockholders[d]	n/a	n/a	10,000.0	10,000	50,000	100.0%	33.3%	22.9%	20.0%
Totals	$164.3	$163.9	20,000	6,415	13,585	100.0%	100.0%	100.0%	100.0%
	n/a	$7.3	$50.0						

Source: TEI July 1989 Reorganization Plan.

Notes: All claims below Note Claims were not treated according to the Bankruptcy Code's absolute priority rule. This rule requires that the most senior note holders be paid in full first. Thus the less subordinated note-holders and the old common stockholders should not have received anything.

[a] To be paid primarily to lawyers and accountants who worked on reorganization plan.

[b] To be paid to the U.S. Department of Energy, Baker Hughes, Inc., Arthur Lipper Corp., and others who hold TEI promissory notes.

[c] These bonds matured in 1984 but were never redeemed.

[d] Old common stock outstanding was approximately 80 million shares.

Table 7.2

Required Components of a Plan of Reorganization

1. A plan must designate classes of claims and interests.
2. A plan must identify claims that are unimpaired.
   A class is impaired unless one of these is true:
   a. The plan does not alter the legal, equitable, or contractual rights of the class.
   b. The plan reinstates all aspects of the claim: interest owed, maturity date, and (a) above.
   c. The class is cashed out.
3. A plan must describe the treatment of each impaired class of claims.
4. A plan must provide uniform treatment for each claim in a class.
5. A plan must provide means to implement the plan.
6. A plan must not issue nonvoting stock and must insure that voting rights are equitable distributed to securities.
7. A plan must contain a disclosure statement that includes the debtor's financial condition, how the bankruptcy occurred, the plan's motivation, and a plan summary. It should inform a creditor and allow him or her to vote on the plan.

Source: Compiled by the author from the Bankruptcy Code.

sell securities; however, the disclosure is a document prepared by a recovering failed company.

In some cases, the plan emanates from the debtor; in other cases, the plan is the product of creditors, the trustee, or an external third party. The hierarchy of repayments in bankruptcy is contained in Table 7.3 and for Chapter 7 liquidations in Table 7.4. Notice that in a liquidation, secured creditors move ahead of administrative and tax claims as a result of the company's terminal status.

Claim holders who are less than fully repaid are designated as "impaired." Only members of impaired classes vote on the adequacy of a proposed plan of reorganization. A class approves a plan when half in number and two-thirds in dollar amount vote to accept it. When alternate plans are presented, voting is not exclusionary, for one plan and against the others; positive or negative votes may be given to all plans. A plan is not approved if even a single class of claims votes to reject. However, if the judge deems a plan to be fair and equitable to a class voting no, the plan can still be confirmed by a "cram-down." If the dissenting class contains secured creditors, the plan may be crammed down if the class retains its lien and receives deferred cash payments equal in value to the security. To cram down unsecured creditors, the plan must provide them with at least as much as they would receive in a liquidation and not make any payments to lower classes of claims. Equity may be crammed down if the plan provides them with an interest in property with a value equal to what they would receive in a liquidation and junior classes receive no payments.[5] Cram-downs are likely when senior creditors undertake to receive full payment of their claims while junior creditors and equity interests receive negligible payments. One factor reducing the number of cram-downs is the fact that the process of evaluating

Table 7.3

Chapter 11 Bankruptcy: Typical Repayment Hierarchy

1. *Expenses* to preserve or sell collateral.
2. *Superpriority liens* authorized by the court for post-petition financing.
3. *Secured claims* up to value of collateral and liens granted by the court for post-petition financing.
4. *Administrative expenses.*
5. *Wage* claims.
6. *Employee benefit* claims.
7. *Consumer deposits.*
8. *Tax* claims.
9. *Trade* claims, i.e., suppliers.
10. *Senior unsecured debt.*
11. *Subordinated debt.*
12. *Preferred* stock.
13. *Common* stock.

Source: Compiled by the author from the Bankruptcy Code.

Table 7.4

Chapter 7 Liquidation: Distribution Priorities

1. *Secured claims* using the proceeds from the sale of pledged assets; however, excess claims are unsecured and fall into number 8 below.
2. *Administrative expenses* in liquidation (notably trustee, attorneys, and accountants).
3. *Claims of creditors* arising in the ordinary course of business from the time the petition was filed until the appointment of a trustee.
4. *Wages and salaries,* up to 90 days prior to filing, to a $2,000 limit per employee.
5. *Employee benefit plan claims,* up to a $2,000 limit per employee.
6. *Customer claims* for deposits, up to a $900 limit per claim.
7. Certain *government taxes.*
8. *Unsecured claims* in order of priority.
9. *Preferred stock.*
10. *Common stock.*

Source: Compiled by the author from the Bankruptcy Code.

liquidation values is time consuming and costly. Recent research findings indicate that a sizable proportion of Chapter 11 reorganizations deviate from the absolute priority rule and provide some payment to lower classes before more senior classes are fully paid off, indicating a desire to avoid delays associated with a cram-down.[6]

When all classes vote to accept a plan or a plan has been crammed down, the plan is said to be confirmed. Confirmation takes about twenty months for the median case and two years for the average.[7] Reorganization plans necessitate subsequent actions: issuance of new securities, cash payouts, and abrogation of old securities. When all actions stipulated in a plan have been completed, the plan is consummated.

Not all bankrupt companies reorganize. A second option is to liquidate and distribute proceeds to claimants according to the absolute priority rule. The Bankruptcy Code's absolute priority rule results in the more senior claim holders being paid in full prior to any distribution to less senior claim holders. Liquidation is unlikely to generate maximum values for corporate assets. Turnaround experts estimate liquidation values for assets such as inventories, supplies, and receivables at fifteen to twenty cents on the dollar. Liquidation values of long-term assets such as plant and equipment vary greatly depending on industry conditions (excess production capacity) and economics (depressed product prices). Several notable investors of the 1980s, including Irwin Jacobs, acquired great wealth by buying the assets of liquidating companies and reselling them at a profit. A liquidation of TEI was hindered by low oil prices and a continued natural gas bubble. With estimated liquidation proceeds of less than 15 percent of total pre-petition debt (see Table 7.5), many creditors would receive nothing with this option.

A third strategy, known as "new value," involves a claim holder—a creditor, or more likely an equity holder—who invests additional equity into the company. Japonica Partners applied this scheme to acquire Sunbeam, Inc., in 1990 and made tremendous profits.[8] The principle of new value in bankruptcy dates back to the 1930s when it was argued that an investor who adds new money and management skills, making the company healthier, deserves a disproportionate piece of the pie.[9] The new-value investor gains leverage by injecting capital.[10] Gains for the new investor come at the expense of other creditors and equity shareholders. For example, junk bond holders anticipating 90 percent ownership in a new company might instead receive only 25 percent. None of TEI's creditors attempted this strategy. However, an equity shareholder made a similar attempt.

In a fourth alternative, another company enters the bankruptcy arena and acquires the failed enterprise. The new owner would try to acquire all of the outstanding claims; recent examples of this approach include General Cinema Corporation's purchase of Harcourt Brace Jovanovich, the acquisition of Southland Corporation by a Japanese firm, and Delta Airlines' bankruptcy court purchase of the Eastern Shuttle. An outside company would want to buy TEI for two reasons: first, to obtain low-cost new reserves and desirable exploration rights; second, some of TEI's operating tax loss carryforward might survive the acquisition (if the deal were structured right) and offset the combined taxable income of the new company. An expected bid from Conoco never materialized. In fact, Conoco was searching for a buyer for its share of the concession.

While the Bankruptcy Code places bonds in a single class, indenture agreements of specific bonds may delineate intrabond seniority and bankruptcy payment priorities. This repayment hierarchy is normally indisputable, but here it

Table 7.5

Liquidation Analysis for TEI As of March 31, 1989 (in $ thousands)

Assets	Book Value	Estimated Liquidation Proceeds
Cash/Cash Equivalents	$8,186	$8,068
Accounts Receivable	$5,629	$5,500
Oil & Gas Properties	$12,355	$43,385
Other Property	$3,475	$3,595
Other Assets	$6,010	$650
Total	$35,655	$61,198
Estimated Proceeds Available for Distribution		$61,198

Less Liabilities: [a]

World Bank Loan	$23,353	
Real Estate Mortgages	$2,979	
Accounts Payable/Accrued Liabilities	$1,944	
General & Administrative Expense	$3,500	
Administrative Claims	$4,200	
Taxes Owed	$2,217	
Trade Claims	$130	
Note Claims[b]	$750	
Total		($39,073)
Net Proceeds for Other Claims		$22,125
Estimated Remaining Claims		$155,131
Percentage of Other Claims		14%

Source: Derived from TEI July 1989 Reorganization Plan.

[a]Liabilities are paid according to the Bankruptcy Code's absolute priority rule.

[b]Includes Department of Energy, Arthur Lipper Corporation, Baker-Hughes, Inc., and promissory note claims.

became controversial. Certain junior bond holders argued (as a result of the exchange offers) that they warranted an elevated position in the repayment hierarchy because they were and had always been cash-pay bonds, while the other instruments had agreed to accept stock in lieu of cash. These holders of original-issue notes asserted that by accepting stock, other note holders had already agreed to be converted into equity, and therefore their hybrid debt/equity security belonged below cash-pay bonds in the debt hierarchy. The fact that the conversion was incomplete was immaterial, they argued, since the terms and conditions of the conversion had been clearly defined. By accepting the exchange offers, the "pseudo equity holders" anticipated benefiting from a recovery in TEI's financial conditions as would a stockholder. Consequently, it was argued, they belonged in their own, lower, committee. The equity committee grasped the idea and intimated that the equity bonds were in reality equity, too, and thus should *not* be elevated above the common equity class in the bankruptcy proceedings. Management indicated that it would not support this challenge, and the argument was dropped before the court ruled on its merits, but it may resurface in future exchange/bankruptcy situations.

The equity-pay notes were partly held by investors carrying the moniker "vulture investors." The vultures descended on TEI once the debt-exchange offers decimated the value of the bonds and the company began to exhibit the classic signs of a dying company: asset sales, a critical cash shortage, and unfavorable industry conditions. Vultures fall into two phylums: one flock pursues immediate and dramatic returns on their investments; the other strives for corporate control. However, both groups operate by paying distressed prices, often as low as twenty or thirty cents on the dollar, to acquire large stakes in the debt of distressed companies. Their goals in the bankruptcy proceedings are often incongruous with the desires of original investors who paid full value for their bonds.

Equity is normally subordinate to debt, since owners must bear additional business risk. Creditors assume that loans will be paid in full. In part, creditors lend to companies knowing that the Bankruptcy Code and bond covenants demand reimbursement of bond principal before resources go to preferred or common stock.

The equity committee contended that Drexel, the underwriter of TEI's bonds, had engaged in practices not in the company's best interest. Judge Richard L. Bohanon agreed with the premise and allowed the committee to pursue Drexel in court. This action paid off handsomely after the plan had been consummated, as discussed in chapter 8. However, by that time, TEI and its equity holders were extinct.

A unique aspect of this case was the absence of secured debt. The banking syndicate that had loaned TEI nearly $300 million had been fully repaid. Secured lenders have the right to be repaid in full before other creditors can receive payment. Moreover, secured creditors continue to receive or accrue interest while the firm is in bankruptcy provided that the assets securing the loan are worth more than the indebtedness.

The Egyptian subsidiary, Phoenix Resources of Egypt, had borrowed money from the International Finance Corporation (IFC) in the World Bank and had fully secured the debt using the concession as collateral. Phoenix of Egypt was not part of the bankruptcy filing nor were several other solvent subsidiaries. Had Phoenix of Egypt filed for bankruptcy, the Egyptian government might have invoked a clause in the concession agreement that would have rescinded the award of the property to TEI and returned it to the EGPC. With this secured position, the World Bank had a special status in the bankruptcy: not a claimant but more a restrained observer. The IFC became a key player when it objected to certain clauses in the indenture of a new class of debt created in the final plan of reorganization; as a result, the clauses were modified to meet the IFC's objections.

A preliminary reorganization plan was floated. It proposed preferential payments to certain subordinated debentures. A private investor threatened a lawsuit against the trustee of his lowly bonds "if any unsecured creditor's share was disproportionately greater than that received by his debentures." He argued that "unsecured is unsecured." Following this threat, the bank trustee held steadfast in the negotiations, the unequal distribution plan was dismissed, and a plan with equal payments (except for bonds whose indentures provided for seniority) was recommended.

Lender liability has recently become a critical factor in bankruptcy cases. Borrowers have sued lenders, claiming that lenders acted "improperly under the explicit terms of the loan agreement or under terms implied by contract law."[11] The basic idea is that by calling a loan or by not renewing a credit line, lenders unfairly caused the failure of the borrower. Settlements have been astronomical and may obstruct the banking sector's ability to perpetuate relationships with borrowers of limited creditworthiness. This issue did not arise in the course of TEI's bankruptcy, however.

Conducting Corporate Business in Bankruptcy

Managers of a bankrupt company accede certain powers to the bankruptcy judge and to creditors. Spending is the area most affected. Although permission is required for any spending, a blanket "ordinary course of business" approval facilitates spending to maintain the business. TEI received this. Capital investment projects require the consent of the court and creditors. All investments are risky. Creditors may propose instead that resources remain in the estate and settle their claims.

An oil company dies unless it acquires new assets through exploration or acquisition. At 1989 production rates, proven reserves in the Khalda Concession would be exhausted in four to five years. Management recommended continuing the exploration and development strategy. Existing commitments included $9 million for construction of a natural gas facility in the Khalda Concession and $3 million in exploration commitments in Malaysia. Egyptian expenditures were low risk, since the EGPC authorized increased oil production to coincide with the start of construction. Malaysia seemed to have enormous potential, given results from a first test well. The court approved both expenditures.

Judge Bohanon was unenthusiastic about new indebtedness. Instead, the company raised cash by selling assets. In March 1988, just prior to the bankruptcy filing, TEI's interest in the junk bond fund, the PT Corporation, was sold for $3 million, generating a $2.9 million gain. PT Corporation had been funded jointly by Drexel and TEI to create a tax shield for junk bond interest payments. TEI contributed its $300 million tax loss carryforward; Drexel contributed over $200 million in cash. A tax loss carryforward is accumulated when a company loses money in one year and may be used to offset profits earned in a future year. From inception, the PT Corporation was a clever transaction; TEI earned hundreds of thousands of dollars each quarter, generated a $2.9 million gain when sold, and the fund was terminated a year before the junk bond market collapsed.

In May 1988, a small producing property in Louisiana was sold for $2 million. In December 1988, a small nonproducing property in Alaska's Cook Inlet was sold to Amoco for $1.5 million. Competition among bidders enabled Kishpaugh to demand a 0.5 percent overriding royalty interest in future production. In 1993 Amoco reported that 750 million barrels of crude oil had been discovered in the first phase of an exploration program on the property. Wall Street speculated that the tiny override might someday be worth as much as $20 million.

Still more money was needed to meet commitments. Nothing was left to sell except the Khalda Concession itself. Kishpaugh pulled a rabbit out of his hat. Samsung, the Korean multinational, agreed to buy 20 percent of the remaining half interest in the Khalda Concession. The purchase price was $12 million up front with further bonus payments to be made by Samsung depending on growth over the next five years in "proven and probable reserves as determined by independent petroleum engineers." Bonus payments were estimated in the range of $8 million to $63 million. In the first and second annual reviews, no additional payment was required; however, in the third review, $4 million was owed to The Phoenix Resource Companies. The Khalda Concession collateralized the World Bank loan; hence, 20 percent of the Samsung payment reduced the IFC loan. Residual funds were escrowed out of the hands of creditors and earmarked for construction of the gas pipeline.

Administration of the bankruptcy also needed cash, to compensate lawyers, accountants, and investment bankers servicing the case. Administrative expenses are a top bankruptcy priority claim (see Table 7.3). Six million dollars were paid in administrative expenses (see the first row of Table 7.1). Certain observers contend that providing legal, accounting, and investment banking services to each bankruptcy committee is a serious flaw in current bankruptcy practice.[12] Expenses are borne by the estate not by the committees. Much of the work effort is duplicative, and, still worse, the practitioners have little incentive to foster a speedy resolution.

The Initial Plan of Reorganization

Once the administrative and cash-flow problems were resolved, it was time to craft a reorganization plan. A plan has two principal purposes: to satisfy creditors' claims and to establish a reorganized company with sufficient capital and cash flow to ensure survival and prosperity. All pre-petition claims must be settled in the plan. Naturally, claims are not all repaid in full; if the debtor had adequate funds to redeem its indebtedness, it would not have resorted to a bankruptcy filing.

The Bankruptcy Code requires that a plan be fair and equitable to all claim holders. Fairness does *not* mean that all claimants share equally in the proceeds of the bankrupt estate; rather, it means that all claims with equal stature receive equal treatment and that each class receives its due. Recently, a judge rejected MCorp's reorganization plan on the grounds that it was "unfair to equity holders."[13] The fairness requirement partially explains why classes of claims maneuver when it is time to establish committees.

A plan must also be feasible. Feasibility refers to a company's condition following emergence from bankruptcy. It is sometimes described as a state wherein the debtor is unlikely to become insolvent during the ensuing three years. There are no exact tests for feasibility, although it is possible to evaluate whether a plan provides the debtor with sufficient resources and future promise to have little likelihood of failing over the foreseeable future.

Crafting a reorganization plan is a formidable task. The architect must possess a variety of talents, including financial expertise, knowledge of operations management, insight into corporate strategy, and extraordinary patience to negotiate with combatants. Cases are prolonged for an assortment of reasons: friction among claimants, personal jealousies, incompetence, and self-dealing. Incredibly, some small firms have been bankrupt for more than ten years. Even some larger companies, such as Wheeling-Pittsburgh Steel and LTV, required five years or more to create a plan of reorganization that obtained bankruptcy court approval. TEI's case was not delayed; in fact, Judge Bohanon aggressively pushed the debtor and committees for resolution.

Plans of reorganization are not inexpensive to produce. For a mid-sized company, plan-development costs may exceed $250,000. Externally developed plans receive expense reimbursement only if the plan is approved. While the debtor has the exclusive right to file a reorganization plan, no other plan is put to a vote. Vote taking is time consuming (as much as several months) and expensive. Ruling on the admissibility of imperfectly filed ballots is critical and subject to vote fraud.

Senior secured-debt holders, a source of conflict because of their usual insistence on a transfer of all assets to themselves, had been repaid before the bankruptcy. Yet discord prevailed concerning the legal challenges discussed above and during the specification of a reorganization plan.

Management crystallized a preliminary plan, which it delivered for review and comment to the committees. By circulating a nascent plan, committee sentiments can be gauged; most groups are presupposed to want more. Kishpaugh's goal was to forge a viable oil and gas exploration company, called The Phoenix Resource Companies, Inc., which would have access to capital markets. His plan proposed issuing $25 million in new debt plus new equity including a preferred stock and warrants (an option to buy equity cheaply in the future) in exchange for $170 million in pre-petition debt and the old common stock. The creditors' committee aggressively condemned the plan and insisted that they receive more debt. Their aim was the creation of a royalty trust that would make no new investments and would pay out all future earnings to new bond holders.

Management argued that the higher interest burden associated with additional debt would produce an infeasible plan, one that would bankrupt the company. It also argued that the plan created an eviscerated company that merely cashed checks issued in Egypt, a company with no future. It campaigned to find a compromise settlement with creditors, but strangely their differences were irresolvable. This was a critical juncture. Other companies in similar positions dig in and do battle with creditors; management proposes an endless succession of reorganization plans, which creditors routinely reject, while the managers remain entrenched in their offices.[14] Kishpaugh was a better man than that. He allowed the exclusive period to expire; his aim was to get the thing done, and he discerned that creditors would never endorse his concept.

The creditors' committee authored its own plan, which was endorsed by the equity committee and the bankruptcy examiner. The plan was mailed for votes with ballots due back by October 16, 1989. It included a $50 million senior note and new equity and warrants and retained the new name, The Phoenix Resource Companies. More troubling than the size of the new debt were its covenants that required that all free cash flow generated in Egypt retire the new debt at face value. Moreover, they decisively restricted The Phoenix Resource Companies' operating flexibility. The covenants proscribed corporate actions in the following ways:

- If Phoenix Resources of Egypt accumulates more than $4 million of unrestricted excess cash after April 9, 1992, then 75 percent of the excess must be used to redeem notes.
- If the non-Egyptian portion of the company has annual cash flows in excess of $4 million, then 33 percent of the excess would be used to redeem notes.
- If cumulative losses from May 1, 1990, forward exceed $12 million, then the notes would immediately be due and payable.
- If company assets are sold, then 33 percent of the proceeds would redeem the new notes.

Most important, the covenants restricted the company's access to new capital. A shortage of capital might jeopardize the Khalda Concession. Management did not endorse the plan and instead let it proceed on its own accord. Possibly this was the response that creditors desired, since they dropped Kishpaugh from the plan and proposed to hire a new CEO.

Not every institutional investor (mutual funds and insurance companies) behaved offensively. A good example was the manager of the high-yield bond funds at Massachusetts Financial Services (MFS), a large Boston-based mutual fund manager. MFS is usually a passive investor, meaning that it does not attempt to influence management. Its investment in TEI dated back to the original-issue bonds, prior to the exchange offers. MFS did not join the creditors' committee but worked from the outside to synthesize a plan that would return its invested principal. MFS accepted the obvious: that a feasible plan of reorganization could not issue sufficient new debt to redeem old debts entirely; hence, MFS advocated the issuance of debt, equity, and warrants to compensate old debtors. MFS's goal was to hold the equity until it recovered its funds and possibly even earned a profit. James Swanson, MFS's fund manager, is interviewed in chapter 9.

Several long-term equity investors regarded TEI without Kishpaugh as a formula for disaster. They viewed him as a key employee; after all, he was responsible for the discovery of the Khalda Concession, had saved the company three times from bankruptcy with successful exchange offers, and had negotiated advantageous transactions with Conoco and Samsung. In addition, they grasped the outrageousness of the covenants attached to the senior notes to be issued by the new plan. Among the most egregious items was the provision that stated that if The Phoenix Resource Companies lost more than $12 million after 1990, the senior debt would immediately become due and payable in full. In that event, a new bankruptcy would be declared, and presumably those TEI debtors and equity holders given stock or warrants in the new company would be wiped out. Incredibly, the $12 million loss calculation included amortization of the new debt; that is, if the $50 million senior note initially traded at forty cents on the dollar, the company would be legally required to report a $3 million annual accounting loss on the bonds. Within several years the cumulative-loss indenture provision could easily be violated, especially if oil prices remained at $15 per barrel. If that happened, the company would be owned entirely by the senior notes. A second harmful covenant earmarked virtually all monies earned in the Khalda Concession for redemption of the new notes *at par* instead of investing the funds to strengthen the company.

These investors scoured the globe seeking players with fresh cash. Mostly, they were ignored, because they lacked a corporate affiliation, because they had little money of their own to invest, or because TEI was bankrupt. At the last minute, they discovered a small oil producer on the American Stock Exchange (Global Natural Resources or GNR) whose exploration strategy complemented TEI's, which had previously acquired oil assets in the bankruptcy court (Galvest, Inc.), and which had a $50 million pool of unallocated funds. More amazingly, GNR and Phoenix Resources had a doppelgänger relationship; they had been created concurrently from the same bankruptcy, King Resources Company.

GNR's balance sheet carried little debt (long-term debt was 33 percent of total assets), and the company had strong profits and a substantial cash horde (derived from an investment by General Electric in GNR preferred stock). On September 29, 1989 (seventeen days before votes were due in on the creditors' plan), GNR proposed a transaction wherein it would invest $25 million dollars in exchange for 51 percent of the new equity. Kishpaugh would continue as CEO, and $25 million of debt would be created and distributed to creditors with GNR's $25 million. Management visited with GNR and concluded that the offer was in the best interest of all parties. It appeared that there would be no difficulties in the bankruptcy court. However, two days before a disclosure statement hearing, GNR canceled the deal. No reason was given. It was hypothesized that a vulture investor had sabotaged GNR's plan by threatening to bring up GNR's sordid history: a former chairman had been accused of stealing corporate assets, an opponent in a proxy battle had mysteriously fallen down an elevator shaft, and it was alleged that at one time GNR's principal owner had been Robert Vesco, the fugitive. Perhaps the vulture investor had plans of his own, either to increase the distribution to his bond or to take control.

One of the largest vulture investors was Goldman Sachs (Goldman). Historically, Goldman had been a financial adviser to blue chip corporations and had refrained from hostile takeovers. This corporate philosophy abruptly changed in early 1989 when Goldman acquired a majority stake in Wheeling-Pittsburgh Steel, a bankrupt company, and then used its equity leverage to attempt a highly favorable (to Goldman) reorganization plan. The plan was rejected by the steel company's creditors, but it was a clear signal of the new Goldman strategy.

Goldman's involvement with TEI was bursting with allegations of illegal activity. At the end, however, Goldman had majority control of TEI. Goldman began accumulating the bonds early. Allegations surfaced that Goldman's bond trader knew the outcome of the reorganization plan before it was finalized, even though he was not a member of the committee. If true, he would be able to buy bonds knowing approximately what they were to be worth in the future. *Forbes* magazine stated that Goldman's partners "frequently discussed the case, including potential plans for reorganization of the company, with unsecured creditors' committee counsel Fried Frank Harris," a well-known large corporate law firm in New York City.[15] This behavior was curious and potentially illegal.

Kishpaugh resigned in a private letter to the judge in November following the withdrawal of the GNR plan. He resigned in support of the creditors' committee plan but would not participate in it. Kishpaugh's actions may have established a new standard for CEOs of bankrupt companies. In July 1992, Edward Beauvais, founder and chairman of America West Airlines, resigned, saying, "[I] hope that it will improve the prospects for a successful emergence."[16] Meanwhile, the World Bank, Phoenix Resources of Egypt's secured creditor, objected to the debt covenants written into the new plan and threatened to foreclose on its loan. TEI was in technical default as a consequence of having filed a Chapter 11 petition. If the World Bank fulfilled its threat and demanded repayment, the Khalda Concession would have to be sold. Between Christmas and New Year's the committee changed several covenants and endorsed the provision that all the covenants could be eliminated with the approval of 66 percent of the new debt.[17] These changes mollified the World Bank.

Kishpaugh was asked on several occasions to remain, but he refused because of the liquidating trust aspect of the plan. George Lawrence, TEI's vice-president, chief financial officer, and general counsel, was appointed CEO. Lawrence had been with TEI since 1985, beginning as a deputy general counsel. Prior to that, he worked in the Justice Department in environmental affairs.

Slightly more than a year after the Chapter 11 bankruptcy petition had been filed, a single plan prepared by the creditors' committee remained on the table. The Bankruptcy Code requires a plan to satisfy two criteria. First, is the plan fair? A plan is fair if it abides by the absolute priority rule and if it pays each claimant as much as they would receive in a liquidation. A liquidation analysis was prepared (the "best interest of creditors" test), reproduced in Table 7.5, to compare the plan with the alternative. A Chapter 7 liquidation would generate $61 million, of which $39 million would pay claims preceding bond holders. The remaining $22 million would partially repay senior unsecured bond holders. Other bond holders and the equity class would receive nothing. Unquestionably, the reorganization plan, with its allocations to all classes of creditors, was better than a liquidation. Second, is the plan feasible? A plan is infeasible if another restructuring is likely. Tables 7.6a and 7.6b reproduce cash-flow projections reported in the plan, based on alternative scenarios for oil prices and production. Even with oil at $12 per barrel, the new TEI would be healthy over the next few years, because the new debt paid no cash interest for three years.

Following a multi-week voting period, the plan was accepted on January 10, 1990, but as usual, another dispute emerged.[18] An investor who still objected to several covenants on the new debt had received incorrect ballots. Moreover, vote totals were not disclosed, as they should have been, to the court or to the parties of interest. Subsequent to an effort to force a recount, Lawrence persuaded creditors to change several additional covenant provisions. Specifically, $6.5 million to be repaid from pipeline construction costs would be moved from an escrow account established to redeem new notes into a general purpose corporate account.

The battle was over. The issue was never TEI's financial well-being but who would control it. Goldman emerged with over 50 percent ownership. However, should the A warrants distributed in the bankruptcy plan be exercised, it would lose its absolute control. Its equity share would be diminished to 35 percent. The A warrants would not be exercised unless the new stock traded above $1 per share within one year from the plan's consummation date. A $1 share price seemed unlikely given the low oil prices, but a gas clause had finally been received for the Khalda Concession.

The Final Plan of Reorganization

Most creditors in a bankruptcy reorganization are repaid with new securities, debt or equity, issued in exchange for securities in the old firm. The senior-most securities might receive some cash, but dollars are generally reserved for the IRS

Table 7.6a

Projected Net Cash Flows (in $ millions)

	Pessimistic Scenario ($12 Barrel)					Current Events Scenario ($15 Barrel)				
Revenues	1989	1990	1991	1992	1993	1989	1990	1991	1992	1993
Khalda Concession Profit[a]	$8.2	$7.3	$10.0	$11.6	$11.6	$8.2	$9.1	$12.5	$14.5	$14.5
Gas Revenue from Khalda Concession	$1.0	$1.0	$1.0	$1.0	$1.0	$1.0	$1.0	$1.0	$1.0	$1.0
Domestic Properties Profit	$0.5	$1.5	$1.5	$1.5	$1.5	$0.5	$1.5	$1.5	$1.5	$1.5
Sale of 20% of Khalda Concession	$12.0	$0.0	$4.0	$0.0	$0.0	$12.0	$0.0	$4.0	$0.0	$0.0
Gas Sales Credit	$2.6	$0.0	$0.0	$0.0	$0.0	$2.6	$0.0	$0.0	$0.0	$0.0
Cash Collateral Release[b]	$3.5	$1.1	$0.0	$0.0	$0.0	$3.5	$1.1	$0.0	$0.0	$0.0
Total Revenues	$27.8	$10.9	$16.5	$14.1	$14.1	$27.8	$12.7	$19.0	$17.0	$17.0
Expenses										
Reorganization Costs[c]	($4.9)	$0.0	$0.0	$0.0	$0.0	($4.9)	$0.0	$0.0	$0.0	$0.0
General & Administrative Costs	($3.5)	($3.3)	($3.3)	($3.3)	($3.3)	($3.5)	($3.3)	($3.3)	($3.3)	($3.3)
Khalda Concession—Capital Expenditures for Gas Pipeline	($2.3)	($4.7)	($1.1)	($1.4)	$0.0	($2.3)	($4.7)	($1.1)	($1.4)	$0.0
Exploration Costs—Non-Khalda[d]	($2.1)	($0.5)	($1.6)	($1.0)	($0.2)	($2.1)	($0.5)	($1.6)	($1.0)	($0.2)
World Bank Debt Service[e]	($9.7)	($4.5)	($4.2)	($3.9)	($3.5)	($9.7)	($4.5)	($4.2)	($3.9)	($3.5)
Senior Notes Interest	$0.0	$0.0	$0.0	($1.7)	($6.7)	$0.0	$0.0	$0.0	($1.7)	($6.7)
Tax Payments[f]	($0.2)	($0.4)	($0.4)	($0.4)	($0.4)	($0.2)	($0.4)	($0.4)	($0.4)	($0.4)
Total Expenses	($22.7)	($13.4)	($10.6)	($11.7)	($14.1)	($22.7)	($13.4)	($10.6)	($11.7)	($14.1)
Projected Net Cash Flow	$5.1	($2.5)	$5.9	$2.4	$0.0	$5.1	($0.7)	$8.4	$5.3	$2.9

Source: TEI July 1989 Reorganization Plan.

[a] Profit data is derived from the Khalda Concession Finance Model.

[b] Cash that is restricted by exploration commitments to various joint ventures.

[c] Primarily administrative claims payable to bankruptcy lawyers and accountants.

[d] Includes funds scheduled for Malaysia, the Natrun Concession—Egypt, Australia, and Dutch North Sea.

[e] Includes principal payment of $4 million upon receipt of 20% Khalda sale proceeds.

[f] The federal government requires companies to pay an alternative minimum tax in lieu of having to pay income taxes. Note: company has tax loss carryforwards.

Table 7.6b

Projected Net Cash Flows (in $ millions)

	Oil Supplies Tighten ($18 Barrel)					An Oil Shock Scenario ($25 Barrel)				
Revenues	1989	1990	1991	1992	1993	1989	1990	1991	1992	1993
Khalda Concession Profit[a]	$8.2	$10.9	$15.0	$17.4	$17.4	$13.7	$15.1	$20.8	$29.6	$32.1
Gas Revenue from Khalda Concession	$1.0	$1.0	$1.0	$1.0	$1.0	$1.0	$1.0	$1.0	$1.0	$1.0
Domestic Properties Profit	$0.5	$1.5	$1.5	$1.5	$1.5	$0.5	$1.5	$1.5	$0.0	$1.5
Sale of 20% of Khalda Concession	$12.0	$0.0	$4.0	$0.0	$0.0	$12.0	$0.0	$4.0	$0.0	$0.0
Gas Sales Credit	$2.6	$0.0	$0.0	$0.0	$0.0	$2.6	$0.0	$0.0	$0.0	$0.0
Cash Collateral Release[b]	$3.5	$1.1	$0.0	$0.0	$0.0	$3.5	$1.1	$0.0	$0.0	$0.0
Total Revenues	$27.8	$14.5	$21.5	$19.9	$19.9	$33.3	$18.7	$27.3	$32.1	$34.6
Expenses										
Reorganization Costs[c]	($4.9)	$0.0	$0.0	$0.0	$0.0	($4.9)	$0.0	$0.0	$0.0	$0.0
General & Administrative Costs	($3.5)	($3.3)	($3.3)	($3.3)	($3.3)	($3.5)	($3.3)	($3.3)	($3.3)	($3.3)
Khalda Concession—Capital Expenditures for Gas Pipeline	($2.3)	($4.7)	($1.1)	($1.4)	$0.0	($2.3)	($4.7)	($1.1)	($1.4)	$0.0
Exploration Costs—Non-Khalda[d]	($2.1)	($0.5)	($1.6)	($1.0)	($0.2)	($2.1)	($0.5)	($1.6)	($1.0)	($0.2)
World Bank Debt Service[e]	($9.7)	($4.5)	($4.2)	($3.9)	($3.5)	($9.7)	($4.5)	($4.2)	($3.9)	($3.5)
Senior Notes Interest	$0.0	$0.0	$0.0	$1.7	$6.7	$0.0	$0.0	$0.0	$1.7	$6.7
Tax Payments[f]	($0.2)	($0.4)	($0.4)	($0.4)	($0.4)	($0.2)	($0.4)	($0.4)	($0.4)	($0.4)
Total Expenses	($22.7)	($13.4)	($10.6)	($11.7)	($14.1)	($22.7)	($13.4)	($10.6)	($11.7)	($14.1)
Projected Net Cash Flow	$5.1	$1.1	$10.9	$8.2	$5.8	$10.6	$5.3	$16.7	$20.4	$20.5

Source: TEI July 1989 Reorganization Plan.

[a] Profit data is derived from the Khalda Concession Finance Model.

[b] Cash that is restricted by exploration commitments to various joint ventures.

[c] Primarily administrative claims payable to bankruptcy lawyers and accountants.

[d] Includes funds scheduled for Malaysia, the Natrun Concession—Egypt, Australia, and Dutch North Sea.

[e] Includes principal payment of $4 million upon receipt of 20% Khalda sale proceeds;

[f] The federal government requires companies to pay an alternative minimum tax in lieu of having to pay income taxes. Note: company has tax loss carryforwards.

and administrative expenses. The value of cash, new debt, and new equity received need not equal the claim against the bankrupt estate, though no class should receive more than it was owed. However, since months may elapse between a plan's construction and consummation dates, a class may receive extra; for example, certain claimants in the Storage Technology case recovered 130 percent of their claim amounts due to stock price appreciation.[19] The amount of debt and equity issued is constrained by the feasibility criteria and by the underlying value of the bankrupt estate.

There were too few assets to repay in full all of TEI's debts. Thirty percent of creditors received full payment, in the form of new debt, as seen in columns four through ten of Table 7.1. Other creditors took new common stock and warrants in lieu of new indebtedness. If the value of the new equity rises, then these old creditors might recoup their investment in TEI or even see a profit.

Toward the end of the bankruptcy, the discourse resembled the scene in George Orwell's *Animal Farm* when the pigs alter the rules by proclamation. With both the GNR bid and Kishpaugh out of the way, the senior-most unsecured creditors firmly controlled the process. A final edition of the plan inserted a new type of warrant (Series C), which was awarded to the senior bond holders. The extra dispensation did not result in the class receiving an excess distribution and, thus, was acceptable.

Newly Distributed Securities

The new securities issued in the Chapter 11 reorganization were $49.25 million of debt securities,[20] 20 million shares of common stock, and three classes of warrants enabling holders to purchase 27.5 million common shares. The debt carried a 10 percent interest coupon, which for the first three years was to be paid in kind, i.e., as new bonds. Quarterly cash interest would commence on July 9, 1993. If all the notes remained outstanding, these interest payments would amount to approximately $1.5 million per quarter. The notes matured April 9, 2000.

The three warrants are described in Table 7.7. Series A warrants, referred to as "equity warrants," were distributed to old equity holders in a ratio of one for eight and expired one year after confirmation unless they were exercised. Unless Phoenix Resources' stock sold above $1 per share by the expiration date, the A warrants would not exercise. The Series B warrants, called "creditor warrants," were distributed as additional compensation to the bond holders who accepted shares of The Phoenix Resource Companies for discharged TEI obligations. The Series C warrants were created at the end of the bankruptcy process and were distributed only to senior bond creditors receiving the new senior notes; these were called new senior note holder warrants.

The A warrants were awarded to TEI equity holders as absolution for their not receiving shares in The Phoenix Resource Companies. Such benevolence to disenfranchised equity holders is customary, though a payment of perhaps 1–3 percent of the new shares is more frequent. The senior bond holders probably did

Table 7.7

Comparison of Warrants

Series	Number Outstanding	Exercise Price	Expiration Date	May Be Accelerated If Price Exceeds
A	10.0 million	$1.00	4/9/91	—
B	11.7 million	$1.00	4/9/95	$1.50
C	5.8 million	$1.75	4/9/95	$2.50

not anticipate that the A warrants would ever be executed. In their minds, they had given away something with no value, and in the exchange they had forestalled a bitter confrontation with equity holders who might have delayed the resolution of the bankruptcy.

Both the B and C warrants had five-year terms. If The Phoenix Resource Companies' stock price exceeded $1.50 (for the Bs) and $2.50 (for the C warrants) for twenty consecutive days, the company could accelerate their expiration and force holders to exercise the warrants sooner. The exercise price for the A and B warrants was $1 per share; $1.75 per share for the C warrants. If all three warrant series were fully executed, the company would raise nearly $32 million of new capital.

Who Got What

The distribution of securities to each class of claimants from the confirmed plan of reorganization varied according to ranking in the claims hierarchy. The *total* allocation to each class is presented in the middle section of Table 7.1, p. 110–11. Table 7.8 lists the distribution *per dollar* for bonds and *per share* for stocks. Overall, the plan made these final settlements:

- *Administrative claims*—$1.6 million
  An additional $4 million was paid to this class in interim compensation.
  Received face amount of allowed claim in cash.

- *Trade claims*—$130,000
  Received face amount of allowed claims in cash.

- *Note claims*—$750,000
  Received $1 principal amount of Series A new senior notes for every $1 principal amount of allowed note claim. In addition, received 128 new senior note holder's warrants (Series C) per $1,000 of allowed claims.

- *Bond claims*
  Received a package of securities consisting of $49.25 million of new senior notes (Series B, C, D, and E), 20 million shares of common stock in The Phoenix Resource Companies, 13.5 million creditors warrants (Series B), and 6.4 million new senior note holders warrants (Series C).

Table 7.8

Distribution of Securities from Chapter 11 (per $1 or 1 share of old security)

			Warrants		
Old Security	10% Senior Notes	Common Shares	Series A	Series B	Series C
14% Bonds	$1.057				0.1294
9% 2nd Bonds	$0.973				0.1193
9% 3rd Bonds	$0.999				0.1223
10% 2nd Bonds	$0.067	0.1662		0.1153	0.0080
10% 3rd Bonds		0.1778		0.1234	
$12^7/_8$% Bonds		0.1753		0.1216	
$14^1/_8$% Bonds		0.1722		0.1195	
12% Bonds		0.1757		0.1219	
9% Oil Bonds		0.1856		0.1289	
$13^1/_8$% Bonds		0.1693		0.1174	
$11^1/_2$% Bonds		0.1875		0.1300	
$8^1/_4$% Bonds		0.1860		0.1291	
Common Shares			0.1250		

Source: TEI July 1989 Reorganization Plan, p. 11.

The senior-most bonds were the 14 percent and the 9 percent second and 9 percent third bonds. Each received new senior notes nearly equal to the full face value of their claims, plus 129, 119, and 122 Series C note holders warrants, respectively, per bond. Variation resulted from interest owed to the bond holders before the bankruptcy filing.

The next most senior notes, the old 10 percent second bond claim, were allocated some of the new bonds ($66.82 par amount of the new senior notes), 166 shares of The Phoenix Resource Companies stock, 115 Series B warrants, and 8 Series C warrants for every $1,000 par amount outstanding. Had a larger new bond issue been feasible, this bond would have received more of the senior notes and fewer common shares.

Other bond claims received no new bonds. Their claims were settled for new shares of common (between 169 and 187 shares of common stock) and creditor warrants (between 117 and 129 Series B creditor warrants) for every $1,000 par amount of their claim, depending on owed accrued interest. The 11½ percent notes, for example, received 187.5 shares of The Phoenix Resource Companies and 130 Series B warrants; after exercising the warrants, the 11½ percent notes would control 2.2 million shares, or almost 5 percent of The Phoenix Resource Companies. The 10 percent third delayed converts could own 3 percent of The Phoenix Resource Companies upon exercising the warrants.

- *Class-action claims*
  $100,000 was put in an escrow account for class-action claims pending the outcome of the court case.

- *Old stockholders*
  Received for every eight old shares, one Series A warrant (totaling almost 10 million warrants) to purchase one new share at a price of $1 per share. These warrants expired one year following the consummation of the plan—on April 9, 1991.

The Phoenix Resource Companies would initially have 20 million common shares. An additional 30 million shares would be issued if all the warrants were exercised (10 million Series A, 13.6 million Series B, and 6.4 million Series C). TEI's equity holders would own 20 percent of The Phoenix Resource Companies if they exercised the A warrants by investing an additional $10 million. However, two-thirds of TEI's 80 million shares had been paid to creditors in lieu of cash interest beginning in 1985. Thus, pre-1985 shareholders, who at one point had owned the entire company, would own 6 percent of The Phoenix Resource Companies for an additional investment of $3 million.

- *Other interests*
  Stock Purchase Claims—These claims, mostly from Baker Hughes Corporation, concerned losses arising from a stock-for-services arrangement instituted when cash flow was limited. The claimant argued that by the time stock certificates were received it was impossible to sell the stock and receive full value of their services.
  Claims would receive no distribution under the accepted plan.

The right-hand side of Table 7.1 (p. 110–11) describes ownership of the new company under four scenarios: all warrants expire unexercised, Series A warrants exercise, Series A and B warrants exercise, and all warrants exercise. Warrants will only exercise if the price of the underlying shares of The Phoenix Resource Companies rises above the exercise price. Consider the Series A warrants: each warrant can buy one share of The Phoenix Resource Companies for a price of $1. If the price of the stock exceeds (falls below) $1, each warrant exercised earns an immediate profit (loss). Before the warrants, the intermediate and junior bonds (the 10 percent second delayed convertible notes down to the 8¼ percent notes) held 100 percent of the stock. If the Series A warrants alone exercised, former TEI stockholders would acquire 33 percent of The Phoenix Resource Companies. However, since the A and B warrants had the same exercise price, it is more realistic to consider both A and B warrants exercising; then the percentage owned by former TEI stockholders drops to 22.9 percent. Finally, if the Series C warrants exercise, the ownership of former shareholders falls to 20 percent.

Table 7.9

Immediate Value of Securities Issued from the Reorganization Plan
(per $1 or 1 share of old security)*

Old Security	Value of All Securities
14% Bonds	$0.45
9% 2nd Bonds	$0.41
9% 3rd Bonds	$0.42
10% 2nd Bonds	$0.18
10% 3rd Bonds	$0.13
$12^7/_8$% Bonds	$0.13
$14^1/_8$% Bonds	$0.13
12% Bonds	$0.13
9% Oil Bonds	$0.14
$13^1/_8$% Bonds	$0.13
$11^1/_2$% Bonds	$0.14
$8^1/_4$% Bonds	$0.14
Common Shares	$0.01

*Based on a $400 price for the senior notes, $.625 for the common stock, $.0625 for the A warrants, $.1875 for the B warrants, and $.1875 for the C warrants.

Value of Distributed Securities

The value of the securities received by the major classes of claim are reported in Table 7.9 as of the consummation date of the plan, April 9, 1990. The three senior-most notes each received about forty-two cents on the dollar. Original security investors incurred a significant loss. Vulture investors, who may have paid less than forty-two cents, earned a profit. The junior bonds each returned about thirteen cents on the dollar. Some of these notes had traded under ten cents during the bankruptcy, so some later investors may have earned an immediate profit.

Common shareholders held warrants worth about 1 cent per TEI share. Before the reorganization plan was announced, TEI's common stock traded for approximately $0.125, while in fact its value was closer to $0.01. Discrepancies such as this arise in many bankruptcies from speculative fervor or ignorance. Recently, the common equity in Continental Airlines traded at $1.50 per share despite an announced plan of reorganization which proposed to terminate the old common stock.[21]

Following the distribution of stock, warrants, and bonds, an active market developed for the securities of the new company. Some original holders chose to sell out, while some new investors bought the issue.

Notes

1. Management perceived itself as lean, having winnowed its ranks until "there were no executives, only a few professionals."

2. At the time, Kishpaugh's salary was $300,000, considerable but not excessive, given his responsibilities and capabilities.

3. See Alison Leigh Cowan, "Ringside Seat on Corporate Disaster," p. D1.

4. Ibid.

5. See Mark S. Summers, *Bankruptcy Explained: A Guide For Businesses.*

6. See Julian R. Franks and Walter N. Torous, "An Empirical Investigation of U.S. Firms in Reorganization," 747–69.

7. See Edward Altman, *Corporate Financial Distress*; or Allan C. Eberhart, "Chapter 11—Surprisingly Good for Shareholders."

8. See *Wall Street Journal* (July 31, 1992): C2.

9. Linda Sandler, "Revco Case Tests Junkholders' Edge Over Stockholders," pp. C1–C2.

10. During December 1991, an appeals court case reversed a bankruptcy decision approving a new-value settlement in a real estate bankruptcy. Ramifications of this decision may be far reaching.

11. See Benjamin E. Hermalin, "The Negative Effects of Lender Liability."

12. See Sol Stein's *A Feast for Lawyers* to hear one man's bitterness for the process.

13. See *Wall Street Journal* (January 8, 1992): B6. Coincidentally, MCorp was the trustee of several TEI bonds.

14. Revco's, Sunbeam's, and LTV's bankruptcy cases dragged on through a series of votes on alternate plans. In part, acrimonious relationships between management and creditors precipitated these delays.

15. Mathew Schifrin, "Seller Beware," pp. 36–38.

16. *Wall Street Journal* (July 20, 1992): C11.

17. Finding itself in a cash-rich position during 1991, Phoenix Resources acquired many outstanding bonds at a substantial discount: from 70 percent to 90 percent of face value. The June 1991 10-Q report to the SEC stated that the company intended to vote these bonds against the covenants; the September 1991 10-Q report contradicted this statement.

18. While not a speed record, the plan emerged swiftly compared with the average reorganization.

19. I am indebted to Rand Askog for this observation and calculation.

20. The five classes of debt, Series A through Series E, differed in order of redemption.

21. Some of this may be due to short sellers closing out their positions. Eventually, the exchange delisted the equity.

8

A Restructured Company

During the one year, eleven months, and fifteen days of bankruptcy, TEI's management, creditors, and external parties jockeyed for position. Each sought to control the committees and the court-appointed examiner in hopes of steering the final plan of reorganization. Underlying these stake-holder maneuvers was the belief that tremendous value remained in the asset.

Prior to the bankruptcy-supervised restructuring, TEI reported having approximately $37 million of assets (at book value), $195 million of debt, 80 million common shares, and a net book value of negative $158 million. The debt holders assumed control of the company, a common outcome in bankruptcy cases with similar imbalances.

In exchange for expunging all claims against TEI, the reorganization plan created $50 million in new debt, 20 million new common shares, and three classes of warrants. The warrants entitled holders to purchase up to 30 million additional common shares in the new company, The Phoenix Resource Companies.

The Settlement with Drexel

Drexel had been a financial adviser to TEI in connection with the issuance of bonds and debt restructurings and had owned and traded TEI securities since 1977. Drexel was a claimant in the bankruptcy case, as an owner of approximately $14 million face amount of TEI's debt securities. Drexel may have held these securities as unsold remnants from original public offerings, as an investment, or they may have been acquired in a distressed purchase, possibly from a failing Drexel client. Soon after TEI's bankruptcy filing, Drexel itself filed for bankruptcy. The TEI bonds, at face value, represented nearly 1 percent of Drexel's reported assets.

The equity committee representing TEI's stockholders accused Drexel of engaging in activities (during past relations between the companies) that resulted in multimillion-dollar damages. This wild-goose-chase claim surfaced prior to

Drexel's bankruptcy filing. Drexel's bankruptcy case was a morass of claims and accusations including allegations of illegal and quasi-legal conduct on the investment banker's part. Overshadowing the proceedings were criminal and civil charges rendered against Michael Milken. In comparison, the TEI case is simple. This climate was ideal for a speedy resolution of TEI's claims. Following the emergence of The Phoenix Resource Companies, George Lawrence, the company president, and Drexel designed a settlement wherein claims against Drexel would be dropped in exchange for Drexel vacating its claims to The Phoenix Resource Companies securities to which it was entitled. In addition, The Phoenix Resource Companies received an allowed claim in the face amount of $100,000, payable solely from the Civil Disgorgement Fund created in the Drexel/SEC settlement. Had Drexel received its due, it would have totaled $2.8 million of senior notes, 2 million common shares, and 1.75 million warrants to purchase additional common stock.

Several other disputed claims were disallowed by the bankruptcy court or were settled. These settlements reduced the number of new securities issued. Debt had a face value of $47 million, not $50 million; 16.9 million shares of common stock rather than 20 million shares; 27.5 million warrants, not the original 30 million.

Ready to Emerge

The reorganization plan was consummated, that is, all parts were implemented, on April 9, 1990. TEI had been a debtor in possession since April 26, 1988.

In early 1990, after being relatively static for nearly two years, production in the Khalda Concession began to expand and ended the year at more than 27,000 barrels per day. Oil prices were weak and pierced the $20 level. Revenues were sufficient for short-term survival, but the new debt's $12 million cumulative-loss indenture provision remained a genuine concern.

On the positive side, the Vermillion field's natural gas discovery offshore Texas was entering production. Revenue reached nearly $1.5 million. The reserve was estimated to have a value in excess of $4 million.

The Phoenix Resource Companies' capital structure continued to display negative net worth of $24 million; that is, the book value of debt, $63 million, exceeded the book value of assets, $39 million. Most of this deficit resulted from the underestimation of asset values by book accounting method. At the end of 1989, for instance, Egyptian reserves were estimated to have a market value of $67 million, with oil priced at $17.86 per barrel; the corresponding figure for 1988 was $52 million, with oil at $13.11 per barrel.

On the effective day of the plan of reorganization, the 10 percent senior notes due April 9, 2000, were estimated by a Wall Street market maker to have a fair market value of $400 per $1,000 bond. There are several reasons for this sizable discount. First, the bonds were unrated, which restricts many institutional investors from trading them. Second, cash interest would not be paid until July 9, 1993. Interest earned but unpaid during the first three years would be distributed on April 9, 1993, in the form of additional senior notes. Third, the 10 percent interest coupon was approximately 400 basis points beneath the interest paid on similar oil and gas company bonds. Fourth, the notes were tightly held: $29 million by one registrant, Goldman, and an additional $8 by Reliance Insurance.

In preparing the 1990 annual report, the accounting firm of Arthur Andersen & Co. extended the financial records back to December 31, 1989, as if that were the date of the reorganization. Following established accounting rules, the senior debt was delineated on the balance sheet at market value and not par value, market value of $18.88 million versus a maturity value of $47.20 million. The difference between the two figures, $28.3 million, called the "unamortized discount," gradually reaches the balance sheet in a process called "accretion," which occurs steadily through maturity. At maturity, book value equals accreted principal value. Table 8.1 describes the expected growth in senior debt resulting from: (a) accretion and (b) interest due, assuming that all of the bonds remain outstanding. In July 1993, when cash interest payments began, there was $61.76 million in senior notes, with a quarterly cash interest burden of $1.54 million.

Table 8.1

Changes in Senior Notes Due to Accretion and Interest (in $ thousands)

Date	Book Value*	Original Principal	Interest Accrued to Principal	Principal + Accrued
4/9/90	$18,840	$47,100		
12/31/90	$23,255	$47,100	$2,698	$49,798
12/31/91	$30,149		$4,980	$54,777
12/31/92	$37,541		$5,478	$60,255
4/9/93	$39,525		$1,506	$61,761

Date	Book Value	Principal + Accrued	Cash Interest
4/9/94	$42,701	$61,762	$6,762
4/9/95	$45,877	$61,762	$6,762
4/9/00	$61,762	$61,762	$6,762

Source: Compiled by the author from The Phoenix Resource Companies, Inc., 10-K reports.

*These figures are approximations due to uncertainty regarding the discount amortization schedule.

In fact, the company has steadily repurchased senior notes at a significant discount with funds raised from the exercise of Series A, B, and C warrants. Table 8.2 lists the bonds bought between April 9, 1990, and the end of the third quarter of 1991. Consider the $407,000 of senior notes purchased during the first quarter of 1991. With $34,000 in interest accrued since April 9, 1990 (at a rate of 10 percent per annum), these securities were owed $441,000. At issuance, they had a book value of $163,000 (0.4 × $407,000), which had grown to $209,000 as a result of interest owed ($34,000) and accretion of the discount ($12,000). The purchase was transacted at 48 cents per dollar of accreted value and resulted in a loss for accounting purposes equal to the difference between the purchase price and the book value, $2,000. Transactions in the second and third quarters resulted in additional accounting losses of $829,000 and $2,739,000 respectively. These losses are noncash charges like depreciation; that is, the company does not actually suffer a loss of cash. The loss reflects the difference between the current value of senior notes purchased and their accreted value based on their market value as of April 9, 1990. The loss results from a *strengthening of the company*. Moreover, repurchasing debt will increase cash flow starting in 1993 when the notes begin to pay cash interest.

Table 8.2

Repurchases of Phoenix Resources' Debt (in $ thousands)

Date	Original Principal	Principal + Accrued	Purchase Price	Price to Principal + Accrued	Book Value
1991 Q:1	$407	$441	$211	0.48	$209
1991 Q:2	$3,647	$4,081	$2,881	0.71	$2,052
1991 Q:3	$7,966	$9,198	$7,618	0.83	$4,879
Notes Accepted for				0.70	$729
B&C warrants*	$1,240	$1,411	$991		

*The C warrants accounted for $12,000 of the total.

The future was not completely sanguine. First, production on the Khalda Concession was not under The Phoenix Resource Companies' control; Repsol, the State Oil Company of Spain, had acquired Conoco's interest in the concession and was the operator. Moreover, Repsol itself did not have free rein: the EGPC, the Egyptian oil authorities, observed its own agenda. Second, oil prices remained unpredictable and volatile. In fact, during the first half of 1990, Egyptian crude oil prices fell by 25 percent from slightly more than $20 per barrel to less than $15 per barrel. Third, an $18 million loan (called a prepayment of exploration expenses) that TEI had procured from Conoco at the time of the farm-out agreement was coming due in April 1991. On the confirmation date, over $14 million of the loan remained outstanding. Fourth, a new concession in Egypt, Natrun, was awarded to The Phoenix Resource Companies in May of 1989. Lawrence increased its 25 percent interest in the concession in 1990 to 37.5 percent through a trade with Banque Lambert (the parent of Drexel) for a similar 12.5 percent interest in a Malaysian field that both The Phoenix Resource Companies and the Banque had invested in. The trade was made to conserve cash. The Malaysian field was not carried for expenses as was the Khalda Concession; it was offshore (more expensive), additional overhead would be required, and the commitment was open ended. To obtain the Natrun concession, the company committed to drill two wells. Monies to explore Natrun had to be raised despite the restrictive covenants on the senior notes.

Iraq Invades Kuwait

Tensions in the Middle East are always near the boiling point even on cool days. American businesses operating there must remain ever vigilant to protect their interests. Egypt in particular is susceptible to instability, with its large population and limited resources. Fundamentalist sympathies hover invisible below the surface.

In April 1990, The Phoenix Resource Companies was created. In August 1990, Saddam Hussein sent Iraqi troops into Kuwait. The price of oil skyrocketed. The United States sent massive quantities of troops, armaments, and technical gear into the region as it prepared to rescue Kuwait. This show of force altered the ostrichlike behavior of conservative Arab regimes such as Saudi Arabia and created a joint American-Arab counterforce to Hussein's brutality. The price of oil continued to rise, reaching over $40 per barrel, twice what it had been a year earlier.

Events were perfectly timed for The Phoenix Resource Companies. As its production escalated, so did the price of oil. In fact, by the end of June 1991, the Conoco loan was reduced to just $2.8 million; without Saddam Hussein it would have exceeded $11 million. Of course, as Conoco is paid off, the company reacquires exploration expenses that it will collect out of cost-recovery oil.

The Iraqi conflict improved the business climate for American companies doing business in Egypt. Tens of thousands of Egyptian workers were driven out of Kuwait and returned home to unemployment. The Egyptian government was a staunch supporter of United Nations resolutions against Iraq and backed its position with troops. The U.S. government sealed this alliance after the conflict by writing off an older Egyptian debt of $7 billion.

When the conflict ended in January 1991, the price of oil retreated. Yet for The Phoenix Resource Companies, 1990 was very profitable; the firm earned $6.97 million or 30 cents per share on revenues of $27 million. Approximately $2.3 million of net income was attributable to an extraordinary income item, an operating loss carryforward, which sheltered income from taxation. With $235 million of these benefits in reserve, The Phoenix Resource Companies is unlikely to pay taxes in the near future.

For the year, operating cash flow approached $13 million; investment activities produced another $5 million. Almost $8 million of debt was retired, and the cash and cash equivalents accounts increased by approximately $10 million, which substantially increased financial flexibility. Capital expenditures consumed $6.5 million. All in all, 1990 was quite a year for the recently bankrupt company.

Cash flows were diminished by the decrease in oil prices in 1991, but a surge of fresh capital was received when warrants issued in the bankruptcy exercised. Series A warrants were scheduled to expire on April 9, 1991, one year to the day after confirmation of the plan. The key issue in deciding whether or not to exercise a warrant is the difference between the exercise and market prices: if a profit can be earned, the warrant should be exercised. The Phoenix Resource Companies' equity was initially valued by the market at $.625 on April 10, 1990. The Iraq situation and the improved cash flows sent the stock up as the A warrants' expiration approached: the stock settled at $1.365 per share after reaching $1.50. Exercising of the warrants was rational, since a $1.365 stock could be bought for just $1, and an immediate profit could be earned. Yet only 7.5 million out of 10 million warrants were exercised, raising $7.5 million in new money for The Phoenix Resource Companies. Presumably, the 2.5 million unexercised warrants were in small accounts for whom the commission expense exceeded the trading profit.

The equity continued to increase in value after April 9, 1991, stabilizing near $1.75. At the beginning of June, after the equity traded above $1.50 for twenty consecutive days, the company accelerated the expiration of the Series B warrants to the end of July. With a cash horde in excess of $22 million, the company was less interested in raising cash than in reducing indebtedness; hence, on July 2, Series B warrant holders were given the option to exercise their warrants with either $1 in cash or $1.25 of the senior notes. The real targets of this offer were owners of the former TEI 10 percent second bonds who had received senior notes and B and C warrants in the reorganization. The company believed that they would want to dispose of the notes since they were illiquid, noncash generating, and yet produced an income tax liability as a result of the accrued interest. All 11,704,510 of the Series B warrants exercised, of which 783,000 did so by exchanging senior notes.

A similar offer was extended at the same time to the Series C warrants. They were permitted to exercise their warrants early by trading in $2.19 of senior notes instead of the $1.75 exercise price. The only justification for accepting this offer rather than waiting was the liquidity issue. Only 5,479 of the warrants accepted.

In September of 1991, the equity reached $2.87 per share and traded for twenty consecutive days above $2.50. After twenty days, expiration of the Series C warrants could be accelerated, yet the company waited. By this time, only $40 million of the senior notes were outstanding, and of this amount Goldman owned $29.5 million. Moreover, Goldman owned 3.6 million of the C warrants. Presumably, during the respite, a negotiated settlement was sought with Goldman. None was reached. After a two-week hiatus, expiration of the Series C warrants was accelerated, giving holders the required sixty days' notice. The pressure being applied to the investment bank was the $6.3 million cost of exercising the 3.6 million warrants at $1.75. Goldman retaliated by announcing that it would register its Series C warrants for sale. The company reciprocated with a wallop of its own: all the senior notes owned by Reliance Insurance would be repurchased in the third quarter (see Table 8.2) for $7.8 million. The pressure exerted on Goldman by this announcement related to the senior note's indenture; specifically, the note requires that after April 1992, 75 percent of the excess free cash flow generated in Egypt beyond $4 million be used to redeem senior notes at full accreted value. However, the notes purchased by an affiliate of The Phoenix Resource Companies were not canceled (though they were not deemed outstanding for the purposes of preparing consolidated financial statements) and thus were available for redemption ahead of Goldman's bonds. Thus, Goldman, which owned $29.5 million of the remaining $32.3 million in senior notes, might not be able to cash out of its bonds until 1997 or beyond.[1]

By this time, Goldman's investment in The Phoenix Resource Companies exceeded $26.75 million, with the prospect of having to spend an additional $6.3 million to exercise the C warrants (as detailed in Table 8.3). By one account, this amount exceeded 5 percent of Goldman's entire free investment capital. Given the turn of events, it is likely that the partners at Goldman decided not to invest any more money in this situation. The potential balance of power really shifted when the Series A warrants were exercised. Absolute control of The Phoenix Resource Companies had escaped Goldman. Prior to that, Goldman owned 52 percent (8.8 million) of The Phoenix Resource Companies' 16.9 million shares. After the As exercised, Goldman's share fell to 36 percent; when Goldman exercised 6 million out of a total of 11.7 million Series B warrants, its ownership share rebounded to 41 percent. Purchasing shares with the C warrants would raise Goldman's share to 44 percent; taking no action would allow its ownership share to fall to 35 percent.

Goldman's announcement that it was registering its Series C warrants for sale caused the stock to tumble. The SEC was unable to review the offer expeditiously. The company cooperated by extending the sixty-day exercise period. Soon the stock was priced at $1.75 per share. At this price, Goldman was unable to find a buyer for its warrants. Eventually, Goldman exercised the warrants at $1.75 each and then immediately sold the shares to investors at $1.75, earning no profit. All but 100,000 of the Series C warrants were exercised.

Mr. Leon Gross, an American investor, reported in a 13D filing that he now owned nearly 12 percent of The Phoenix Resource Companies as an investment.

Table 8.3

Goldman Sachs' Investment (values are approximate, dollars in millions)

Security	Unit Cost	Gross Cost	Received in Exchange
Senior TEI Bonds	0.45	$13.25	$29.5 of senior notes
Junior TEI Bonds	0.15	$7.50	52% of Phoenix Resources
Series A Warrants*			
Series B Warrants	1.00	$6.00	6 million shares
Series C Warrants	1.75	$6.30	3.6 million shares
Total		$33.05	

*These warrants were sold and not exercised.

Mr. Galal Doss, a director and chairman of The Phoenix Resource Companies, bought 350,000 additional shares, bringing his ownership beyond 700,000 shares, more than 1.5 percent of the company. Other major holders were Goldman at 35 percent, State Street Research at 9 percent, and Massachusetts Financial Services at 7 percent.

Improved Operations

The Phoenix Resource Companies bore little resemblance to TEI. In April 1993, Phoenix had fewer than twenty employees; by contrast, employment at TEI had peaked at 3,500 in 1977. Diminutive size does not mean dormancy, however. The developed fields in the Khalda Concession—Salam, Khalda, Yasser, Hayat, Saffir, Kahraman, and Tut—are cash cows. Discovered but not yet developed Khalda Concession fields—Amoun and Tarek—are being tested. Each undeveloped field has had one discovery well.

In the last quarter of 1992, production in the Khalda Concession exceeded 30,000 barrels of oil per day, up from annual averages of 28,900, 26,600, 21,600, and 20,800 in 1991, 1990, 1989, and 1988, respectively. The increase was due in part to the development of low gas-to-oil ratio reservoirs (EGPC limited the amount of natural gas that could be vented) and the completion of a condensate recovery plant. Sales of natural gas began during 1991 at 1.9 million cubic feet.

The Khalda Concession is operated under a farm-out agreement, originally between Conoco and TEI, but later between Repsol and The Phoenix Resource Companies. The agreement provided that approximately 10 to 12 percent of the proceeds from the concession, net of production expense, belong to the company. Phoenix pays no operating costs.

In January of 1989, TEI had sold 20 percent of its remaining share of the Khalda Concession to Samsung Company Limited, a Korean corporation. Kishpaugh had worked nearly eighteen months ironing out the details. The Egyptian government approved the sale in November 1989 and it became effective January 1, 1990. TEI immediately received a payment of $12 million. However, in Kishpaugh's master stroke, the Koreans agreed to additional payments depending on the amount of reserves developed over a five-year period, up to $63 million.

After the sale, the concession was split among the three concessionaires: Phoenix Resources of Egypt 40 percent, Repsol 50 percent, and Samsung 10 percent. The concession is operated by Khalda Petroleum Company, an Egyptian company that is owned jointly by the contractors (50 percent) and the EGPC (50 percent) and employs approximately 500 people. The Khalda Concession is located 50 miles from the Mediterranean coast and 190 miles west of Alexandria, the nearest population center. (See the map in Figure 5.2.)

The December 1991 issue of *Investor* magazine reviewed all U.S. oil and gas companies. It noted the improvement in The Phoenix Resource Companies' results, at the time the ninety-third largest oil and gas company. Phoenix received the following accolades compared with all other U.S. energy companies.

- First place for most improved cash flow,
- Third place for most improved income,
- Eighth place for strength of current ratio,
- Twentieth place for relative growth in natural gas reserves.

Whether these good fortunes will extend into 1994 and beyond depends on exploration success in Egypt.

Details of the Khalda Concession Agreement

Concession revenues are split into two categories. The first is cost-recovery oil: 40 percent of total production revenues available to recover the contractors' costs. Production costs are recoverable immediately, while capital costs are amortized, using the straight-line method, over four years. If cost-recovery oil is insufficient to recover all costs, unrecovered costs are banked and recovered out of future cost-recovery revenue after current charges are recovered.

The remaining 60 percent of production is profit oil. Profit oil plus unused cost-recovery oil is split 75 percent to EGPC and 25 percent to the contractors until production reaches 25,000 barrels per day, after which the split moves progressively in EGPC's favor, ultimately reaching a maximum of an 85–15 percent split at 100,000 barrels per day. All Egyptian taxes are paid by the EGPC, so that the contractors' share of income is completely free of Egyptian taxes. A foreign tax credit is available to shield foreign income against U.S. taxes.

The original concession agreement designated natural gas production as belonging entirely to Egypt. However, that arrangement gave little incentive to the contractors to expend monies to gather and transport gas. And since oil and gas are produced synchronously, the EGPC has the power to curtail oil production if "gas is being wasted." In fact, such a gas/oil dispute partially explains TEI's bankruptcy: oil production was lower than it might have been had Conoco not spent years negotiating a gas contract with EGPC.

In parts of the concession where crude oil is being produced, the contractor maintains concession rights for twenty-five years from the time of a commercial discovery. Areas with natural gas can be operated up to twenty-five years but no more than thirty-five years from the time of commercial discovery. Areas not producing by certain dates must be relinquished to the Egyptian government unless significant gas discoveries are known and development plans are pending.

The contractors share profit oil according to their respective ownership percentages: Repsol 50 percent, The Phoenix Resource Companies of Egypt 40 percent, and Samsung 10 percent. Repsol collects virtually all cost-recovery oil, since it pays these costs.

Approximately $365 million in capital expenditures had been made in the Khalda Concession through 1992. Only $248 million of these funds have been recovered to date, with Repsol, Phoenix Resources of Egypt, and Samsung waiting to collect $98 million, $9 million, and $1 million, respectively. Twenty-seven million dollars in additional spending is projected for 1993, of which Phoenix Resource of Egypt will pay $1 million.

Thirty-seven wildcat exploratory wells in the concession have yielded commercial discoveries in twelve major areas, nearly all of which have multiple reservoirs. Another seventy-three wells have been completed for production and service. In 1991, of thirty wells drilled, twenty-three were development wells. Thirteen additional wells were drilled in 1992 including three exploratory wells and further drilling is planned for 1993. Facilities have been designed for an eventual 40,000-barrel-per-day capacity and include a condensate recovery plant, employee living quarters, administrative buildings, and a 100-mile oil pipeline.

The Egyptian government constructed an electricity-generating plant in the coastal town of Matruh, which is being supplied with natural gas from Khalda shipped through a fifty-mile pipeline constructed by the contractors. The approximate three billion BTUs per day delivered to Matruh beginning in 1991 were the first commercial outlet for the concession's very significant potential gas output. However, the concession is not near to any other significant industrial or consumer markets for natural gas. The principal natural gas market is in Alexandria and Cairo, but a new natural gas pipeline would have to be constructed to serve that market.

Egypt's continued natural gas flaring constraints and the lack of economic access to gas markets have caused many potential crude oil production sites to be placed on hold (especially Amoun, Tarek, and the deeper zones of the Salam field) due to their high gas-to-oil ratios. To fully exploit the concession's potential, especially in deep Jurassic formations, a pipeline to population centers along the Nile would be necessary.

Signs are surfacing that there will be enough natural gas in the vicinity of the concession to allow a major new pipeline to be constructed. Major natural gas discoveries were reported by other producers in 1991 and 1992: Phillips/Repsol to the west of the concession, Shell Oil approximately 15 kilometers to the west of the Tarek field and 35 kilometers north of the Kahraman; Norsk Hydro 15 kilometers northeast of Tarek, and International Egyptian Oil Company (a subsidiary of AGIP) to the east of Tarek. A line can easily be drawn connecting the Tarek and Amoun fields and all the new discoveries. It appears that a unified natural gas project to ship gas to the population centers will happen. Repsol is responsible only for paying for oil development costs. Natural gas costs are shared. The Phoenix Resource Companies would probably need to raise at least $25 million to pay for its share of the costs. These developments could impact the total payments from Samsung for 20 percent of the concession.

Valuation

The company's reserves in physical units increased in 1992 to 9.4 million barrels of oil (from 8.7 million) and 20.3 billion cubic feet of natural gas (from 14.7).[2] On a *net, discounted* basis (at 10 percent as prescribed by the SEC), future cash flows should approximate $73.5 million. If oil prices had remained at 1990 levels, future cash flows would have been $32.5 million higher.[3] An additional asset is The Phoenix Resource Companies' tax carryforward (in excess of $250 million), which might be worth 5 to 10 cents per dollar.

The company's value is impeded by an inability to produce and sell all the natural gas on the concession. Until another pipeline is built, most of the natural gas on the concession will remain in the probable category and not be included in the value estimates.[4]

Political Risks

With virtually all its income-producing properties located in the Western Desert of Egypt, The Phoenix Resource Companies is exposed to profound political risk. Egypt's government confronts sizable poverty and growing fundamentalist sentiment. The government has been known to harass foreign companies in exchange for benefits, and in the extreme case a new government could nationalize the oil industry. The company is also subject to the risks inherent in the exploration and production of oil and gas.

From 1988 through 1990, all of the company's operating revenues came from the sale of crude oil and natural gas. Fluctuations in price and output, neither of which the company has any control over, can have a major impact on the company's financial performance and survivability. At present, all of the production is sold to EGPC on a month-to-month basis at the "posted price" for Gulf of Suez–blend crude oil.

Mitigation of these political or country risks requires diversification into other countries with more stable environments. However, financial constraint in the new debt's covenants may preclude the acquisition of new non-Egyptian properties.

If the price of natural gas should move up and/or if a pipeline were constructed that could economically transport the gas reserves to major population centers along the Nile or elsewhere, the company would experience a potential bonanza. At this time, most gas is being flared (burned on site), and known oil reserves are not being accessed because of their high gas-to-oil ratios. Because gas is so plentiful in this area, many more wells could be put into production should the demand and transportation facilitation be in place.

Recent Developments

In February of 1992, after lengthy negotiations, the company reached an agreement with Goldman to repurchase Goldman's senior notes. At the time, only $32.2 million original face amount of the senior debt remained outstanding, of which Goldman owned $29.5 million, or 92 percent. With accreted interest, approximately $38 million was owed. Goldman and minority bond holders would receive 90 percent of the accreted obligation, or $34.2 million. Of this amount, $27 million would be paid in cash and $7.2 million would be a 9 percent note given to Goldman. The new note was repaid in full in August 1992.

The company stated that its objective was to "reduce the Company's interest costs"[5] but equally important was a desire to permanently abrogate the onerous covenant provisions of the senior notes that related to corporate existence, sale of assets, cancellation of indebtedness, and capital structure. In order to change the covenants, two-thirds of bond holders, other than Goldman and the company, had to agree, after which they might sell their notes to the company. There would be little incentive to keep the notes if the covenants were changed.

On February 28, 1992, the company announced that all but $700,000 of the notes had agreed to change the covenants and cash out. A loss of $13.5 million was recorded on the transaction, since the price paid for the bonds exceeded the accreted value of the notes (indicating a strengthened financial position of the company). Goldman remains as the largest single shareholder, with 14.29 million shares, or 34.4 percent of the total.

To date, Goldman has received nearly $38.24 million from its investment of approximately $33.05 million. This includes $250,000 for the Series A warrants (at 50 cents apiece), $59,000 from Series B warrants (at 65 cents apiece), $6.3 million on the Series C warrants (at $1.75 apiece), $305,000 from sale of common stock, and $31.33 million from the sale of bonds. Goldman may receive more than $35 million when its remaining common shares are sold.

Shareholders approved a 1 : 10 reverse stock split and expanded the number of authorized shares to 10 million in May 1992. By increasing the price of the stock above $20 per share, institutions may purchase the stock and investors can margin their security. Both would increase the market for the stock.

Notes

1. The 10-Q issued for the third quarter of 1991 reported that between $4 and $6 million of the senior notes might have to be repurchased in 1992.

2. Production in the Salam field reached 30 million barrels in October 1992, at which point the allocation of oil between Phoenix Resources of Egypt and Samsung switches more favorably toward the company.

3. For TEI the sum is a net-net calculation, since Repsol is responsible for capital expenditures and operating expenses on the concession.

4. Yet the contract with Samsung requires additional payments to be based on both proven and probable reserves.

5. See *TEI's Offer to Purchase and Solicitation of Consents,* February 1992, page 9.

Part IV
Financial Lessons

9

Interview with a Fund Manager

James Swanson is a well-regarded mutual fund manager at Massachusetts Financial Services, in Boston, where he is the co-portfolio manager of two closed-end high-yield funds with invested capital in excess of half a billion dollars. After receiving his B.A. degree from Colgate University in 1971 he worked at Chemical Bank for a year. He then attended the Harvard Business School, receiving an M.B.A. degree in 1974. Following graduation, he worked in the private placement department of New England Mutual Life.

Swanson agreed to be interviewed for this book in part because his funds bought and sold TEI's securities for many years and because he was willing to share his insights. He recalled meetings conducted by the company's managers for security analyst, as well as conversations with members of the creditors' committee. The interview took place on March 22, 1991. We gratefully acknowledge his candor and his willingness to speak with us.

The transcription has been edited mostly for space considerations with an effort made to preserve content and meaning.

Harlan Platt: How would you characterize TEI from its inception until its demise in August 1988?

James Swanson: Exchange offers without precedent in number. Exchanges were coming out of Drexel Burnham. About a year earlier, another energy company, Anglo Energy, had done an exchange. It was a section 3(A)9 exchange, where investment bankers cannot contact holders. Wilbur Ross, with Rothschild, was brought in to represent creditors.

Several other distressed oil situations were similar at the time. TEI was more complex than others. We were not sure of what we were doing, due to the newness of exchanges. It was preferable to a Chapter 11 filing. In retrospect, I think at the time Drexel placed a lot of pressure on us to accept the exchange.

I came into the high-yield area right about this time. TEI was one of the first exchange offers. I was relatively unfamiliar with the exchange-offer process. At the time, it seemed pretty rudimentary. In retrospect, it seems pretty complicated.

HP: What was your background?

JS: Previous experience first was at a bank as a credit analyst, then New England Life, where I was involved with private placements and was an oil and gas specialist for a while. I started a public bond fund (high-yield).

Educationally, my background was liberal arts, then the Harvard Business School. I worked with Conoco on an oil and gas deal while with the insurance company.

HP: What can you tell us about Kishpaugh?

JS: Kishpaugh? Yes, I went to the dog-and-pony shows [marketing meetings conducted by a company and its investment banker designed to aid in the sale of securities]. What did I feel at the time? Nothing pernicious. He seemed to be more of a salesman than a hands-on operator. Looking back, I was dazzled by a heavy sales pitch; he could convince you that the next effort would be successful. You came away from meetings highly encouraged by the prospects. This was very important to the completion of the exchange offers. I have a memo that the road show [was] very successful.

Underlying all this was a Chapter 11 threat. [I] totally believed in the equity exchange part of it, was a proponent and still would be, especially with our outlook on oil at the time. We saw oil moving up strongly. Long-term orientation: value in Egypt, Khalda.

When a company gets in trouble like this, let's admit that we have equity. Equity is ultimately where we're going to get value out of the company. Subordinated debt really is equity, and that's coming out more and more today.

Now what is confusing things is Judge Lifland's decision [LTV]. When new securities are taken in an exchange offer, they must be valued at a market price on day of exchange for future bankruptcy claims purposes. Some go Chapter 11 a second time, for example, Crystal Oil. Then your new claim [that had been worth $1] may be 10 cents on the dollar.

At the time, I was a proponent of some debt, since we're a fixed-income operation, but mainly I was looking to the equity to do the trick. Today [I] would rather have both to retain a claim in the company. In August 1988, let's face it, we were equity holders. [We] saw a favorable oil scenario.

HP: Tell me about the strange role of Goldman Sachs in the meetings of the creditors' committee.

JS: The Goldman high-yield desk, not the Water Street Workout Fund, was involved. I thought the desk was trading to work out their position but [was] unaware of how they accumulated [their bonds] or [the extent of] their influence. I was surprised and a little disturbed that they had this position, because we have an ongoing relationship with Goldman. We would have to disclose it, but would they have shown their cards to us? No, I doubt it.

Very disturbing when the filings occurred, and I became aware of the extent that they were involved. [We] knew they were maneuvering in the restructuring, and if I had my eyes open, would have picked up where we were in the capital structure. They played this game to the hilt. We were not positioned as well.

HP: You mean they elevated themselves in terms of seniority?

JS: They knew what they were doing. They got control of one issue and put themselves above everyone else.

Rumors around the time of the bankruptcy were that Kishpaugh was taking too much out for himself. People whispering in our ear: this Kishpaugh has got to go. What the hell, this thing is going into the ground again. They're living high on the hog. I didn't up front see it. I still believed in Kishpaugh up until a little later than this. He always answered my phone calls. Jim Gregory would be a real good conduit. Gregory left about mid-1990. At or just before the bankruptcy people around here thought we should start getting a hold of the situation because he would take everything out. We didn't have any evidence of that, because expense ratios were going up, but revenues were going down.

An [internal] memo dated November 1986 tells where the trouble with Kishpaugh started. Selling off U.S. operations for $100 million. Just after that, we started hearing the Kishpaugh stories.

I inherited TEI issues across the spectrum. I think Milken called [us] on these. He convinced me that this was a good vehicle. I thought this was a Section 3(A)9 exchange. But I'd have to check if he called. I know we were talking to Drexel.

HP: How did you react to the change in accounting methods?

JS: From an analyst's point of view . . . it never affected us. We go by production schedules, discount out what I think are the yields, do present value analysis and net out the debt. . . . [We] recommended buying more of [the] bonds in September 1985, while TEI had a $135 million negative net worth, based on the Phoenix prospects. Didn't buy any. Based on prospects of Conoco purchase.

[The] Conoco deal gave a lot of credibility to Phoenix and Kishpaugh. Agreement with Conoco amounted to a commitment that eight wells be drilled with a maximum dry-hole cost of $150 million. The negative was that Conoco could back out after four dry holes had been drilled. Basic sharing arrangement [was] 50/50 till 70 million barrels had been found, in which case TEI would [get] back another 25 percent. However, the fact that the Egyptian project was being run by

[Charles] Reimer, former head of domestic exploration, and . . . that Conoco is involved in these reservoirs, and . . . has said that the pay zones may have some value, [gives] a vote of confidence in these fields. We were worried about the company's reliance on Egypt, however. The program must not only be successful but must pay off relatively soon to relieve the company's predicament. Conoco's participation was certainly welcome for two reasons; it lent credence to national reports of a major find, and it supplied TEI with four infusions of cash during the next year.

The logic of our doing the exchange, being involved, and even picking up more [was based on] our outlook for oil at the time. [That was what] made sense and that Conoco was the key element in our going along [with the exchange offers]. If it were not for Conoco, I think we would have asked for a liquidation. Without Conoco, this didn't make operational sense. Otherwise, push for liquidation and take whatever you can get as these companies tend to just bleed cash.

[Managers] stay on [for] their salaries. I remember this was a big issue. They just pay themselves and run the company into the ground, with the creditor left with nothing. Stop the music when you know they're not going to do anything to add more value.

HP: What about all the rumors on Egypt? Were you hearing reports of 100 million, 500 million, 1 billion barrels?

JS: Kishpaugh didn't dissuade us from that, by the way. Pretty much we discount the rumors. Having an oil and gas background with the insurance company, I had heard a lot of promoters. I would discount most of the rumors, but again it was my experience with Conoco. I thought they had a lot of credibility, because I had worked with them on an exploration project before I came here. Typically, we dismiss the positive rumors. Also, there were rumors that there was nothing there. The shorts were trying to get us. Negative rumors about Egypt were late (don't remember exactly when). Many rumors of a big find. We dismissed them, as we have no way to access it.

HP: During exchanges what was your focus: seniority, maturity, cash interest? Did your focus change during the course of the exchange?

JS: First focus was that creditors should get control of the stock. [We] wanted the equity or warrants. Ultimately, that's where the value is. Also, new notes, since they could get in trouble again. Most important to get equity but retain some fixed-income instruments even if at a lower coupon, as we are running a yield fund. Bond holders wanted control of company. At this point we really were holders of equity. When bonds are significantly impaired, more than a 20–30 percent discount, it's clear to us that impairment should wipe out the equity ownership or almost all of it. We have become the owners, as legally we have the controls. We can dictate a lot of the terms, and once they're in default we pretty much can drive the machine.

Long-term outlook: maximize value in credits. We believed in TEI, versus the vulture funds that buy debt at 20 cents on the dollar and want to get out at 30 cents. Believe in the dream. Get a call option on the future.

HP: I asked Mike Milken about TEI: "How many of the bonds did Drexel own, $10 million?" He answered, "No, we don't have a single one." As it turns out, they had nearly $15 million. Earlier in the day in a speech he gave at Northeastern University, he told me this story: "Let me explain the TEI problem. I sat down with Kishpaugh when the stock hit 6 and said let's go into the market and sell some equity. Enough to pay off all the debt. Kishpaugh said, sell stock at 6?! This is a $30 stock!"

What is your position in The Phoenix Resource Companies?

JS: We have 1.66 million shares, 0.23 million A warrants, 1.15 million B warrants, 0.15 million C warrants, and $1.5 million debt. We own about 10 percent of the company. About 90 percent is in institutional hands.

HP: How do you play this one now?

JS: If we could get 50 to 60 for the debt, take it, as it's better to invest it somewhere else. The majority holders can screw us if we stay in and everyone else turns their debt in and stirs the covenants.

HP: When the company achieves a certain level of net worth, the cash will be used to redeem debt.

JS: Should have been more involved in details of covenants. Only concerned with getting the equity at the time.

HP: You potentially got screwed by people on the inside with other plans. They weren't divulging those plans. Did Goldman devise the covenants?

JS: I thought at the time that they were fighting for us. Their debt holders, too, know their stuff and should protect us. Now should sell debt. Debating whether to sell or exercise warrants.

HP: Thanks very much for taking time out to talk with us.

10

Interview with a Stockholder

We agreed to provide this stockholder with anonymity. In the transcription of our interview, from January 21, 1992, we refer to him as Mr. Confident. He agrees with the following description:

Mr. Confident is a college-educated (B.S. and M.B.A.) corporate manager whose knowledge of financial markets includes both textbook and hands-on experience. He first bought TEI stock in March 1982; eventually he invested virtually everything he owned in it. Even after the bankruptcy and reorganization, he remains confident and now owns stock in The Phoenix Resource Companies.

Harlan Platt: Why did you first buy stock in TEI?

Mr. Confident: I love to read the *Wall Street Journal*. One day in 1982 I noticed the price jump $10 a share. After that, I began watching it, read up on it in *Value Line*, and waited my chance.

One day it fell $10 a share, [from a level] of about $40 a share. When it hit $12, I called my broker and told him to buy me 100 shares. He said, "Are you crazy? It's going to zero." Naturally, I listened to him, and the next day it went back up $10 a share. Several months later I got a new broker and bought 100 shares when it fell again to $12.

In fact, about a year ago I documented that I had bought the stock at this time for a class-action lawsuit. I got back $140 from a $1,200 investment. It's the lawyers who win these cases.

HP: What did you find appealing in TEI?

MC: The volatility mostly, but also the story. Every investor dreams of discovering the sure thing. I thought this was it. I felt they had found a new Saudi Arabia.

HP: My friend John Edmunds talks about the fundamentalist's vice: someone who says, "It was a good buy at $12, so it's a better buy at $9." Did this apply to you?

MC: It didn't *apply* to me, it *was* me! I bought 100 shares at $12, another hundred at $10, 200 shares at $7.50, 500 shares at $5, 1,000 at $2.50, and 2,500 shares at $1.

HP: So your investment was about $11,000, and you owned about 4,500 shares with an average cost of $2.50 a share.

MC: That's right. I was out about $1.50 a share or $6,000–$7,000. But that was only the beginning.

One day I was at home during the day sick. With nothing to do, I watched the Financial News Network, which had a ticker tape and a Reuters news wire. Suddenly, across the tape came news that TEI had discovered oil in its first Egyptian well. I couldn't believe my good fortune. I was going to be rich. I was among the first to read the news. Then I considered how much quicker I would be rich if I bought more stock. So I called and doubled up: I bought 4,500 shares at $1. Now I had invested over $15,000 for 9,000 shares. I figured I would get $10 a share, or $90,000.

HP: What happened?

MC: At first it was a dream come true. The stock slowly rose and soon reached $2. Then I did something that I regret more than losing my own money. I told friends and relatives about the stock, and they invested.

HP: Did you do this to get the stock to go up?

MC: No, of course not! My friends aren't [Donald] Trump. No, I wanted them to be rich, too.

As the stock rose to $6 [a share], I kept buying. Eventually I had about 20,000 shares at a cost of about $75,000. At $10 I might have sold out, but I never got the chance.

HP: How did you get so hooked?

MC: Greed mostly. My broker tells me that markets are only moved by fear and greed. I also got hooked [on] information. I believed that one reason why some people did well on stocks was that [they had] information. So I started to call TEI every month. I talked with the information people, the financial people, and even with Kishpaugh.

In fact, I was just getting public information from a voice and not from a newspaper. I thought I could detect little nuances in their voices. I thought I knew something that no else did. I became an information junky.

Finally, I suppose I got caught up in the excitement. I'd never before owned a stock that doubled in a month and quintupled in a year.

HP: How did the bankruptcy treat you and other shareholders?

MC: We was robbed! For my 20,000 shares I got warrants to buy 2,500 shares of The Phoenix Resource Companies for a buck a share. That's it. If the stock hadn't risen, I would have been wiped out—Zippo.

HP: Did you exercise when the stock went up?

MC: Of course! Not only that, but I had bought 8,000 more warrants for $1,000. I figured that with so much lost already, what was another $1,000. If I had waited longer, I could have gotten 32,000 warrants for my money. When the expiration date came, I converted my warrants into 8,000 shares of The Phoenix Resource Companies. At $2 a share I'm still out, but $10,000 richer than I was at $1, and I'll be even at $7 a share.

Analyzing the Company with a Bankruptcy Prediction Model

A recent innovation in modern corporate finance is the development of models to predict bankruptcy. Early warning models, as they are called, compile and compare financial ratios to estimate the likelihood of corporate failure. Harlan and Marjorie Platt recently developed an oil-and-gas-sector early warning model. This chapter is based on their model.[1]

The early warning model seeks systematic differences between bankrupt and nonbankrupt companies. While it should be easy to find data on bankrupt oil and gas companies (Dun & Bradstreet report that 2,139 independent oil and gas companies failed from 1985 to 1988), the task is complicated, because most of the companies were privately held and never released their financial or reserve data. For the expanded time period 1982–1988, sixty-eight independent oil and gas companies are listed in the SEC list of Bankrupt Publicly Traded Companies. Data are available for only thirty-five of these bankrupt companies.

The comparison group of nonbankrupt American oil and gas companies included eighty-nine companies found in the Arthur Andersen *Reserves Disclosure* Database. The total sample, then, included 124 companies—35 failures and 89 survivors. Table 11.1 lists the companies in the sample by group, failures versus survivors.

Financial data were obtained from Compustat files or from 10k reports. Oil and gas reserve data were obtained from 10k reports for bankrupt companies and from the Arthur Andersen *Reserves Disclosure* Database for nonbankrupt firms. Data were obtained for the year prior to bankruptcy. Each company's accounting method was determined from footnotes to the 10k reports or from Compustat footnotes.

Many financial and reserve ratios were compared in a search for the optimal set of bankruptcy predictors. The best *set* of ratios is:

Table 11.1

Companies in Sample

Bankrupt Companies	Nonbankrupt Companies	
Amarex, Inc.	Adobe Resources Corp.	MCO Resources, Inc.
Arapaho Petroleum	Alexander Energy Corp.	Mitchell Energy
Buttes Gas & Oil Co.	American National Petroleum	Moore McCormack
Cambridge Oil Co.	American Quasar Petroleum Co.	MSR Exploration Ltd.
Century Oil & Gas Corp.	Apache Petroleum Co.	Newhall Resources
Crystal Oil	Barnwell Industries	Norris Oil Co.
Dalco Petroleum	Baruch-Foster Corp.	NRM Operating Co.
Energy Exchange	Basic Earth Science Systems	Nugget Oil Corp.
Energy Sources, Inc.	Basix Corp.	OKC Ltd. Partnership
Galaxy Oil Company	Beard Co.	Park-Ohio Industries
Gasoil, Inc.	Bellwether Exploration Co.	Pauley Petroleum
Gulf Energy Corp.	Blackgold Energy Resources	Pennzoil Co.
High Summit Oil & Gas	Bogert Oil Co.	Petrol Industries
Holiday Resources, Inc.	Brock Exploration Corp.	Petroleum Development
Magic Circle Energy Corp.	Cabot Corp.	Petrotech, Inc.
Marlin Oil Company	Cenergy Corp.	Plains Resources
Marline Oil Corporation	Chapman Energy, Inc.	Pogo Producing Co.
MGF Oil Corporation	Coastal Corp.	Premier Resources
Nicklos Oil & Gas Company	Cobb Resources Corp.	Presidio Oil Co.
Nucorp Energy, Inc.	Consolidated Oil & Gas	Pyramid Oil Co.
Oklahoma Energies	Convest Energy Corp.	Pyro Energy Corp.
Partners Oil Company	Damson Oil Corp.	Reading & Bates
Peninsula Resources	Dekalb Corp.	Sabine Corp.
Petromac Energy, Inc.	Egret Energy Corp.	Sage Energy Co.
Seneca Oil Co.	Energy Development Partners	Saxon Oil Development
Southland Energy	Energy Oil, Inc.	Seahawk Oil International
Taurus Oil Co.	Energy Ventures, Inc.	Snyder Oil Partners
Texas General Resources	Enex Resources Corp.	Southdown, Inc.
Texas International	Ensource, Inc.	Summit Energy, Inc.
Tomlinson Oil Co., Inc.	Equity Oil Co.	Sunshine Mining Co.
Towner Petroleum Company	Evergreen Resources, Inc.	Templeton Energy
Transcontinental Energy	Falcon Oil & Gas Co., Inc.	Texon Energy Corp.
UniOil	Forest Oil Corp.	Tipperary Corp.
Xenerex Corporation	Global Natural Resources PL	Tom Brown, Inc.
XO Exploration	Golden Oil Co.	Total Petroleum (NA)
	Graham Mccormick O&G Partnership	Triton Energy Corp.
	Hadson Corp.	Usenco, Inc.
	Hamilton Oil Corp.	Valex Petroleum
	Harken Oil & Gas, Inc.	Wainoco Oil Corp.
	Helmerich & Payne	Wright Brothers Energy Co
	Homestake Mining Co.	
	Kencope Energy Co.	
	Kimbark Oil & Gas Co.	
	KRM Petroleum Corp.	
	Louisiana Land & Exploration	
	Magellan Petroleum Corp.	
	May Petroleum, Inc.	
	Maynard Oil Co.	
	Mcfarland Energy, Inc.	

(a) real net cash flow relative to real total assets,
(b) real total debt relative to real total assets,
(c) exploration expense relative to real total reserves,
(d) current liabilities relative to real total debt,
(e) accounting method interacted with variable (a),
(f) the prime interest rate, and
(g) the oil price relative to the change in oil prices.

Table 11.2 contains the model's actual parameters.

Table 11.2

Oil and Gas Early Warning Model

Independent Variable	Coefficient
Constant	−26.66***
	(3.52)
Net Cash Flow/P	−9326.78***
Total Assets*P	(−4.06)
Total Debt/i	1340.04***
Total Assets*P	(4.26)
Exploration Expense	63.37***
Total Reserves*P	(3.77)
Current Liabilities	0.43***
Debt/i	(2.94)
ACCT * NCF/P	7026.40***
TA*P	(3.41)
Prime Interest Rate	1.87***
	(2.75)
Oil Price	−0.04*
Change in Oil Price	(−1.74)
ANALOG R^2	74.0%

Notes:
1. ***, **, and * denote statistical significance at the 0.01, 0.05, and 0.10 levels, respectively.
2. P and i in the list of independent variables are abbreviations for crude oil prices and the prime interest rate, respectively.

The model correctly classified as bankrupt or nonbankrupt 94.3 percent of the bankrupt companies and 95.5 percent of the nonbankrupt companies. The model's prediction should be accurate for about 95 out of every 100 companies analyzed.

Inputting TEI's data into the early warning model provides a quantitative assessment across time of the company's financial health. Estimated probabilities of bankruptcy are reported in Table 11.3. Several early years are missing from the table due to data unavailability. Estimated failure probabilities start out

Table 11.3

Probability of Bankruptcy for TEI

Year	Probability of Bankruptcy
1969	0.3%
1970	0.3%
1971	n/a
1972	2.8%
1973	n/a
1974	n/a
1975	n/a
1976	0.5%
1977	0.9%
1978	0.5%
1979	9.7%
1980	0.2%
1981	16.7%
1982	26.7%
1983	82.7%
1984	45.3%
1985	77.2%
1986	91.2%
1987	100.0%
1988	100.0%

low, less than 1 percent. Even the sale of junk bonds in 1977 does not create a high failure risk. It has been argued that Michael Milken sold "good junk bonds," while investment banks that entered the market five or ten years later sold "bad junk bonds" in a frenzy to grab market share from Drexel.[2]

An estimate of bankruptcy probability equal to or greater than 40 percent suggests a likely failure. TEI's bankruptcy risk jumped into the danger zone in 1983. Which ratio was responsible? Many factors are simultaneously considered in an early warning model, so that it is impossible to singularly assign "blame." Yet much of the increased risk came from the ratio of long-term debt to total assets. Starting in 1983, this ratio became dangerously high. A second episode of high bankruptcy risk began in 1985 as a result of high debt and an excessive exploration budget. The latter factor may be more responsible.

Based on the results of the early warning model, it is hard to comprehend how so much money could have been invested after 1982 in so distressed a company. Several explanations are possible, however. First, by combining many factors, the early warning model may have seen what others missed. Second, magic created by the Khalda Concession discovery may have overwhelmed reason. Third, oil price volatility ultimately destroyed the company; investors who had survived the 1973 bout with OPEC may have mistakenly believed that oil prices would never crumble. Whatever the reason, investors and company managers are encouraged to fall back on the fundamental analysis that lies at the heart of any early warning model.

Notes

1. See Harlan Platt and Marjorie Platt, "Bankruptcy Discrimination with Real Variables."
2. See Harlan Platt, "Underwriter Effects on High Yield Bond Default Rates."

What Have We Learned?

The story of the first junk bond takes many unexpected turns but ultimately follows a well-trodden path. The sojourn provokes intellectual inquiry into a number of critical business issues. Four key questions are:

(1) What was the optimal strategy regarding exchange offers?
(2) Could the bankruptcy have been avoided?
(3) When should the bankruptcy have been declared?
(4) What can be achieved in bankruptcy negotiations?

There is room for many viewpoints; my thoughts are as follows.

Strategy for Exchange Offers

Each of TEI's three exchange offers accomplished something different: the 1985 exchange gave the company the right to pay interest with common stock, the 1986 offer delayed bond maturity dates, and the 1987 exchange did both. The winners and losers followed different strategies, but the outcomes depended as much on the particular events that ensued as on their decisions. Generally though, free-ridership, refusing all offers and benefiting from the sweat of others, may actually backfire because of the importance of seniority in bankruptcy. Also, small issues playing the squeaky wheel may gain relative to others, since settling their claims may be the least-cost approach. Finally, exchange offers are a transfer from equity to debt holders; that is, bond holders gain relative to shareholders. The chief question is the size of the transfer.

The four original-issue debt securities received approximately 65 percent of the common equity in TEI in the exchange offers and from the payment of interest in stock. This outcome parallels what may have ensued in an early bankruptcy filing without any bankruptcy-related costs. Later, after the bankruptcy, a small group of bond holders initially acquired all of the new company.

Avoiding Bankruptcy

TEI failed for three reasons. First, it took titanic risks with borrowed money. While the expected value of a strategy that has a 10 : 1 payoff and a 20 percent chance of success may be that you will double your investment, eight out of ten practitioners are likely to go bankrupt. Prodigious risk taking is best left to the very rich, the very young, or the foolish.

Second, when the price of TEI's common stock rose to $6 per share in response to the Egyptian discovery, new equity should have been issued and the debt paid off. Instead, greed kept the leverage high. The adage that "half of something is better than all of nothing" is often hard to implement.

Third, oil prices collapsed. Unstable product prices affect more than just natural resource companies; price declines contributed to the bankruptcies of Coleco (Cabbage Patch Dolls), Midway Airlines, Prime Motor Inns, and many others. However, in the petroleum market, market forces alone do not set prices; government regulations and OPEC play critical roles. Not surprisingly, oil prices have followed a roller coaster course. Companies might protect themselves against this risk by hedging.

Timing of the Bankruptcy

TEI filed for bankruptcy at the last possible moment. This decision adhered to Kishpaugh's conception of business ethics. However, other solutions were possible: an earlier filing or a Savin solution.

A bankruptcy filing would not have been propitious while there were secured creditors. After the deep drilling fiasco, assets were valued below liabilities, and the secured creditors would have taken everything. However, after the banks were paid off, and before the number of common shares had grown from 20 to 80 million, a bankruptcy filing might have better protected shareholders.

Savin Corporation took a different tack. Instead of filing for bankruptcy protection, management received from shareholders the right to issue 500 million shares of stock. Had TEI gone this way, the stock could have been used to pay interest and even principal on the debt. An obvious advantage is that the $6 million dollars spent on professional fees in the bankruptcy would have been saved. Ultimately, the bond holders would have owned most of the company, but the original shareholders would have retained a small fraction of the firm without additional cost.

Bankruptcy Negotiations

The two relevant issues in a bankruptcy are money and control. In this case, the senior-most creditors eventually got their money back and more, the middle securities achieved control and made money, and the junior securities simply made money. However, as of the day the bankruptcy reorganization plan was consummated, the three top senior notes received about 42 cents on the dollar and junior bonds each returned about 13 cents on the dollar. Common share holders held warrants worth about 1 cent per share.

Appendix A[1]
Oil and Gas Industry Basics

Origin

The creation of fossil fuels (i.e., crude oil, natural gas, oil-bearing sands, condensate, tar sands, etc.) is usually described as the result of a decomposition process stretching over millions of years. A chemical reaction among vegetation, animal matter, water, and sediments is thought to create these hydrocarbons. Oil and gas are captured beneath rock structures in the earth. Natural gas rises above the oil layer, creating a gas cap, which is why oil and gas are discovered in the same well. In fact, if the gas : oil ratio is high enough, natural gas separation equipment may be required.

However, Dr. Thomas Gold may soon disprove this accepted paradigm. Dr. Gold believes that hydrocarbons are abiogenic; that is, they were formed at the time of the earth's creation. To test his theory, he has drilled two wells in Sweden in areas at least twenty-five miles from any sediment. In both cases, he discovered oil where none should have been found according to the biogenic fossil theory: at depths of 6.7 km and 2.8 km. Should Dr. Gold's theory be true, the aggregate reserves of oil and gas in the world would be infinitely greater than currently believed.[2]

Searching for Oil

Initially, there was no science to oil discovery, only accidental discovery. The first domestic oil discovery in Pennsylvania and some discoveries in the Middle East followed evidence of surface seepage. Oil discovery has been revolutionized by sophisticated discovery tools, including computer models and infrared satellite photography that tell searchers where to look and how deep to drill.

There are three types of drilling. The first type, known as exploratory or "wildcat" drilling, comprises drilling with a limited probability of discovery.

Wildcatters are not reckless oilmen who drill anywhere; rather, they are astute gamblers who make a big bet on subjective data. Natural selection thins the ranks of wildcatters; only those wildcatters who on occasion make a discovery can afford to keep drilling. Approximately one out of every ten wildcat wells yields commercially viable oil and gas reserves. Step-out and deep-testing wells are exploratory wells, which have a higher probability of success. A step-out well is drilled in an unproven location near a proven area in the hopes of extending the proven reservoir. A deep test is an exploratory well drilled in an existing field but to a deeper zone where no proven reserves yet exist.

Development wells are the second type. They are drilled in proven oil fields into known reservoirs to increase production and improve the likelihood that the oil or gas will continue flowing. In older fields, a development well may be drilled to *maintain* net production, not to increase it. Most wells drilled in the United States fall into this category.

The third type is a production well. They are drilled into proven reserves to prepare the well to retrieve the oil. The well then becomes a working well.

After a desirable drilling location has been pinpointed, drilling rights must be obtained. The land may be purchased outright or leased, or only the mineral rights may be acquired. Depending on the property's location, drilling rights are obtained from private property owners, states, local governments, or national governments.

Production

The average well is productive for ten to fifteen years, though some produce for forty years. The life cycle of an oil well includes three stages. In stage 1, spontaneous pressures from the natural gas push oil out the drill pipe. James Dean is engulfed by oil in the film *Giant* when he makes such a discovery.[3] Technologies have since been developed to control the flow rates.

Stage 1 wells are described by initial flow rates. In the United States, acceptable stage 1 wells yield about 50–100 barrels per day; in the Middle East a stage 1 may yield 10,000 barrels per day. Reported flow rate is affected by the choke equipment at the mouth of the drill pipe plus the circumference of the pipe. A loose choke and a wide pipe can cause the oil to flow faster but shorten the well's life. The industry standard is to operate the well at a slow flow rate and thereby prolong the well's life. Unscrupulous companies may distort reported flow rates from discovery wells by tinkering with the choke and pipe.

Stage 2 wells lack spontaneous pressure and require artificial inducement such as pumped air. In stage 3, continuous pumping has created a viscosity problem. Chemicals or detergents may reduce viscosity. Stripper wells are stage 3 wells common in the United States. They average less than 10 barrels per day.

Only 30 percent of oil reservoirs are recovered with current technologies. The abundance of unrecovered oil has lead to the development of enhanced oil recovery

(EOR) techniques. Perhaps 10 percent of oil reserves can be recovered through EOR.

Natural gas recovery is more delicate and capital intensive. Large containment vessels are required at the surface. Transportation is also a problem. Natural gas is bulkier than oil unless it is liquefied. Originally, a pipeline had to be constructed in order to make a gas field viable. Today, end users may receive natural gas in a liquefied form, albeit at a substantially higher cost. End users include gas utilities, large manufacturing concerns, and pipelines.

Notes

1. This and subsequent appendices were coauthored with Chris Decker and Pierre Poulin.

2. *The Economist*, "Black Gold."

3. Blow-out control equipment was developed about fifty years ago, though blow-outs still occur.

Appendix B
Oil and Gas Accounting

Accounting practices for oil and gas companies have two unique features. First, key expenses are either capitalized or expensed. Capitalization, as opposed to expensing, spreads certain expenses across several years and may provide an inflated impression of income. Second, noncash expenses include depreciation, depletion, and amortization charges. Noncash charges reduce income but do not affect cash flow.

Full Cost versus Successful Efforts

Oil and gas companies may report their income following either full-cost or successful-efforts methods. Full-cost accounting capitalizes virtually all costs, reporting them over time; consequently, reported costs do not exactly parallel the time of expenditure. Moreover, a portion of current costs are not reflected on the income statement until the future. With successful-efforts accounting, expenditures are capitalized only if the costs incurred are likely to lead to revenues in the near future.

Most but not all major oil companies use successful-efforts accounting. Many smaller companies choose full-cost accounting. One reason for this dichotomy is that smaller oil and gas companies are more concerned about the implications of unsuccessful drilling efforts. In contrast, multinationals are protected by their diversification in location, riskiness of exploration efforts, and type of business.

Both accounting methods have been and are still acceptable in the accounting community. However, the differences between the methods complicate comparison of oil and gas companies using different methods.

Regulatory Skepticism

In the mid-1970s the Financial Accounting Standards Board (FASB) attempted to force all oil and gas companies to use successful-efforts accounting, since it capitalized only those expenditures predicted to have an economic value and did not conceal failed drilling attempts behind a capitalization cloak. The Security and Exchange Commission (SEC) objected. Instead, it proposed the Reserve Recognition Approach (RRA); this form of accounting features current values and adjusts assets to their discounted present value and reflects the adjustment in income. That proposal failed. In 1982 the issue was permanently settled; companies may now use either method. However, multiple additional disclosures are now required concerning:

- quantity of reserves,
- related capitalizations,
- costs and results of production, and
- discounted value of expected cash flows.

TEI Accounting Practices

TEI had never reflected the effect of deferred income taxes resulting from deductions from intangible drilling and development costs on its balance sheet. At year-end 1975, deferred taxes equalled $25.5 million. This practice was acceptable (FASB No. 9 net method) under current generally accepted accounting principles for companies in the oil and gas industry; however, the company could have disclosed the item. The IRS examined TEI's 1974 tax return over the deferred tax issue. Beginning in 1974, the company disclosed how deferred income taxes would have altered earnings if they had been expensed.

In December 1978, the FASB issued Statement of Financial Accounting Standards No. 19, requiring adherence to a form of successful-efforts accounting in which costs incurred in the acquisition, exploration, and development of oil and gas are expensed. In addition, previously capitalized economically impaired properties were to be written off as a loss. Statement #19 also mandated comprehensive tax allocation accounting; that is, deferred taxes on the balance sheet would reflect the difference between reported financial statement tax and actual taxes paid. In the past, the figure was merely disclosed.

In 1978, TEI's 1977 financial statements were restated due to the deferred tax change and discontinued operations, primarily the energy services division. In 1979, the 1978 financial statements were restated due to discontinued operations. In 1980, 1979 and prior years were restated due to even more discontinued operations.

Oil and gas companies influence gross revenues in two ways: (1) by modifying the rate at which they exploit known hydrocarbon reserves, and (2) by altering the rate of spending on new exploration and development activities. Obviously, drilling success is important, but that factor is out of a company's control. TEI pursued both means as detailed in Tables B.1 and B.2.

The reserve report (Table B.1) begins with 1982 and describes a major natural

Table B.1

Changes in Reserves (in millions of barrels, gas in billion cubic feet)

	Proved Reserves Oil	Proved Reserves Natural Gas
Beginning 1982 Reserves	16.5	146.9
Reserve Additions/Reductions		
Reserve Estimate Revisions	3.1	84.5
Reserve Discoveries	2.8	78
Sales of Producing Properties	−2.2	−14.2
Production	−2.6	−23.6
Ending 1982 Reserves	18.3	291
Beginning 1983 Reserves	18.3	291
Reserve Additions/Reductions		
Reserve Estimate Revisions	−2.1	−58
Reserve Discoveries	1.9	1
Sales of Producing Properties	−1.9	−63.9
Production	−2	−17.6
Ending 1983 Reserves	14.2	152.5
Beginning 1984 Reserves	14.2	152.5
Reserve Additions/Reductions		
Reserve Estimate Revisions	0.3	−1.6
Reserve Discoveries	3.6	5.6
Sales of Producing Properties	−0.1	−13.1
Production	−2.6	−15.2
Ending 1985 Reserves	15.4	128.2

Source: TEI 10-K reports.

Table B.2

Drilling Operations

	1984	1985	1986
Net Developments Wells			
Oil Wells	52.38	13.32	9.37
Gas Wells	1.75	2.29	7.13
Total Producing Wells	54.13	15.61	16.5
Percent Dry Holes	6%	26%	4%
Net Exploratory Wells			
Oil Wells	15.94	6.48	6
Gas Wells	1.38	0.04	4.35
Total Producing Wells	17.32	6.52	10.35
Percent Dry Holes	83%	27%	67%

Source: TEI 10-K reports.

gas discovery in the Eloi Bay region of Louisiana and an upward revision in "proven" reserves attributed to prior discoveries. Together the two factors added 111 percent to total reserves measured at the beginning of the year. The value of those reserves, using the average price received by the company in 1982 ($3.09 per thousand cubic feet of gas), was approximately $502 million. Crude oil reserves rose, too, though by a smaller percentage amount.

Appendix C
TEI's Four Divisions

Oil and Gas Division

The raison d'être of small oil and gas firms is to grow. They pursue the lost Dutchman's oil field as the key to the world of big oil. Realistically, it would be easier to find a needle in a haystack than to make a sizable hydrocarbon discovery in the continental United States. The Seven Sisters[1] (who together controlled a majority of crude oil reserves, oil refining capacity, and final crude oil sales to consumers) long ago locked up the most attractive U.S. properties with leases or outright purchases. Small oil firms had two remaining options:

1) The conservative approach, followed by most small firms, involved obtaining leases and drilling rights in geographic locations shunned by the majors, areas with relatively small potential for large discoveries. The predilection of major oil companies is to work virgin tracts that might yield a major discovery and thereby have a significant impact on financial performance.

2) The aggressive approach required ambitious bidding against the majors in risky areas such as coastal U.S. waters, Alaska, or outside the United States.

The first strategy offered limited profits with modest risks. The second strategy was risk intensive. If the gamble was successful and yielded significant new reserves, then the firm evolved into an intermediate-sized energy enterprise. If the wager miscarried, the firm was likely to drift into bankruptcy.

The oil business was unusually tranquil in the early 1970s: few mergers, no foreign reserve expropriations, and no industry-shattering hydrocarbon discoveries. Oil prices and production were firmly under the control of the Seven Sisters. Structurally, the industry was an oligopoly. Economists designate an industry as oligopolistic if competition is based on nonprice variables such as advertising and packaging.[2] Without price competition, industry profits increase. Cooperative behavior among firms, whether tacit or by covenant, allows participants to share industry profits rather than compete for them. But for small firms, finding money to grow remained a problem. (Appendix E describes sources of finance to oil and gas companies.)

TEI's oil and gas division comprised domestic and foreign operations; however, for many years the domestic division was paramount. The majority of the company's production originated from the Eloi Bay and Half Moon Lake fields, located in shallow waters in St. Bernard Parish, Louisiana. Most of the company's leases were in Louisiana, but exploration sites were planned in Alaska, Canada, and abroad.

The year 1969 was typical; TEI participated in drilling nineteen gross domestic development wells. Ten wells proved to be successful oil wells, six were commercial gas wells, and three were dry holes. Table C.1 presents TEI's drilling results, while Figure C.1 illustrates the corresponding industry results. In terms of success rate, TEI exceeded the pack. However, a high success rate normally indicates a drilling strategy favoring extension of known oil reserves versus exploratory drilling.

In oil company parlance, the name of the game is reserve acquisition. Companies unable to increase in-ground oil and gas reserves are self-liquidating dinosaurs. TEI pursued reserves aggressively: it purchased proven reserves, bought or leased untested parcels for future drilling activities, and organized a joint venture with Humble Oil (a big oil company at the time) to buy and operate F.A. Callery, Inc. The joint venture was small, valued at $1.6 million, and included TEI as a 32 percent participant. Callery's properties contained nine producing wells, yielding 1,200 barrels of oil per day, and possessed 460 undeveloped acres in the Darrow field, Ascension Parish, Louisiana.

The company's largest field was in the waters of Eloi Bay, Louisiana. The Eloi Bay leases controlled a 23 percent interest in 12,000 acres and sixty offshore wells. When three New York investors filed suit on February 16, 1970, claiming ownership of leases being worked by a subsidiary, J.C. Trahan Drilling, trading in TEI's common stock and warrants on the Pacific Stock Exchange was halted. The United States District Court in New Orleans ruled against the plaintiffs and awarded TEI clear title to the properties; however, the plaintiffs were granted an interest in the first eleven wells that had been drilled in 1962. A settlement was reached after the company appealed the decision. TEI exchanged $550,000 for clear title. At the time, there were 2.5 million barrels of oil and 2.8 Bcf of gas on the properties.[3]

The oil and gas division adhered to the conservative strategy during the early 1970s. In 1973, for example, it participated in drilling seventy-three wells in the Gulf Coast area, the West Texas–New Mexico area, and Canada. Nearly 58 percent of these wells yielded commercial quantities of hydrocarbons. By contrast, a company engaged in wildcat drilling (seeking substantial new discover-

Table C.1

TEI Drilling Results

Net Wells*	1964	1969	1976	1980
Development	24.7	5.8	30.2	69.2
Exploratory	6.0	0	3.1	36.5
Dry Development	6.8	1.0	3.9	6.1
Dry Exploratory	4.6	0	2.6	14.4
% Dry	37.1%	17.7%	19.4%	19.3%

Source: TEI 10-K reports.
*Net wells is derived by summing the company's share of each well drilled.

Figure C.1. **U.S. Oil and Gas Drilling Success Rates**

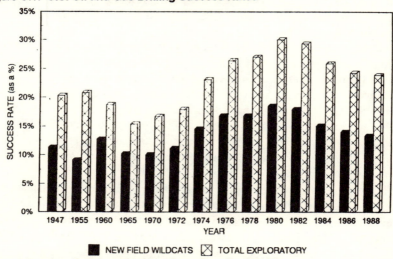

Source: American Petroleum Institute, *Basic Data Book 1990.*

ies) might have a 10 percent drilling success rate. A hard-working firm following the safe strategy can achieve steady growth, as seen in Table C.2, where TEI's energy sales are reported (reserve disclosure data were not required at this time and therefore are not available).

Firms in the oil patch entered a watershed period in 1973, and in the process TEI discovered what it wanted to be when it grew up. The year began uneventfully, with the economy growing strongly at a real rate of 5.8 percent through September. Then, in October, war erupted in the Middle East, and the Arab oil embargo began. The embargo is indelibly etched in the minds of Americans who

Table C.2

TEI Net Oil and Gas Sales

Year	Oil-Bbls	Gas-MMCF
1969	789,735	5,267
1970	844,152	5,721
1971	989,572	6,910
1972	1,052,482	7,111
1973	1,254,335	8,463

Source: TEI annual reports, 1969–1973.

Figure C.2. **U.S. and Middle East Oil Prices**

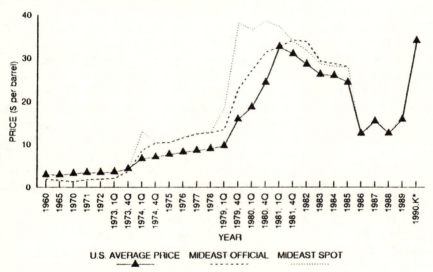

Source: Monthly Energy Review, 1990.
* After Iraq invaded Kuwait.

endured endless lines, often waiting an hour or more for gasoline. Prices for energy needs escalated, causing great discomfort. Moreover, the reversal in the cost of this basic commodity precipitated two major worldwide economic recessions in 1974 and 1979, and unrelenting waves of inflation, unemployment, and industrial dislocation.[4]

The energy crisis was manna to oil companies. The year 1973 began a golden era of rapidly escalating values for all energy forms. The U.S. price of a barrel of crude oil in October 1973 (seen in Figure C.2) was roughly $4. A year later U.S.

oil prices were $7 per barrel, a 75 percent increase. Still later, when the Shah of Iran was deposed in 1979 and the flow of oil was disrupted, oil prices ratcheted upward again. From a U.S. average price of $9.66 per barrel in the first quarter of 1979, the price reached $35 per barrel in the first quarter of 1981. In the eight years 1973–1981 oil prices jumped by nearly 750 percent.

World and United States oil prices diverged as seen in Figure C.2, until President Reagan deregulated oil prices in 1981. Prior to 1981, U.S. prices lagged behind Mideast prices because of oil-price controls; after 1981 Mideast prices were artificially too high, as OPEC failed to recognize the new market-place reality.

History had never before witnessed such a dramatic increase in the price of a basic commodity. Even the Black Death during the Middle Ages, which killed off nearly a third of the world's population, only doubled real wage rates.[5] Bankruptcy vanished from the oil business; it was said that any fool with a drill and a lease could make money.

An unprecedented decade of high profits and cash flow created prosperity for established oil companies. Oil company chief executive officers became modern-day Roman emperors. Like the Romans, oil companies pursued novel methods for spending their newfound largess. Some, such as Mobil, purchased businesses they knew nothing about: Montgomery Ward, a retailer. In most cases, it would have been more expedient simply to burn the money. Other oil companies pursued costly energy supply strategies. Many, including Standard of Ohio, ARCO, and Phillips, purchased coal or exotic fuel companies, usually earning little or no profit from the ventures. Others, such as Dome Petroleum and later Exxon, drilled Arctic wells with princely budgets in excess of $100 million. At least the emperors of Rome left behind architectural legacies; more often than not, oil companies bequeathed to their survivors only waste.

TEI could endure the siren's song of easy money for only so long before abandoning the conservative strategy that had prudently stewarded the division. Eventually, the aggressive approach, with its associated higher risks, was embraced. The following steps were taken:

1. In the last quarter of 1973, an exploration program was initiated in Alaska.

2. A greater share of a growing total capital pool was devoted to investment in exploration. During the first half of 1973, $4 million was spent on exploration; an additional $9 million was spent in the second half of the year. The budget continued to expand.

3. In 1976, TEI moved to be exclusively an oil and gas exploration and development firm.

The future had been inextricably altered. The successful idea of being a mini-conglomerate was dropped. TEI would now pursue the stars.

Energy Services Division

A second way to earn profits in the oil patch is to provide aid and assistance to oil and gas exploration companies. The energy services division had expertise in:

(a) repairing and servicing producing wells,
(b) completing new wells drilled to their final depth,
(c) transporting oil field liquids, and
(d) constructing oil field structures.

Well servicing flourished and grew profitable when energy prices escalated in 1973.

New government regulation (see Appendix F, "Oil and Gas Regulation") sought to increase energy supplies impeded by the oil embargo in 1973 and counterproductive federal regulations by permitting incremental production from reworked oil fields to be priced at market levels, well in excess of the regulated price for existing fields. Oil companies responded to these incentives and invested in mature and previously closed-in fields. Speculative fever permeated every corner of the oil patch and rekindled the quest for oil and gas.

TEI was prepared for the crisis. The energy services division, which functioned primarily in West Texas, began an ambitious expansion plan in 1969, culminating in the acquisition of Skytop Rig Company and Bighorn Well Servicing, Inc., and investment in existing businesses such as Snyder Well Servicing, Tucker Well Servicing, and Tracer Surveys. Combined, the companies operated seventeen well-servicing rigs, eleven double derricks, two single derricks, three well-swabbing units, two roustabout gang trucks, and two heavy-duty hot-oil units. TEI's energy service divisions sold products and services that on average accounted for 69 percent of direct drilling expenditures.[6]

TEI built its first ultra-deep rig in 1972 at a cost of approximately $500,000. The rig drilled to a depth of 25,000 feet. Deep drilling was more costly both per foot drilled and cumulatively, as seen in Table C.3, and yielded higher profit margins for drilling companies. The count of well-servicing and swabbing units surpassed fifty by 1974. The service division continued to expand throughout the mid-1970s; it nearly doubled in 1974 with the purchase of R&R Equipment Company of Grand Junction, Colorado, for $1 million cash, $4 million in long-term notes, and 306,000 shares of TEI stock. With sixty-eight well-servicing units, TEI had grown into one of the largest well-servicing companies in the United States. The division provided services in six western states. Numerous acquisitions of small well-servicing companies (between $1 and $4 million) increased the division's size to include ninety-three onshore well-service rigs, nine barge-mounted rigs, and ten crew boats, which serviced rigs off the Texas and Louisiana Gulf coasts. The major firms in the industry are identified and ranked in Table C.4.

Table C.3

Costs of Drilling and Equipping Wells (in dollars per foot)

Region	Depth			
	1,250–2,499	10,000–12,499	15,000–17,499	20,000+
Alaska	$591	$278	$1,058	$1,492
Appalachia	38	—	218	—
Gulf of Mexico	—	429	624	400
Louisiana	22	157	293	485
Texas	33	112	229	276

Source: American Petroleum Institute, *1980 Joint Association Study.*

The energy services division was well positioned. The oil field services and equipment manufacturing businesses grew rapidly; however, profits earned by exploration firms were an intoxicant that led TEI to refocus itself on oil and gas exploration and production.

Energy Equipment Manufacturing

The energy industry is capital intensive both in the field and in processing. Field work requires drilling rigs, well rigs, derricks, and heavy-duty carriers. TEI acquired Skytop Rig Company for $1.7 million in 1969 to manufacture these machine needs. With facilities in Odessa and Victoria, Texas, and Edmonton, Canada, Skytop was a market leader in this specialized market niche. Skytop held a valuable patent right for a speedkit system used in manufacturing well-servicing rigs. The company also rebuilt and modernized older drilling and well-servicing rigs; it manufactured a unique tilt right that could drill directional holes from an offshore platform; and it was one of the world's largest manufacturers of portable oil-well-servicing masts.

TEI continued to acquire manufacturing companies: Mechanical Seal and Service, Inc. (a producer of seals for pumps that transfer liquids), Midway Manufacturing and Supply Co. (a manufacturer of drilling rigs for shallow holes), and Regal Tool and Rubber (a producer of swabcups, drill pipe protectors, and a patented shock absorber system to protect offshore rigs). The division ventured into the foundry business by acquiring Newcastle Foundry in January 1971 (for $683,000, the assumption of $1 million of debt, and an option to buy 100,000 shares of TEI stock at $6) and Pentex Foundry Corporation in August 1974. Newcastle produced wear-corrosive and heat-resistant high-strength irons used in the auto and petroleum industries. Pentex was a dormant company; it was hoped that it could produce castings to be sold to the chemical and refining industries.

Table C.4

Major Oil and Gas Service and Supply Companies

Industry Segment as a Percent of Firm's Revenue

Firm	1975 Total Revenue ($ millions)	Drilling								Contract Drilling		Pipelaying		Platform Fabri-cation	Profit Margins	
		Wire-log	Oil Well Servicing	Work-over	Bits	Muds	Other Drilling Tools	Rig Equipment	Well Completion Equipment	Off-Shore	On-Shore	Off-Shore	On-Shore		1975	1976
Baker International	510			11%	14%	18%	9%		24%						8.0%	8.3%
Chicago Bridge & Iron	564														7.3%	9.1%
Dresser Industries	2,012	5%			3%										6.2%	6.7%
Global Marine	105									76%					2.5%	6.6%
Halliburton	4,210	1%	16%			2%						13%	12%		5.3%	6.0%
Helmerich & Payne	64										56%				23.2%	21.2%
Hughes Tool	348		21%		42%		12%								12.4%	10.6%
Marathon Manufacturing	294														5.1%	6.1%
McDermott (J.Ray)	1,102											46%	46%		12.3%	5.4%
Ocean Drilling & Exploration	208									70%	10%				17.8%	11.2%
Offshore	172									100%					16.9%	NA
Parker Drilling	112										100%				11.6%	13.0%
Reading & Bates	191										44%			31%	14.1%	11.2%
Rowan	65									32%					NA	NA
Rucker	161			19%	5%		13%	20%							9.9%	10.2%
Santa Fe International	332		5%							22%	21%	39%		8%	8.7%	18.7%
Schlumberger	1,566	33%								5%	6%				14.0%	7.4%
Sedco	227				30%					81%				8%	18.5%	11.6%
Smith International	293				30%		50%								11.6%	NA
Universal Oil Products	825														-4.2%	NA
VETCO	171							78%							NA	NA
ZAPATA	336									26%					1.1%	8.6%
Industry Composites[a]	13,868	$659	$825	$87	$374	$176	$255	$166	$122	$844	$407	$1,184	$1,012	$104		
Oil Well Equipment[b]															8.3%	7.7%
Offshore Drilling[b]															11.1%	10.5%

Table C-4 *(continued)*

Market Share of Firms in Industry Segments[c]

	1975 Total Revenue ($ millions)	Drilling								Contract Drilling		Pipelaying		Plat-form Fabrica-tion
		Wire log	Oil Well Servicing	Work-over	Bits	Muds	Other Drilling Tools[c]	Rig Equip-ment	Well Comple-tion Equip-ment	Off-Shore	On-Shore	Off-Shore	On-Shore	
Baker International	510	0.0%	0.0%	64.7%	19.1%	52.2%	18.0%	0.0%	100.0%	0.0%	0.0%	0.0%	0.0%	0.0%
Chicago Bridge & Iron	564	0.0%	0.0%	0.0%	0.0%	0.0%	0.0%	0.0%	0.0%	0.0%	0.0%	0.0%	0.0%	0.0%
Dresser Industries	2,012	15.3%	0.0%	0.0%	16.1%	0.0%	0.0%	0.0%	0.0%	0.0%	0.0%	0.0%	0.0%	0.0%
Global Marine	105	0.0%	0.0%	0.0%	0.0%	0.0%	0.0%	0.0%	0.0%	9.5%	0.0%	0.0%	0.0%	0.0%
Halliburton	4,210	6.4%	81.7%	0.0%	0.0%	47.8%	0.0%	0.0%	0.0%	0.0%	0.0%	46.2%	0.0%	49.9%
Helmerich & Payne	64	0.0%	8.9%	0.0%	0.0%	0.0%	0.0%	0.0%	0.0%	8.8%	0.0%	0.0%	0.0%	0.0%
Hughes Tool	348	0.0%	0.0%	0.0%	39.1%	0.0%	16.4%	0.0%	0.0%	0.0%	0.0%	0.0%	0.0%	0.0%
Marathon Manufacturing	294	0.0%	0.0%	0.0%	0.0%	0.0%	0.0%	0.0%	0.0%	0.0%	0.0%	0.0%	0.0%	0.0%
McDermott (JRay)	1,102	0.0%	0.0%	0.0%	0.0%	0.0%	0.0%	0.0%	0.0%	0.0%	0.0%	42.8%	0.0%	50.1%
Ocean Drilling & Exploration	208	0.0%	0.0%	0.0%	0.0%	0.0%	0.0%	0.0%	0.0%	20.0%	0.0%	0.0%	0.0%	0.0%
Offshore	172	0.0%	0.0%	0.0%	0.0%	0.0%	0.0%	0.0%	0.0%	14.3%	4.2%	0.0%	0.0%	0.0%
Parker Drilling	112	0.0%	0.0%	0.0%	0.0%	0.0%	0.0%	0.0%	0.0%	0.0%	27.5%	0.0%	0.0%	0.0%
Reading & Bates	191	0.0%	0.0%	0.0%	0.0%	0.0%	0.0%	0.0%	0.0%	12.9%	0.0%	0.0%	0.0%	0.0%
Rowan	65	0.0%	0.0%	0.0%	0.0%	0.0%	0.0%	0.0%	0.0%	2.5%	7.0%	0.0%	57.0%	0.0%
Rucker	161	0.0%	0.0%	35.3%	2.2%	0.0%	8.2%	19.4%	0.0%	0.0%	0.0%	0.0%	0.0%	0.0%
Santa Fe International	332	0.0%	0.0%	0.0%	0.0%	0.0%	0.0%	0.0%	0.0%	8.7%	17.1%	10.9%	25.6%	0.0%
Schlumberger	1,566	78.4%	9.5%	0.0%	0.0%	0.0%	0.0%	0.0%	0.0%	9.3%	23.1%	0.0%	0.0%	0.0%
Sedco	227	0.0%	0.0%	0.0%	0.0%	0.0%	0.0%	0.0%	0.0%	12.6%	12.3%	0.0%	17.5%	0.0%
Smith International	293	0.0%	0.0%	0.0%	23.5%	0.0%	57.4%	0.0%	0.0%	0.0%	0.0%	0.0%	0.0%	0.0%
Universal Oil Products	825	0.0%	0.0%	0.0%	0.0%	0.0%	0.0%	0.0%	0.0%	0.0%	0.0%	0.0%	0.0%	0.0%
VETCO	171	0.0%	0.0%	0.0%	0.0%	0.0%	0.0%	80.6%	0.0%	0.0%	0.0%	0.0%	0.0%	0.0%
ZAPATA	336	0.0%	0.0%	0.0%	0.0%	0.0%	0.0%	0.0%	0.0%	10.4%	0.0%	0.0%	0.0%	0.0%
Industry Composites[a]	13,868	$659	$825	$87	$374	$176	$255	$166	$122	$844	$407	$1,184	$1,012	$1,012

Source: Standard & Poors Estimates, Compustat Data, *Business Week*, (Investment Managers Service).

[a] The composites are only representative of each industry segment. For example, onshore drilling is highly competitive and will include many small participants.

[b] Based on Standard & Poors Industry Group Stock Indexes.

[c] Market shares are estimates.

Table C.5

Exploration and Production Capital Expenditures by Region (in $ billions)

	Average		1973	1974	1975	1976	1977	1978	1979	1980	1981	1982	1983	1984
	1963–67	1968–72												
United States	$3.7	$4.3	$7.3	$11.2	$9.1	$13.1	$14.9	$17.3	$24.2	$32.4	$50.8	$50.9	$36.6	$37.4
Other Western Hemisphere	0.9	1.1	1.8	2.4	2.3	3.0	4.4	5.8	7.8	10.6	12.3	13.8	13.2	13.6
Western Europe	0.2	0.5	1.3	2.4	3.6	4.2	5.3	6.0	7.2	10.5	10.3	10.5	8.1	7.4
Middle East	0.3	0.5	0.9	1.0	1.0	1.4	1.9	1.6	1.7	2.5	3.5	3.7	2.6	2.0
Africa	0.3	0.6	0.5	0.8	0.8	1.0	1.0	1.3	1.7	2.3	3.5	3.8	2.8	2.3
Far East	0.1	0.5	0.7	1.1	1.5	1.2	1.3	1.8	2.1	3.2	5.1	6.2	5.3	5.5
Total	$5.5	$7.5	$12.5	$18.9	$18.3	$23.9	$28.8	$33.8	$44.7	$61.5	$85.5	$88.9	$68.6	$68.2

Source: Arthur Andersen & Co., Oil and Gas Reverse Disclosure.

Capital expenditures for oil and gas exploration and production exploded upward industry-wide, as seen in Table C.5. Compared with 1973, expenditures nearly doubled by 1976, tripled by 1979, quadrupled by 1980, and were seven times greater by 1981. The growth in United States and worldwide expenditures was nearly equivalent.

Driven by market growth, the manufacturing division expanded internally. Skytop added a 63,000-square-foot plant in Victoria, and Regal added a 28,000-square-foot factory in Corsicana, Texas. In 1976, TEI planned a marine fabrication facility for Regal in Hancock County, Mississippi, along the Gulf of Mexico; a plant expansion for Midway Manufacturing; and a new plant for Mechanical Seal and Service. Regal added two 400-ton injection presses to its oil field product line. Later, TEI bought Derricks, Inc., a manufacturer of on-shore and offshore drilling derricks and substructures for 177,500 shares of common stock. A $15 million contract was received in 1978 to deliver ten drilling rigs to the Soviet Union over the next two years.

Such an extraordinary undertaking should have led to expanding profits, growing market share, and a resolve to become the leader in the industry. But that was not the case. Instead, the division drained the total business.

Real Estate Division

The company had diversified into real estate in 1968, partially motivated by a recognition of the approaching environmental movement (see the company literature reproduced in Figure C.3). TEI embraced a new corporate motto: "Energy and Ecology for Man" (see Figure C.4).

In that same year, TEI crafted its best acquisition: The West Aspen Company of Aspen, Colorado, for $1.7 million. At the time, Aspen was an old mining town located at the foot of Aspen Mountain that served as a sleepy hideaway for ski bums, the vacationing rich, and a few local residents. The purchase included a prime 221-acre site in Aspen. In 1991, undeveloped property in town sold for more than $1 million per acre. This property was a "lay-up." A plan was conceived to develop the site into a resort complex with a hotel, a convention center, retail shops, and other assorted services. Supplemental designs included a 300-unit apartment complex, 1,200 townhouse units, 20 duplex houses, parks, and attractive landscaped areas. But the townspeople rejected the idea as out of step with the existing character of the community.

The West Aspen Company then agreed to a 45 percent joint venture participation with an insurance company and C.V. Richardson Development Corporation to develop 537 acres located within Oklahoma City limits. This plan was similar to the Aspen, Colorado, prototype and included commercial and residential developments. In the late 1970s, the company successfully rezoned an area adjacent to a strategically located expressway in northwest Oklahoma City to be developed as a high-rise office tower.

Figure C.3. TEI Corporate Mission

TEXS INTERNATIONAL COMPANY

. . .dedicated to the development
of natural resources for
the environment of man.

Preserving the Ecology

. . . preserving and improving our living environment through extensive and carefully planned development of land . . . our business is to provide people with a pleasant and clean place in which to live and work . . .

The Search for Energy

. . . exploring for petroleum reserves in the United States, Canada, the Arctic, South America and the Middle East . . . manufacturing drilling equipment, well servicing equipment and other heavy oil field equipment used in the search for and production of hydrocarbon reserves throughout the world . . . engaging in the well servicing business which involves the completion of newly drilled oil and gas wells, and servicing them after they are completed to maintain them on a productive capacity . . . our business is the search for petroleum reserves throughout the world . . .

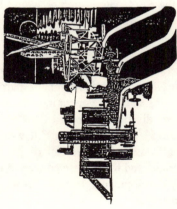

On the Cover
APOLLO 10 View of Earth.
The Arabian Peninsula, Persian Gulf, and other Middle East countries, containing 63 percent of the world's known oil reserves, are seen in center of the picture. Clearly visible is the outline of the African continent. Europe and much of Asia are covered by heavy clouds. Photograph courtesy NASA.

Figure C.4. **TEI Corporate Logo**

ENERGY AND ECOLOGY FOR MAN

A separate joint venture was begun in 1969 that purchased a mobile-home manufacturer for $5,000,000 with the intention of developing mobile-home parks in five cities.7 In 1970, $1.5 million was paid for Consumers Ice Company, whose principal assets were 1,120 acres (500 acres with development potential) of land located in Pacifica, California. This property included the last sizable open areas suitable for development located within twenty minutes of downtown San Francisco and was convenient to the airport as well as to Palo Alto and San Jose.

A subsidiary established in 1971 registered a $20 million real estate limited partnership fund with the SEC. These monies would be leveraged with about $100 million in debt and used to purchase commercial properties. Investors would obtain the full advantage of partnership tax benefits. Similar to its oil and gas partnerships (see Appendix E, "Sources of Finance to Oil and Gas Companies and TEI"), the general partner (TEI) was responsible only for costs that were not immediately deductible or depreciable for tax purposes, but would participate in income, capital gains, and some operating expenses.

In 1971 the real estate division purchased Crown Hill Cemetery Associates of Denver, Colorado, for $3 million. Crown Hill was the largest nonsectarian cemetery in the greater Denver area. Not all of the interment grounds were currently needed for burials, and those were converted for the interim into commercial and multifamily developments. In 1974 Crown Hill added 900 crypts to its impeccably kept cemetery.

In 1974, TEI bought a ninety-four-bed acute-care hospital and adjacent land in Panama City, California, for $7.9 million, primarily as a real estate play. Also, government-sponsored Medicare and Medicaid had recently been approved, and the management of hospitals was becoming a growth area. Another property bought and held for investment purposes contained sixteen acres (1,200 feet of waterfront) in Newport, Oregon, and an area 110 miles south of Portland known as the Twenty Miracle Miles.

The real estate division had terrific long-run ideas and plans; however, in their infancy, many were cash drains, which was anathematic to a company driven to grow via acquisition. Many of the assets were preserved until they were sold at a profit; some were sold when the company became desperate for cash.

Summary

Throughout the late 1960s and early 1970s, TEI launched an enthusiastic diversification program fueled by both acquisition and internal growth. By 1975, oil and gas production had been overshadowed, and the company was a mini–oil conglomerate. The annual report placed manufacturing and well-servicing in premier positions. The report stated that "TEI does complete drilling rigs." The corporation's two mottoes were, "We build rigs and we mean every word of it" and "We have the resources." Skytop/Brewster was a genuine market leader, with sales in France, Argentina, Singapore, and Brazil. Regal Tool and Rubber also was a leader, with 20 percent of the U.S. market for drill-pipe protectors. Overall, TEI had a reputation as a flourishing specialist in all aspects of the petroleum industry, and many people were unaware of its stature as a financial pioneer. Ironically, the company reversed itself in just one year and embarked on oil and gas exploration.

Notes

1. Exxon, BP, Shell, Texaco, Chevron, Mobil, and Gulf.
2. Good examples of oligopolies are soap products, cereals, and beer.
3. *Wall Street Journal* (February 2, 1970): 14.
4. The gross national product declined by 5 percent from the onset of the recession in January 1974 until its end in March 1975. Normally, in a recession, GNP declines between 2 percent and 4 percent. Unemployment peaked at 9 percent; in fact, unemployment did not return to its September 1974 level of 5.9 percent until August 1978. During the remainder of the decade, high inflation was a persistent problem.
5. Charles Maurice and Charles W. Smithson, *The Doomsday Myth: 10,000 Years of Economic Crises.*
6. Based on calculations made by the Independent Petroleum Association of America.
7. *Wall Street Journal*, "Texas Petroleum Corp. Reached Agreement with a New Division of AAA Enterprises Inc. for Development of Mobile-Home Parks in Five Cities."

Appendix D
Industry Segments

Onshore and Offshore Drilling

Drilling occurs on and off shore. Onshore drilling is more customary and easier. Most onshore wells are fairly shallow (less than two miles deep), though some reach depths of six miles. An onshore rig costs between $1 million and $10 million. Most are owned by drilling contractors. The largest onshore rig producers are steel manufacturers.

Most onshore drilling is of development wells, with the United States and Canada accounting for approximately 70 percent of this activity. The Baker Hughes Tool Rotary Rig Count (see Figure D.1) constitutes the best information source for tracking the number of rigs in use.

Offshore drilling is a different breed, requiring a copious capital investment and involving steep risks. Offshore drilling rigs are constructed to endure severe weather conditions such as hurricanes and to include a provision for locomotion. The least expensive are jack-up rigs for shallow-water drilling; recessed legs are lowered to the ocean's floor in depths of 300 to 400 feet. Drillships are self-propelled mini-barges that work depths up to 400 feet. A third type is floating semi-submersible rigs for deep-water drilling.

Offshore production rigs, also known as platforms, increase in cost when their design allows them to work at greater depths. In 1979–1980 during a drilling frenzy, platforms functional to a 200-foot depth sold for $6 to $10 million, 400-foot platforms cost $100 million, and 600-foot platforms (of the type used in the North Sea) sold for $200 million.

Drilling Contractors

For economic and technical reasons, major integrated oil companies and independent oil and gas firms customarily hire drilling contractors to perform drilling

Figure D.1. **Onshore Drilling in the United States and Canada: Baker Hughes Tool Rotary Rig Count**

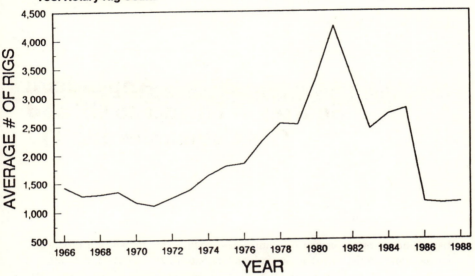

Source: Oil & Gas Journal, 1966–1988.

Note: Approximately 90 percent of rigs are operating onshore.

services. The alternative arrangement would require owning diverse types of equipment in locations around the world.

Barriers to entry and exit are almost nonexistent in the onshore drilling contracting business. Used rigs sell at steep discounts. Contractors compete based on their ability to transport rigs, expertise in operations, and price.

Capital-expenditure requirements impose steep entry barriers to the offshore drilling business. The business is highly cyclical: either feast or famine. In boom times, drillers try to transfer their risk to gas companies by demanding long-term contracts.

Drilling Components and Service

The cost of supplies is insignificant relative to the total cost of drilling. Therefore, suppliers of hardware and rig services compete primarily based on performance and reliability. Many of these segments behave oligopolistically. Services include quick replacement and on-time delivery of rig parts. Table C.4 details the major competitors in the industry.

Appendix E
Sources of Finance to Oil and Gas Companies and TEI

Rising energy prices enrich oil companies twice. First, if they are producers, revenues and profits increase. Second, and perhaps more important, the value of discovered but not yet producing reserves increases. Reserves are an oil company's principal asset. A hypothetical company in 1973 (when oil averaged $3.54 per barrel) with $100 million dollars of proven in-ground reserves, with no incremental effort, would have seen the value of its reserves rise to $450 million in 1979, when oil prices reached $15.89. The extra $350 million of assets are an artifact of price fluctuations.

In-ground oil is not worthless. Lenders will advance oil companies money provided they establish sufficient collateral: proven reserves. Hence, an upswing in oil prices leads to an enhanced ability to borrow money. The late 1970s witnessed oil companies securing ample new money from higher profits and new bank loans. Many companies embraced adventurous schemes including:

(a) exploring in pristine areas despite high costs;
(b) testing new energy sources including shale oil, tar sands, and solar power; and
(c) diversifying into new industries.

Arguably, the companies should have distributed the funds to shareholders, who would then invest or spend the money in whatever manner was in their own best interest. In subsequent years, when oil prices fell, most of these adventures were discontinued.

Oil and gas firms are classified as majors or independents. Majors are distinguished by multibillion-dollar revenues and a high degree of vertical and sometimes horizontal integration; for example, USX owns U.S. Steel and Marathon Oil. More than likely, they have significant international operations that may include downstream marketing, petroleum refining, oil trading, and even petro-chemicals; for example, Mobil owns Glad plastic bags. Other majors include Amoco, Chevron, Royal Dutch, Shell, Exxon, and Texaco. Conversely, indepen-dents range from one-man–one-drilling-rig operations to firms generating multi-billion dollar revenues; they are usually not integrated, and they concentrate on exploration, development, or production.

Financially, majors are among the healthiest of all firms as a result of an extended history of generous earnings, significant reserve accumulation, and the portfolio effect of vertical integration. Neither the business cycle nor vacillations in oil and gas prices jeopardize their future. This autonomy is much appreciated by lenders, for whom the majors are perfect debtors; they have nearly unlimited access to the public and private capital markets as sources of debt and equity financing.

Major oil companies access world capital markets to raise money by issuing debt and equity securities. Consider Exxon in early 1992: It had 475 million shares of common stock listed on the NYSE, worth approximately $28 billion, $8.3 billion of long-term debt, and $19 billion of current liabilities. Its capital structure reflected 51 percent equity and 49 percent debt.

Independents are vulnerable to the vagaries of the national economy and the petroleum market. Consequently, their financial performance vacillates between boom and bust. Not surprisingly, smaller independents are restricted from the public capital market. Their financing comes from owners' invested equity, bank borrowing, and private placements with insurance companies. Banks and insur-ance companies are more difficult lenders than sources of money in the public capital market. They limit management's decision-making power and constrain company spending, dividends, and even overhead, including salaries. Few inde-pendents have hard assets other than their proven developed and undeveloped reserves that a bank would lend against.[1]

The critical factor determining the size of a bank line of credit to an indepen-dent oil and gas company is its "borrowing base." The borrowing base is derived from: (a) procuring an estimate of oil and gas reserves from an engineering consultant engaged by the independent, (b) assigning a market price to value those reserves, (c) discounting the revenue stream to reflect the time until the hydrocarbons are produced, and (d) reducing that amount by a risk adjustment, which gives the bank a degree of security against falling prices, over-optimistic reserve assessments, or natural calamity. Table E.1 contains an example reserve valuation. The borrowing base enables a producer to borrow against future pro-duction revenues.

A lending arrangement predicated on an estimated valuation of an *unobserv-able* hydrocarbon deposit is exposed to unforeseen revisions. Upward reserve revisions are welcome, since the firm can borrow even more money; downward revisions are onerous, since they force the borrowing firm to reduce its debt. Similar problems ensue from movements in crude oil prices. Higher reserve valuations enable firms to grow their bank debt to fund new discoveries, in the

Table E.1

Valuing Oil Reserves

Proved Reserves	Current Year
Beginning balance (barrels)	20,000
Revisions of previous estimates (barrels)	3,000
Purchases (barrels)	2,000
Production (barrels)	(4,000)
Ending balance	21,000
x	
Current market price	$20.00
=	
Revenues	$420,000
x	
Discount factor[a]	0.8
=	
Present discounted value of reserves	$336,000

[a] The SEC requires a 10% discount rate. Companies and their lenders may choose another rate.

hope that a new discovery will lead to higher profits, more reserves, and thus more bank debt.

Another approach to financing utilized by independents has been to farm out promising prospects. A farm-out is essentially a joint venture between a company with reserves or potential reserves and another company with money or expertise. In exchange for advancing either money or expertise, the co-venturer obtains a fixed percentage of production revenues. Table E.2 contains a partial list of farm-outs that took place in the 1970s.

Limited-drilling partnership funds (LPFs) are another funding source for oil and gas companies. LPFs emanated from a desire by oil and gas companies to raise riskless capital and from the desire of investors to benefit from liberal interpretations of the federal Tax Code. The general partner paid tangible drilling costs, which had to be capitalized for income tax purposes; the investor paid intangible (deductible) costs. LPFs were a deal made in heaven: both parties prospered. Originated in the early 1950s, they became a financing staple by the late 1960s.

The tax shelter advantage of LPFs lasted until the 1986 federal tax law. Funds were sold publicly subject to SEC regulations accompanied by a prospectus, or were privately placed. The most common types were drilling funds, royalty funds, and completion funds. Rising interest rates made debt financing infeasible and stimulated LPF sales. Figure E.1 depicts the prime interest rate over this period. By 1970, it was estimated that between a third and a half of the drilling conducted by the 12,000 independents was financed by LPFs.[2]

Table E.2

Farm-Out Agreements in 1974

Independent Operator	End-User	Contract Length (yrs)	Independent's Investment ($ millions)	End-User's Investment ($ millions)	End-User's Percentage Participation
Dome Petroleum Ltd.	Dow Chemical	2–4	30.6	59.4	25%[a]
McCormick Oil & Gas Co.	Dow Chemical	3	18	18	50%[a]
Texas Oil & Gas	Dupont	N/A	N/A	N/A	A portion of 40 wells
Oceanic Exploration	Fluor	N/A	N/A[b]	N/A[b]	13%
Four Small Oil Independents	Coors	N/A	N/A[c]	N/A[c]	25%
Inexco Oil Co.	Gulf Oil	>4 yrs	N/A	30	N/A[d]

Source: Oil & Gas Journal, all issues, 1974.

[a] Dow Chemical holds a call option to buy 100% of the production.
[b] Total investment in an Aegean Sea drilling program is $100 million.
[c] Coors has an interest in 46 wells + a fixed price contract on gas produced.
[d] Gulf Oil made an advance payment in order to retain rights to 6 million barrels of higher priced sweet crude.

Figure E.1. **Prime Rate from 1961 to 1985**

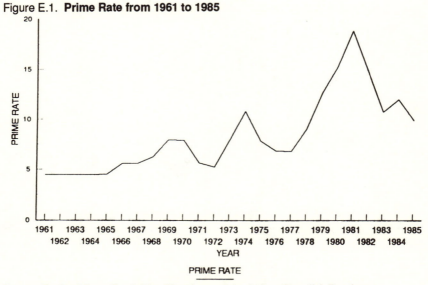

Source: Derived from Cambridge Planning and Analytics, Datadisk Database.
Note: Rate is average per year.

The general partner in a limited partnership assumes unlimited liability, while the limited partners have no liability beyond their original investment. The general partner was often an oil and gas company committed to exploration and development. Unlimited liability was immaterial to the independents since their assets were few and there was limited protection behind their corporate shield. The general partner profited from a multitude of financial and operational advantages in the LPF structure. A major advantage was the general partner's ability to record *all* of the fund's proven reserves on its own balance sheet, which then increased the independent's borrowing power. Moreover, the corporate balance sheet did not reveal the exploration, sunk, or intangible costs. Most important, an LPF was a source of both capital and cash flow due to fees charged to investors.

Exploration funds are a special variety of LPFs that prospered in the early 1970s, driven by the energy crisis. Wildcatters (oil companies specializing in unproven areas) would underwrite the LPF even before acquiring a drilling prospect. Some wildcatters managed to benefit doubly from the exploration fund by having the partnership drill on an unexplored lease adjacent to other unexplored leases owned solely by the wildcat firm. Valuable geologic insights for the firm's other leases could be garnered from the partnership's well.

Drilling fund sales reached nearly $300 million by 1969 and then surged in the early 1980s to nearly $2 billion (see Figure E.2). In the early 1970s, public drilling fund shares were sold to high net worth individuals at prices between

Figure E.2. **Public Drilling Fund Growth in the United States**

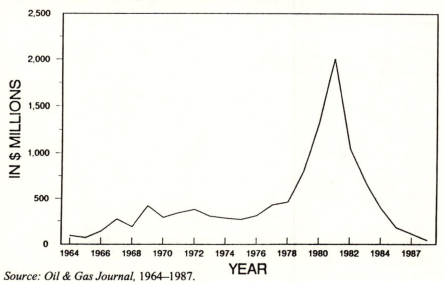

Source: Oil & Gas Journal, 1964–1987.

Figure E.3. **1985 Returns for Oil and Gas Financing**

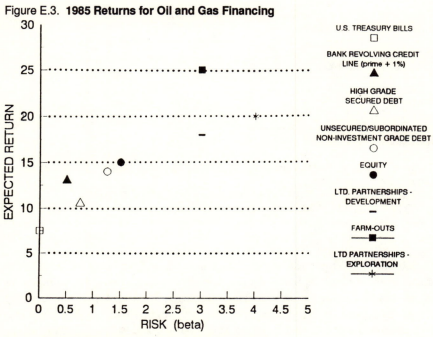

Source: Derived from material in the *Oil & Gas Journal.*

Table E.3

How an Investor Benefits in a Limited Partnership Fund: 1969

Assumptions:
1) Investor is in the 70% tax bracket.
2) Intangible costs are 80% of investment.

Investor Invests in Limited Partnership Fund

	Year 1
Investment	$10,000
Intangible Costs from Drilling[a]	$8,000
Tax Savings (at tax rate = 70%)	$5,600
or Total Investor's Risk Capital	$4,400

Limited Partnership Fund Strikes Oil

	Year 2	Tax Deductions
Revenue	$1,000[b]	275
Operating Expense	$250	
Profit	$750	
Reinvested into Further Drilling	$750	
Intangible Costs from Drilling[a]	$600	600

Total Tax Benefit in Year 2.

Profit	$750
Total Tax Deductions	$875
Net Loss for Tax Purposes	($125)

Source: James C. Tanner, "Investing in Oil Drilling Funds Multiply but Draw Fire for Bid to Lure Less Affluent."

[a] Based on the Federal Tax Code all intangible costs are fully deductable.

[b] Qualifies for a 27.5% deduction under oil depletion allowance.

$1,000 and $5,000 per share. Fund sales slowed, and investors divested older shares in the mid-1970s following revisions in federal tax laws and elimination of the federal oil depletion allowance. Tables E.3 and E.4 describe benefits earned by typical investors. Changing tax laws limited these highly profitable investments to sophisticated investors. Investors returned to these funds when oil and gas prices climbed in 1980.

Table E.4

How an Investor Benefits in a Limited Partnership Fund: 1972

Assumptions:
1) Investor is in the 50% tax bracket.
2) General partner in drilling fund provides a non-recourse loan.[a]

Investor Invests in Fund	Year 1
Investor's Investment	$50,000
General Partner's NonRecourse Loan	$50,000
Total Investment from Investor	$100,000
Intangible Costs from Drilling	$110,000
Tax Savings (at tax rate = 50%)[b]	$55,000
Investor's Tax Benefit After Year 1	
Tax Deduction	$55,000
Investment	($50,000)
Cash Profit	$5,000

Source: James C. Tanner, "Small Investors Lured into Oil Drilling Often Miss the Breaks."

[a] There was a loophole temporarily in the federal Tax Code that allowed an independent oil producer or anyone else to make a loan to an LPF, but the investor could take the full deduction on intangible costs allocated to both the investment and the loan. This loophole was eliminated in 1974.

[b] Based on the federal Tax Code, all intangible costs are fully deductible.

In the mid-1980s, the traditional oil and gas financing sources described above evaporated: banks needed to shore up their capital, falling prices reduced borrowing bases, and investors grew cool to LPFs. Some drilling capital was raised from new sources: venture capital, institutional investors, and master limited partnerships (MLPs), as detailed in Table E.5.

MLPs have several advantages compared with LPFs. They provide the investor with liquidity by being listed on a stock exchange. Equally important, an MLP's cash flow is paid directly to investors, skirting corporate income taxes, and the investor may deduct losses. An MLP not only received drilling capital but also reduced its tax liability. Mesa Petroleum, Unocal, and Diamond Shamrock are firms that applied this financing technique. In the 1990s, some MLPs have converted back into stock companies to regain access to capital markets. Investors have different appetites for risk. Those willing to incur more risk receive, on average, more reward. Figure E.3 compares the financial sources in

Table E.5

The Decline of Traditional Sources of Finance for Oil and Gas Companies

Source	1981	1982	1983	1984[a]
	(in billions)			
Wall Street & Banks	$10	$7	$0	($1)[b]
Public & Private Drilling Fund	$10	$3	$2	$1
Total	$20	$10	$2	$0
Industry Drilling Expenditure	$37	$29	$19	$23
External Funds as % of Total Expenditures	55.3%	32.8%	7.9%	0.0%

Source: Oil & Gas Journal, 1981–1984.
[a]Estimated.
[b]Negative due to accelerated recall of loans and scarcity of new loans.

Table E.6

Limited Partnership Sales to the Public by TEI

Year	Sales	Rank in U.S.
1970	$1,640,000	4
1971	$6,376,250	5
1972	$9,225,250	unknown
1973	$9,900,000	unknown
1974	$11,400,000	unknown

Source: TEI annual reports, 1970–1974.

the oil and gas market on a risk/return basis. There was an investment available for every investor's palate.

TEI's Fund Raising

TEI formed a drilling fund in 1969 as a wholly owned subsidiary, Texas International Drilling Funds, Inc. It registered a $25 million oil and gas investor drilling program with the SEC, naming it the Texas International Drilling Fund —Series A. Limited partnership units were sold in 1970. An additional $18 million would be contributed by the general partner, TEI. Public investors paid all drilling costs currently deductible for tax purposes, and the company paid all costs that had to be capitalized for tax purposes. Limited partners wrote off dry holes and other expenses immediately for tax purposes, while the partnership, which relied on full-cost accounting for financial statement purposes, did not report as a loss costs not directly related to production. In exchange, the company received a 10 percent one-time subscription fee from limited partners and 50 percent of gross revenues. In 1970, the company created a division to actively market units of participation. Twenty-four brokerage and investment firms, including two insurance companies, executed selling agreements with the fund. Table E.6 describes yearly sales. Eighty brokerage firms were participating by 1972. TEI established its own marketing organization in Philadelphia, with regional offices in New York, Tampa, Oklahoma City, Los Angeles, and Seattle.

In early 1971, an offer was filed to redeem the partnership units purchased by the public in 1970 and 1971, thereby increasing the company's share of production and returning capital to investors who had already taken full tax advantage of deductible expenses.[3] The company shared tax benefits and production revenues as a limited partner when it repurchased units. Repurchased limited partnership units were accounted for as a purchase of productive oil and gas properties, since the principal assets of the partnerships were capitalized reserves.

During 1972, the company's share of partnership production was 1.7 Bcf of gas and 143,000 barrels of oil. The program had drilled 176 wells through 1972 at a total cost to the company of only $3.1 million as compared to an industry average of $500,000 per well. These wells resulted in 18 Bcf of gas and 2 million barrels of oil being added to proven reserves. Thirty-four additional partnership wells were drilled in 1973 at a cost to the company of only $2.2 million. An incremental 4.9 Bcf of gas and 0.3 million barrels of oil were added to proven reserves.

Early partnership funds spent 20 percent of their funds on exploratory drilling. Later funds were wildcat funds with 40 percent of monies spent on exploration; revenues were split 70 percent to the public until payout and 50/50 thereafter. Of the $9.9 million raised through partnerships in 1973, $735,000 were in two wildcat funds that made significant discoveries.

TEI's reserve value expanded to $166 million in 1976 from $17 million in 1972. Wall Street ignored these financial gyrations and elevated the equity value from $35 million in 1969 to $107 million in 1974 and $132 million in 1975.

The high-yield debt market also contributed to TEI's growth. Drexel and Mike Milken invented the high-yield bond. A high-yield bond is a debenture, or unsecured obligation of a corporation, which carries a relatively high interest rate to compensate investors for the associated high risk. The risk in owning a junk bond is that future interest and principal payments are not guaranteed, nor are they secured by any of the company's real assets.

TEI was the first junk bond issued by Drexel. In April 1977 a $30 million debenture was issued, which promised to pay investors an 11.5 percent annual rate of interest (versus the 8 percent rate being paid on twenty-year AA corporate bonds) and to return the $30 million of borrowed funds in approximately twenty years. Undoubtedly, some pundits expected the offering to not attract bidders, but TEI and Drexel were ready for success and quickly returned to the market with a second issue, an additional $20 million of 11.5 percent debt, issued in 1978 but also due in 1997.

TEI also borrowed from a consortium of banks. Bank loans to oil companies are typically short-term secured obligations; oil and gas properties serve as collateral to secure the loan. In addition, banks write covenants limiting the borrower's spending discretion and setting limits on its liquidity, additional indebtedness, and executive compensation. Should any loan covenant be violated, the bank can demand repayment.

TEI's total debt grew from $89 million in 1976 to $253 million in 1978. Supporting this debt were total assets "recorded" in 1978 at $378 million. The excess of assets over debt, $98 million, was stockholders's equity obtained from the sale of common stock or retained earnings.

The objective of leveraging TEI was to undertake an aggressive drilling program that would transform the firm. In hindsight, the plan was overly ambitious.

Notes

1. Smaller independents tend to operate by utilizing contract drilling and acquiring drilling rights via leasing.
2. James C. Tanner, "Investing in Oil, Drilling Funds Multiply but Draw Fire for Bid to Lure Less Affluent," pp. 1, 33.
3. By the end of 1972 the company had repurchased $1,000,000 worth of units, which represented approximately 70 percent of the 1970 and 40 percent of the 1971 drilling programs.

Appendix F
Oil and Gas Regulation

Oil Regulation

President Eisenhower was advised by petroleum interest groups that the steady encroachment of foreign petroleum suppliers into the American market constituted a national security risk. He authorized an import quota on oil. By restricting foreign petroleum supplies, the major oil companies gained control over the U.S. supply of oil and its price.

After two decades of harmony, a series of unforeseen events transformed the oil business during the 1970s. First, low-cost domestic petroleum reserves were depleted after years of overproduction. The statutory exclusion of economic foreign oil and adherence to the principle of economic exploitation led to the premature exhaustion of low-cost domestic oil. Remaining reserves had higher production costs. Second, inflation became a persistent national problem. President Nixon contrived an assortment of wage and price controls to limit inflation, but he feared that higher energy costs would contradict these policies. He directed federal agencies to allow increased offshore oil production and imports of foreign oil. The administration believed both actions would lower oil prices.

Not surprisingly, the wage-price controls failed.[1] New inflationary pressures materialized, including the energy crisis in 1973–74, an agricultural products price emergency, and demand pressures subsequent to the 1972 recession. In response, President Nixon's Cost of Living Council requested the Federal Energy Administration (FEA) to construct a new energy price control system.

The FEA devised a two-tier pricing scheme in 1974 designed to maintain a shortfall between the average U.S. domestic petroleum price and the world market price. In a modest concession to supply-siders and economic reality, the FEA decontrolled new discoveries and stripper wells producing less than ten barrels per day. Approximately 25 percent of U.S. production was decontrolled.[2]

The two-tier pricing system worked as follows:

(1) Old oil (oil discovered prior to 1973) was priced at $4.25 initially and $5.25 per barrel at year-end 1974. President Ford later adjusted these prices.
(2) New oil (oil discovered after 1972) was not controlled.

The allocation of oil into the old and new categories was contentious when a single property produced both types. The price differential between the two categories exceeded 100 percent. More regulations were enacted to guide the pricing.

The regulations were not working, however. Price restraints on older oil fields and an elaborate bureaucratic maze had devastated the incentives driving the energy supply complex. President Ford signed the Energy Policy and Conservation Act in 1975 to decontrol prices and thereby stimulate exploration. The plan promulgated a five-year gradual transition to world oil price levels.

President Carter left the phasing-out of controls in place. In 1979 the Iranian disruption again reduced the supply of oil to the United States, and oil prices surged. The United States remained heavily dependent on oil imports. Carter devised a new decontrol plan to combat dependency on oil imports.

Realization that a shift to world oil price levels would cause oil company profits to skyrocket created a specter in Congress of an angry citizens' backlash against members of Congress. Consequently, the Crude Oil Windfall Profit Tax Act of 1980 was enacted to limit big oil's profits. Under the statute, all crude oil production revenue was taxed at the following rates:

Type of Oil	Tax Rate on Well Head Revenue[4]
Old Oil[1]	70 percent
Stripper Oil[2]	60 percent
Incremental Tertiary and Heavy Oil	30 percent
Newly Discovered Oil[3]	30 percent

[1]Oil discovered before 1979.

[2]Oil produced from a well yielding under ten barrels per day.

[3]President Reagan persuaded Congress to reduce this rate to 15 percent by 1986, enabling oil producers to keep an additional $10 billion in oil revenues.

[4]Independent producers paid a reduced rate on the first 1,000 barrels per day produced and sold.

January 1981 commenced a new epoch. President Reagan abolished all price controls on crude oil, propane, and gasoline and eliminated crude oil allocations.

Gas Regulation

Congress regulated natural gas prices in the 1930s to avoid rising prices; instead, they reduced supply. The situation was similar to a famous economics joke:

A man walks into a sporting goods store and asks, "How much do tennis rackets cost?" When the proprietor answers, "$30," the man quips, "But they only cost $15 across the street." The proprietor responds, "Well then, go buy one across the street." To which the man says, "I can't. They're out of them."

The moral of the story, of course, is that artificially low prices dry up supplies.

Prior to 1978, the natural gas market had two segments caused by the limited jurisdiction of federal regulations to only interstate commerce. The intrastate nonregulated marketplace had many producers engaged in active commerce; the regulated interstate market was moribund. Regulations restrained prices in the interstate market to uneconomic levels (as low as $.10/Mcf). Market prices (as much as $1/Mcf) were paid intrastate. Most domestic natural gas is produced in states bordering on the Gulf of Mexico. A shortage of industrial users along the Gulf prior to 1970 led to a surplus of natural gas in the intrastate market.

Regulatory failures during the 1960s and 1970s initiated natural gas shortages. Decontrol of natural gas was launched soon thereafter in the National Gas Act of 1978. The Act was motivated by a desire to lessen America's oil import proclivity by increasing natural gas reserves and production, a policy foreshadowing Egypt's natural gas drive. Natural gas price controls were to be phased out by 1985. This legislation had two weaknesses: (1) it presumed that oil prices would stay below $15 per barrel, and (2) it assumed that natural gas supplies would remain limited. Neither condition held. New natural gas reserves increased by 50 percent from 1978 to 1979 as prices rose to economic levels. Increases in oil prices experienced in 1979 after the Iranian crisis again stimulated natural gas drilling. Deep gas prices accelerated as oil users sought replacement fuels after the second oil price shock. By 1980, deep unregulated gas was selling for $8/Mcf versus $3/Mcf for new controlled gas and $0.25 for some old natural gas.

In 1992, natural gas was overabundant and many producers found it difficult to cover their costs. Shortages developed and natural gas prices rose. Again regulation was at fault. In 1989, Congress authorized a $0.93 per Mcf tax credit to natural gas produced out of coal-seam gas, enabling large oil companies able to use the tax credit to profitably sell natural gas at low prices.

Notes

1. There are very few historical examples of effective wage-price controls; normally, they exert downward pressure on wages and prices for a short period of time. Once consumers and businesses learn how to defeat the regulations, either prices resume their upward spiral or production ebbs.

2. The fact that so much U.S. oil was produced out of stripper wells attests to the sorry state of the U.S. oil industry. The average domestic well yielded about twenty barrels per day; in contrast, in the Middle East the average well flowed approximately 1,500 barrels per day.

Appendix G
Industry Conditions

Control of Oil

The oil business was practically a cottage industry until 1882, when John D. Rockefeller, Sr., consolidated the majority of U.S. oil production and refining capacity under an umbrella trust designated the Standard Oil Trust. The trust dominated the U.S. oil market and established pricing and production levels until the U.S. Supreme Court dissolved it in 1911 by applying the Sherman Act. The trust's dissolution produced a startling array of companies: Standard of New Jersey (now Exxon), Standard of Indiana (now Amoco), Standard of California (now Chevron), Standard of Ohio (now BP America), and Standard of New York (now Mobil). Geology also diminished the trust's significance when oil was discovered in Texas. Rockefeller, who controlled most of the oil east of the Mississippi River, was unable to seize control from independent Texans.

Even with the Trust dissolved, two factors kept oil prices from being set by free-market forces. The first was the Texas Railroad Commission. The commission was created in 1930 as a quasi-public state regulatory agency to establish production ceilings and generally restrict oil output. Texas controlled more than 50 percent of domestic petroleum reserves until Alaska's Prudhoe Bay was developed. The Connally Hot Oil Act, a federal statute, reinforced the commission's power by restricting interstate sales of oil produced in excess of state regulatory levels.

The second factor inhibiting the free market was the oil majors, initially only British Petroleum, Royal Dutch/Shell, and Exxon. They acquired control over international oil production, refining, and marketing. In 1928, the expanded Seven Sisters formulated a cartel with a document known as the As Is Agreement. Members of the cartel agreed to abstain from competitive practices in pricing, production, and downstream functions in international markets in order to keep oil

prices and consumption at profitable levels. Through a series of similar agreements and abetted by U.S. government geopolitical influence, the majors came to
control Middle East oil reserves and thereby the majority of the world's hydrocarbon resources. This influence was sustained until the early 1970s.

In the late 1950s, the majors flooded the Eastern Seaboard of the United
States with low-cost Middle East oil that had production costs about one-tenth of
domestic costs. Independent domestic producers lobbied for protection against
the foreign assault. Their petition argued that national security would be impaired by the elimination of domestic producers.[1] In response, President Eisenhower instituted mandatory oil import quotas.

The U.S. oil industry was reeling under the combined assault of restricted
prices and output and cheap oil imports. Domestic producers went broke, while
energy consumption boomed in response to low prices. During the 1960s, approximately half of the wildcatters who together accounted for 40 percent of
production went bankrupt or left the business.[2] Domestic drilling plummeted by
30 percent from 1958 to 1968.[3]

Mounting political opposition arose to offshore leasing following a major oil
spill in the late 1960s off the Santa Barbara, California, coast. Sales of federal
government offshore oil leases slowed to a trickle. Energy self-sufficiency became an unattainable goal.

U.S. oil reserves stagnated, rising by less than 2 percent annually; meanwhile,
U.S. energy consumption surged. Few important indigenous oil fields remained
to be discovered; the Alaskan North Slope field was a phenomenal exception.
Worldwide oil reserve growth stagnated after 1984 (as shown in Figure G.1), and
the U.S. share of total reserves plunged after 1948 (as seen in Figure G.2) as a
result of the constant level of U.S. reserves (as seen in Figure G.3.). In the early
1970s, it was estimated that domestic oil reserves possessed a ten-year life.[4] The
United States, decline is illustrated by the lowly stature of the largest U.S. field,
the East Texas field, with over 5 billion barrels of proven reserves, which in
1969 was only the twenty-fourth largest field in the world. By comparison, the
two largest fields, both in the Middle East, had 62 billion (Burgan field in
Kuwait) and 45 billion (Ghawar field in Saudi Arabia) barrels of reserves.

U.S. reserve problems derived from geologic and pecuniary causes. The first
principle of resource economics is to exploit the most promising land tracts first.
As a result, residual acreage yields fewer and leaner discoveries. Average U.S.
oil production per well foot drilled declined from 275 barrels per foot in the
1930s to 35 barrels per foot in 1972.[5] This natural phenomenon was coupled
with a damaging accounting change, the reduction and eventual elimination of
the oil depletion allowance, which decreased the earnings potential of drilling.
The depletion allowance authorized drillers to deduct a portion of the *value* of
reserves in the ground against their income. Congress, in pursuit of new revenues, dropped the oil depletion allowance from 27 percent to 22 percent. The
impact was stunning. U.S. reliance on imports as a percentage of domestic oil

Figure G.1. **World Proven Crude Oil Reserve Growth**

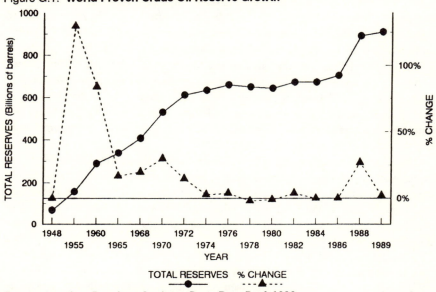

Source: American Petroleum Institute, *Basic Data Book 1990.*

Figure G.2. **World Proven Crude Oil Reserves**

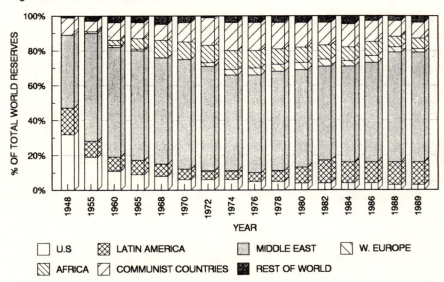

Source: American Petroleum Institute, *Basic Data Book 1990.*

Figure G.3. **U.S. Proven Crude Oil Reserve Growth**

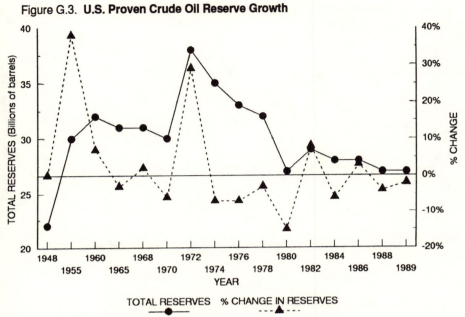

Source: American Petroleum Institute, *Basic Data Book 1990.*

Figure G.4. **Share of Imports As a Percentage of U.S. Consumption**

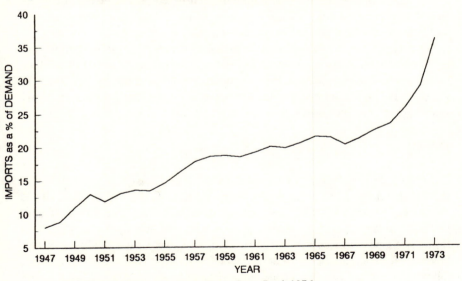

Source: American Petroleum Institute, *Basic Data Book 1976.*

Figure G.5. **Proven Natural Gas Reserves in the United States**

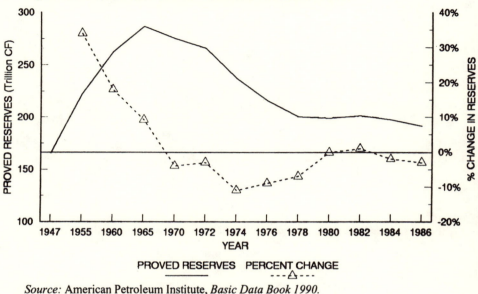

Source: American Petroleum Institute, *Basic Data Book 1990.*
Note: Includes natural gas in storage.

demand climbed steadily from 8 percent in 1947 to 23 percent in 1970 (see Figure G.4). On the positive side, America consumed only 4 percent of its oil from North Africa and the Middle East, despite a total absence of energy conservation and eschewing alternative energy sources.

Natural gas reserves also fell, as depicted in Figure G.5, but the problem in that market was strictly economic. The Federal Power Commission (FPC), which began to regulate gas prices in 1956, chronically depressed natural gas prices. In the early 1970s, unexplored gas was estimated at 1.178 trillion cubic feet, nearly four times the reserve position.[6]

OPEC

The Oil Producing Exporting Countries (OPEC) cartel was founded in 1960, but the cartel did not achieve its economic potential until the 1970s. In 1970 the Persian Gulf branch of OPEC, comprising Abu Dhabi, Iran, Iraq, Kuwait, Qatar, and Saudi Arabia, began nationalizing oil concessions held by the Seven Sisters (initially 51 percent was nationalized). Companies were compelled to sell their holdings at book value plus an adjustment for inflation and capital investment. Oil prices remained low despite the nationalizations.

Growing worldwide energy needs and paltry increases in supply leveraged OPEC's control of the oil market. In August 1973 a representative from Aramco[7] reported the status of the world energy crisis to the State Department: "Even without the specter of political restrictions in Saudi Arabia, the industry supply outlook is tight throughout the period, and is essentially nil during the following winter."[8] Earlier in June, Persian Gulf OPEC members flexed their muscles and enacted the Geneva Accord, which increased the gross price of oil to compensate for devaluations of major foreign currencies. Simultaneously, they increased income tax rates on energy producers. Several months later, in October 1973, a major conflagration erupted between Israel and her Arab neighbors. Persian Gulf OPEC members retaliated against the United States for assisting Israel in the war and imposed an oil embargo. Kuwait and Libya exploited this opportunity to further nationalize their oil.

The embargo strained an already tight energy supply environment. Energy prices in general, and oil prices in particular, exploded upward. Crude oil jumped from $3 to over $11 per barrel in several months' time. The regulatory policies of Presidents Nixon, Ford, and Carter were total failures, like attempts to put out a fire with a bucket of grease.

Regulation focused on controlling inflation. Since energy prices were not permitted to rise, consumption was encouraged, and domestic exploration, production, and conservation were discouraged. Under the tutelage of these failed policies, U.S. dependence on imported oil rose to 35 percent of total consumption. Political fallout from the embargo accelerated offshore lease sales and construction of the Alaskan pipeline. The embargo ended in 1974.

Oil company earnings and balance sheets flourished. Balance sheets for full-cost accounting firms exhibited the increased value of oil in the ground; all energy companies earned windfall inventory profits and earned higher profits due to higher prices. The nation became fiercely anti-oil. Congress assaulted the industry, instituting a windfall profits tax to expropriate "unearned" gains of oil behemoths and, in 1975, totally removed the oil depletion allowance, except for firms producing 2,000 barrels or less per day. This change was estimated to have eliminated $2 billion in investment capital from an industry that needed to respond to a foreign threat by investing funds in domestic energy sources.[9]

Eventually, a new breed of bureaucrat enlightened the energy regulatory agencies to the need to provide incentives to producers. Decontrol of energy prices emphatically stimulated exploration activity, which caused drilling costs to escalate. In November 1979, an insurrection in Iran deposed the Shah and climaxed in the detainment of Americans in the U.S. embassy. The United States froze Iranian assets and banned their imports in retaliation. Disruptions in Iran caused Iranian oil production to virtually halt, eliminating 10 percent of world oil production and further fueling domestic exploration.

Oil prices climbed in 1980 and 1981, pushed by OPEC, shortages, and inflation. Analysts assigned values to in-ground reserves of domestic energy producers of up to $10 per barrel versus only $1 per barrel in 1970. Wall Street oil industry analysts strongly recommended most high-risk energy exploration companies. Domestic oil stocks carried premium prices due to security and geo-graphic considerations. The oil and gas industry, newly invigorated by President Reagan's energy policies, was finally contemplating a rosy future.

Boom and Collapse

Escalating oil prices and decontrol of "deep gas" provoked independents and majors into a drilling frenzy. Land rigs engaged in drilling increased 50 percent from 1977 to 1981; half the growth occurred between 1980 and 1981 (see Figure D.1 in Appendix D). Oil and gas wildcat wells drilled expanded from 7,131 in 1971, just prior to the first Arab oil embargo, to 17,430 in 1981. Deep-gas drilling, led by Standard of California and Standard of Indiana, moved swiftly into new potential areas, including the Overthrust Belt between Wyoming and Utah, the Tuscaloosa Trend in Louisiana, the Austin Chalk in Texas, and the Anardarko Basin in the Texas Panhandle and west of Oklahoma City. Many firms borrowed heavily to fund this deluge of drilling. One independent, NuCorp, stretched its indebtedness from $65 million in 1980 to $525 in 1981. Between 1979 and 1981, a major offshore producer, Global Marine, raised $1 billion in debt to buy twenty-eight sophisticated offshore rigs.

As happens with most speculative bubbles, a crash followed the boom. At the Independent Petroleum Association of America's annual meeting in May of 1982, in Dallas, the crowd was amused by the joke that the "First National Bank of Midland has become, through foreclosures, the largest drilling rig contractor in the United States."[10] The industry's collapse was swift and complete. Oil prices tumbled by $7 per barrel from almost $35 per barrel in 1982. Oil conservation (see Figure G.6) and the elasticity effect of high prices kicked in. Energy use per dollar GNP produced fell by 19 percent from 1973 to 1982. Natural gas demand also decreased 10 percent from 1981 to 1982 (as seen in Figure G.7), and producers began to speak of a gas bubble that lingered throughout the decade. Endusers who had signed "take or pay" gas contracts with independents abrogated them. By December 1982, deep-gas prices fell 50 percent from a high of $11 per Mcf. Some deep-gas holdouts such as GHK/Parker Drilling continued to drill in the Anardarko Basin toward a goal of 33,000 feet. Rampant inflation compounded the effect of falling prices, sending other costs, such as labor rates and insurance, skyward.

Debt ratios of independents had ballooned during the boom years to 50 per-cent of total capital on average in 1982. Most independents lacked access to the long-term debt market; Mike Milken had just begun to develop the high-yield market as a source of long-term capital for smaller firms. Banks had funded most of the independents, viewing them as nearly riskless clients, since they were secured against a "borrowing base" calculated at a fraction of the value of proven reserves. It was assumed that prices and reserve values would rise by 10 percent to 15 percent annually. Interest rates were as low as 10 percent. With a

Figure G.6. **Conservation Trends in the United States**

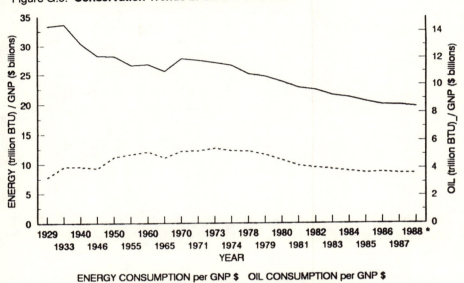

ENERGY CONSUMPTION per GNP $ OIL CONSUMPTION per GNP $

Source: Author derived information from Cambridge Planning and Analytics, Datadisk Database.
Note: Estimated.

Figure G.7. **U.S. Natural Gas Consumption**

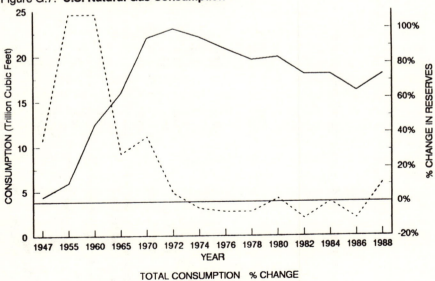

TOTAL CONSUMPTION   % CHANGE

Source: American Petroleum Institute, *Basic Data Book 1990.*

Table G.1

Large Oil and Gas Industry Mergers/Acquisitions

Company Acquired/Acquirer	Year Acquired	Reported Purchase Price[a] ($ billion)	Proven Reserves[b]				Discounted Cash Flows from Proven Reserves after Taxes[c] ($ millions)	
			Oil (million barrels)		Gas (billion CF)		($ millions)	
			U.S.	Foreign	U.S.	Foreign	U.S.	Foreign
Conoco/DuPont	1981	$7.8	403	1,104	2,660	946	$3,148[d]	$2,231[d]
Hudson Bay Oil & Gas/Dome Petroleum[f]	1981	$1.7	261	0	3,458	0	$4,813	$0
Santa Fe/Kuwait	1981	$2.4	138	0	183	0	$1,469	$0
Marathon/U.S. Steel	1982	$5.9	641	488	2,031	1,617	$5,996[d]	$9,791[d]
Cities Services/Occidental Petroleum	1982	$4.0	287	20	2,749	271	$4,295[d]	$370[d]
Natomas/Diamond Shamrock	1983	$1.5	7	74	132	65	$338	$684
El Paso Co./Burlington Northern	1983	$1.3	7	0	479	0	$815[d]	$0
General American Oil/Phillips Petroleum	1983	$1.1	56	24	294	225	$902[d]	$172[d]
Texas Gas Resoures/CSX Corp.	1983	$1.1	6	0	195	0	$267	$0
Gulf/Chevron	1984	$13.3	858	1,199	3,703	1,816	$5,489	$2,682
Getty Oil/Texaco	1984	$10.2	1,189	692	2,440	380	$5,210	$766
Shell U.S.A./Royal Dutch Shell	1984	$5.7	2,166	71	7,434	254	$13,075	$208

Superior Oil/Mobile	1984	$5.7	180	134	1,929	2,321	$2,318	$1,302
Aminioli (R.J.R.)/Phillips Petroleum	1984	$1.7	119	0	397	90	$639	$118
Gulf Canada/Olympia & York	1985	$2.9[e]	0	194	0	1,535	$0	$1,159[e]
American Natural Resources/ Coastal Corp.	1985	$2.4	19	0	306	0	$461	$0
Texas Oil & Gas/U.S. Steel	1986	$3.7	41	0	1,836	0	$1,958	$0

Source: Arthur Andersen/Cambridge Energy Associates, *World Oil Trends 1986–1987.*

[a] Reported purchase price includes all costs of acquiring net assets of the target companies, not just oil and gas reserves.

[b] Proven reserves represent all reserves of the acquired company even if less than 100% of the company was acquired.

[c] Based on SFAS No. 69 criteria, except as noted (pretax for Hudson Bay/Dome Petroleum).

[d] Based on SEC standardized reporting of reserves (after tax for Conoco/DuPont).

[e] Expressed in Canadian dollars.

[f] Most of Hudson Bay's reserves are located in Canada or other foreign locations.

ready supply of cheap capital, the independents accelerated their exploration and development spending to three times cash flow in 1981 from a historical level about 1.33 times internally generated cash flow.[11]

By early 1983, capital funding had dried up. In addition to third world debt, bank problem loans encompassed defaulted energy loans. Energy center banks in Texas and Oklahoma collapsed, as did Continental Illinois of Chicago. Exacerbating the capital shortage was the decrease in the personal tax rate in 1981 from 70 percent to 31 percent, inspired by President Reagan's supply-side economic program. The affinity of wealthy investors for limited-partnership drilling funds waned as tax brackets declined. Consequently, drilling funds became extinct.

An accounting partner at Coopers & Lybrand in Houston expressed this opinion: "They [independents] violated the age-old tradition that you do not borrow drilling money—money you pay back on the success of drilling."[12] With the decline in oil prices, cash flows were inadequate to meet interest payments. No doubt the independents had assumed that the debt would be repaid with cheaper dollars as a result of inflation.

Troubled oil and gas companies littered the countryside. Companies were forced into bankruptcy or "debt compositions," whereby they exchanged new securities for older securities. Securities were parcelled out in rough approximation to the Bankruptcy Code's priority scheme. Farm-outs created drilling capital for some independents. By early 1983, the high-risk, go-for-broke exploration strategy of the late 1970s was forgotten. The industry consolidated. Thousands of oil and gas companies vanished.

The antitrust legal climate veered in the pro-merge direction, reversing nearly a half century of trust busting. Reagan ended the preemptive view that "big is bad" and instead advocated industrial consolidation to combat international business pressures. Nearly $25 billion of oil and gas mergers and acquisitions were completed from 1981 through 1983. Merger activity accelerated in 1984 to $36.6 billion, involving only five major transactions, as seen in Table G.1.

Professor James Tobin at Yale has noted that industrial firms are less likely to invest in *new* sources of physical capital (drilling) when similar capital can be acquired less expensively on Wall Street (buying stocks). Mergers procured reserves at an estimated cost of $4 to $5 per barrel as compared with exploration cost to search for new oil in excess of $10 per barrel. Incentives to drill were not in place. Chevron took advantage of the price disequilibrium to increase proven reserves by 176 percent, and Texaco by 68 percent. However, as bidding for oil company stocks drove up equity prices, new exploration efforts should have commenced.

Some analysts argued that mergers would adversely affect future exploration activities.[13] Companies holding reserves might be satisfied with inventory gains and not drill for oil when prices rose. Others argued that a competitive industry structure would increase the probability of finding new reserves.

Potential OPEC/industry benefits from obstructed exploration were waylaid by a secular downtrend in oil consumption: from 1979 to 1985, worldwide demand declined by nearly 6 million barrels per day, or 11 percent. Factors contributing to this decline included a worldwide recession spanning 1981–1983, energy conservation, and a switch to nuclear and coal power. In addition, between 1979 and 1985 free-world oil production increased by 4.8 million barrels per day, or 27 percent.[14]

Beginning in 1986, Persian Gulf Cooperation Council members, led by Saudi Arabia, implemented a "market share strategy," which flooded the market with crude oil designed to increase market share.[15] Total revenue would hold constant if shipping volumes rose to compensate for the reduced price. Prices plummeted: $7 in the first twenty days of January alone and 55 percent by the end of the second quarter. For the American oil patch, it was like the ten plagues of Moses descending on Dallas. In the next three years, 2,139 oil and gas companies failed. OPEC lacked the cohesiveness required to adhere over the long run to such a radical strategy. Some non–Persian Gulf OPEC members wanted to raise price regardless of demand ramifications.

Throughout 1988, the price of oil hovered between $10 and $15 per barrel. In 1989 the price began climbing, reaching $21 late in the year, but then fell again to $14 in June 1990. In July, the price again began moving upward to $18 in response to Iraq's President Hussein's threats to force Kuwait to raise the price. At the beginning of August, Iraq invaded Kuwait, and the price soared to $24. When a war involving the United States became imminent, the price rose to $33. But battlefield success translated into lower oil prices; the beginning of the United Nations–sponsored coalition's air attack on Iraq on the war's first day in January 1991 caused oil prices to plummet by $10.56 per barrel in volatile oil futures trading, its largest-ever one-day move.

Notes

1. John M. Blair, in *The Control of Oil*, observed that there was very little evidence that quotas addressed a real national security threat. He noted three factors: (a) a journalist's investigation that alleged that the secretary of the treasury benefited from this policy by profiting from a Texas oil field interest; (b) loopholes in the quotas, which allowed overland imports from Canada and Mexico; (c) exemptions that allowed refineries to trade foreign crude oil allocations—thus, a refinery inland relying less on foreign oil supplies would trade its allocations to an East Coast refinery relying more on foreign oil.

2. David Brand and Norman Pearlstine, "Petroleum Hunting Set to Spur Activity As Prices of Crude Oil Are Being Lifted," p. 34.

3. Ibid.

4. Edmund Faltermayer, "The Energy Joyride Is Over," p. 99.

5. Ibid.

6. Standard & Poors, "Oil and Gas Industry," *Industry Survey, 1973.*

7. Aramco is the American–Saudi Arabian Oil Company, organized in 1936. Initially, members included Standard of California (Chevron) and the Texas Company (Texaco). The significance of Saudi Arabian concessions soon became indisputable, and Standard of

New Jersey (Exxon) and Socony-Vacuum (Mobil) came to an agreement to join in 1946.

8. "Summary and Analysis of the Hearing Record and Investigation on Multinational Oil Corporations and American Foreign Policy," prepared in 1974 for the Subcommittee on Multinational Corporations (chaired by Senator Frank Church) of the Senate Committee on Foreign Relations.

9. Standard & Poors, "Oil and Gas Industry," *Industry Survey, 1974.*

10. Peter Koenig, "The Big Oil Field Sell-Off," p. 217.

11. Ibid.

12. Rick Hagar and Marcia A. Parker, "Handful of U.S. Producers Emerges from Bankruptcy," p. 41.

13. Steven Greenhouse, "An Unsettling Shift in Big Oil," p. C-3.

14. The calculation of free-world reserves excludes centrally planned economies, specifically the Soviet Union and China.

15. Daniel Yergin, *The Prize: The Epic Quest for Oil, Money, and Power,* pp. 748–49.

Appendix H
Egyptian Oil and Gas
Production History

The first oil discovery in Egypt occurred at the southern end of the Gulf of Suez in the early 1900s. Development began in the 1930s with investments made by Shell, Standard Oil (now Exxon), and Socony-Vacuum (now Mobil) in the region near the original discovery.

The Western Desert was first drilled in 1946. An early triumph was the discovery of the El Alamein field, about 100 miles from the Khalda Concession, in 1966 by Phillips Petroleum. El Alamein production peaked at 40,000 barrels per day; by 1974 it had fallen to 9,000 barrels per day. Meanwhile, Amoco had two fields producing 20,000 barrels per day. By 1978, industry analysts estimated that the Western Desert would yield 220 million barrels of oil and 2.2 trillion cf of natural gas.[1] Those quantities were too low to attract a major oil company exploration team. TEI was less discriminating and luckier. Its first discovery alone probably exceeded those quantities. In 1982, the EGPC tested a wildcat south of the Khalda Concession at 5.7 million cf gas and 356 barrels per day. The Egyptians estimated reserves at 15 million barrels and 400 billion cf.

Egyptian production peaked at 930,000 barrels per day in 1986. A drought in 1988 exacerbated the production slowdown by cutting hydro-electric power production. Crude oil was the substitute fuel. What was burned to produce electricity could not be exported. Oil export revenues declined by 60 percent between 1986 and 1988.

The EGPC let seventy new exploration agreements involving $750 million in exploration funds in response to this crisis. In the previous decade, only 100 agreements had been written. Policies were legislated to encourage domestic natural gas consumption. A 1,200-mile natural gas pipeline grid was begun in

1990. Most important, the gas clause in oil concession agreements was amended to allow foreign operators to participate in gas production sales.

Note

1. *International Petroleum Encyclopedia,* 1978.

Appendix I
The Khalda Concession
Financial Model

The Khalda Concession agreement defines the distribution of funds between the concessionaires and the EGPC. A basic overview of concession terms includes the following:

1. Oil is produced and sold, creating revenues.

2. Up to 40 percent of this revenue repays operating and capital costs. Uncollected costs are banked and collected out of future revenues after current costs have been fully repaid. Khalda's operating costs were easily repaid, since they were only $2 per barrel; capital expenses were high and had to be banked. By 1989, the bank contained over $140 million of capital charges.

3. Remaining revenues including unneeded cost-recovery monies are classified as profit oil. These funds are split into unequal shares among the EGPC, Phoenix Resources of Egypt, and Conoco of Egypt, depending on the rate at which the oil is produced. The split between Phoenix Resources of Egypt and Conoco of Egypt also varies depending on the cumulative production from the Khalda and Salam fields. (This factor would not come into play during the time range of the model.)

A computer spreadsheet requiring approximately 250,000 bytes of memory was constructed to simultaneously evaluate the impacts of many factors. The spreadsheet simulated the profitability of the Khalda Concession. Conoco's analysis for deciding whether to invest in Egypt and, if so, on what terms can be studied with the output. The study begins with no cumulative production, a 50–50 split of operating expenses (for accounting purposes only), Conoco paying all capital costs, Conoco advancing $18 million to Phoenix Resources of Egypt, fluctuating oil prices (set to actual values), and modest production flow rates (set

Table I.1

The Khalda Concession's Profitability for TEI

	1986	1987	1988	1989	1990/Dream Scenario
Oil Production					
Egyptian Production (bbl)	0	17,700	19,500	21,600	100,000
Price per Barrel	$17.25	$17.25	$13.96	$16.58	$20.02
Cost-Recovery Oil	0	44,577,450	39,801,060	52,286,688	365,000,000
40% of Revenue TEI's Share of Cost	50%	50%	50%	50%	50%
Operating Costs					
Total Expended for Conoco	0	12,533,370	13,541,000	14,460,800	48,800,000
Collected	0	12,533,370	13,541,000	14,460,800	48,800,000
Owed	0	0	0	0	0
Total Expended for TEI	0	12,533,370	13,541,000	14,460,800	48,800,000
Collected	0	12,533,370	13,541,000	14,460,800	48,800,000
Owed	0	0	0	0	0
Total Collected	0	25,066,740	27,082,000	28,921,600	97,600,000
Total Uncollected	0	0	0	0	0
Capital Costs					
Conoco					
1986	26,250,000	26,250,000	26,250,000	26,250,000	26,250,000
1987		18,750,000	18,750,000	18,750,000	18,750,000
1988			3,750,000	3,750,000	3,750,000
1989				10,500,000	10,500,000
1990					13,250,000
1991					
Total	26,250,000	45,000,000	48,750,000	59,250,000	69,750,000
Total Due	26,250,000	71,250,000	102,784,668	150,640,799	199,190,157
Collected	0	17,215,332	11,393,868	21,200,642	187,463,410
Uncollected	26,250,000	54,034,668	91,390,799	129,440,157	11,726,747
TEI's Prepayment from Conoco					
1986					
Total Due	4,500,000	4,500,000	4,500,000	4,500,000	0
Collected	4,500,000	9,000,000	11,325,432	14,569,987	12,519,460
	0	2,174,568	1,255,445	2,050,527	11,782,412

Uncollected	4,500,000	6,825,432	10,069,987	12,519,460	737,047
TEI					
1986	0	0	0	0	0
1987		0	0	0	0
1988			0		
1989				562,500	562,500
1990					1,250,000
1991					
Total	250,000	250,000	250,000	250,000	250,000
Total Due	250,000	500,000	629,191	809,444	945,526
Collected	0	120,809	69,747	113,918	889,860
Uncollected	250,000	379,191	559,444	695,526	55,665
Concession's Capital Costs Collected	0	19,510,710	12,719,060	23,365,088	200,135,682
Excess Cost-Recovery Revenue	0	0	0	0	67,264,318
Profit Oil					
60% of Revenue	0	66,866,175	59,701,590	78,430,032	547,500,000
Excess Cost Recovery	0	0	0	0	67,264,318
Total Revenue	0	66,866,175	59,701,590	78,430,032	614,764,318
Barrels per day					
<25,000/day	1	1	1	1	0
$	0	8,358,272	14,925,398	19,607,508	38,422,770
25–50,000/day	0	0	0	0	0
$	0	0	0	0	34,580,493
50–75,000/day	0	0	0	0	0
$	0	0	0	0	30,738,216
75–100,000/day	0	0	0	0	0
$	0	0	0	0	26,895,939
>100,000/day	0	0	0	0	0
$	0	0	0	0	0
TEI Profit Oil	0	8,358,272	7,462,699	9,803,754	65,318,709
Summary for the Khalda					
TEI Revenue	0	21,012,451	21,073,446	24,378,472	115,008,569
TEI Cost	0	12,654,179	13,610,747	14,574,718	49,689,860
Annual TEI Profit	0	8,358,272	7,462,699	9,803,754	65,318,709

Note: Conoco's capital costs are amortized over 4 years.

to actual values). For the final, catchall year 1990, a "dream scenario" evaluated a high production rate of 100,000 barrels per day and a relatively high oil price, $20.02 per barrel. Table I.1 presents the simulation results.

Each concessionaire's profit equals approximately $9 million per year through 1989, as seen at the bottom of Table I.1. In addition, Conoco would recover $50 million out of a $237 million capital investment and $4 million of the $18 million loaned to Phoenix Resources of Egypt. The gain to TEI is obvious; the advantage to Conoco is harder to decipher.

The final column in Table I.1 describes the outcome of the dream scenario: output at 100,000 barrels per day and oil prices averaging $20.02. Conoco's (and TEI's) annual "dream" profit of $65 million would increase by an additional $20 million once uncollected capital expenses are recovered.

Conoco's expectations for the Khalda Concession can be surmised. Clearly, it did not expect what happened. At an output level of 100,000 barrels per day and a price of $20, annual return on investment exceeds 35 percent; if oil prices had escalated, the return on investment would have gone higher. Table I.2 presents annual 1990 profits for a range of possible prices and outputs.

Table I.2

Potential Annual Returns to Both TEI and Conoco

Daily Production (bbl)	Price Per Barrel	Annual Profit to Each Contractor
50,000	$20.00	$33,000,000
50,000	$28.00	$49,000,000
50,000	$35.00	$63,000,000
100,000	$20.00	$62,000,000
100,000	$28.00	$90,000,000
100,000	$35.00	$115,000,000

Appendix J
Original Khalda Concession Terms

KHALDA PETROLEUM CORPORATION

Participants

Egyptian Petroleum Corporation
Conoco Egypt }   CONTRACTORS
Phoenix Resources of Egypt

Drilling Rights

Conoco Egypt = 50%
Phoenix Resources of Egypt = 50%

Cost-Recovery Oil

Conoco Egypt = 50%
Phoenix Resources of Egypt = 50%

Up to a maximum of 40 percent of oil production revenue is allocated to concessionaires according to the following:

(a) *operating costs*—recovered in period incurred; unrecovered costs are banked for later recovery if funds are insufficient; current expenses are recovered first, then the oldest year's unrecovered funds.

(b) *capitalized costs*—including exploration and development costs amortized on a straight-line basis over four years; unrecovered costs are banked for later recovery.

Profit Oil

Egyptian Petroleum Corporation = 75% of total
Conoco Egypt = 50% of 25%
Phoenix Resources of Egypt = 50% of 25%

Includes the following:

(a) *production oil*—60% of total oil production revenue.
(b) *excess cost recovery*—any oil not allocated to cost-recovery oil is added to profit oil.

Production Escalation Allocation (applies only to Salam field)

Production Level (barrels/day)	EGPC	Contractors
25,000 or less	75%	25%
25,000–49,999	77.5%	22.5%
50,000–74,999	80%	20%
75,000–9,999	82.5%	17.5%
100,000 or greater	85%	15%

Total Expenditures to Date (as of 1988)

Conoco Egypt spent approximately $210 million for 59 wells, an airstrip, 30 roads, storage tanks, a dormitory for over 100 people, and a 10-mile pipeline from the main Conoco-operated pipeline to the Salam field.

(a) Khalda and Salam fields: an estimated $150 million was spent on exploration and development.

Other Potential Expenditures

(a) Oil production revenues are split 50–50 except: (1) cost-recovery oil is allocated according to proportion of expenditures made by each partner; (2) if cumulative production exceeds 30 million barrels, Conoco gives up 5% of production revenue for every 10 million barrels until cumulative production exceeds 70 million barrels, when 75% of concessionaire's share goes to Phoenix.

(b) Further field discoveries: Conoco Egypt pays 85% versus Phoenix's 15% share of exploratory and development costs; Phoenix has the option to pay no costs beyond the costs of one well completed and tested per field; if Phoenix continues to fund 15%, then the allocation of profit oil is 57.5% for Phoenix and 42.5% for Conoco; otherwise, all proceeds go to Conoco.

Production Pre-Payment on Crude Oil Production

Conoco advanced $18 million for future oil production in 1985; at the end of 1990 Phoenix still owed $14 million of that money; Phoenix's oil revenues were diverted to that account beginning April 1991; however, the account was cleared in May 1991.

Other Farm-Outs

In any future concession rights north of the 29th parallel in the Western Desert acquired by either Phoenix or Conoco, the following allocation of drilling-rights interests will occur:

If Conoco acquires rights, Phoenix is entitled to a 10% interest in Conoco's interests.
If Phoenix acquires rights, Conoco is entitled to a 50% interest in Phoenix's interests.

Bibliography

Abdine, Shawky, and Kanes, William. "Egyptian Exploration, Background, and Future Potential." *Oil & Gas Journal* (August 29, 1983): 71–73.

Altman, Edward. *Corporate Financial Distress.* New York: John Wiley, 1985.

American Petroleum Institute. *Basic Data Book 1990.* Washington, D.C.

———. *Basic Petroleum Data Book 1976.* Washington, D.C.

———. *1980 Joint Association Study.* Washington, D.C.

Anderson, Leonard. "Seagram to Seek 41% Conoco Stake at $2.55 bil, Cities Service Out." *Wall Street Journal* (June 26, 1981): 2.

Arthur Andersen & Co. *Oil & Gas Reserve Disclosure: Survey of 375 Public Companies 1980–1983.* Chicago, IL.

Arthur Andersen/Cambridge Energy Associates, *World Oil Trends 1986–1987.* Cambridge, MA.

Benoit, Ellen. "Seagram's Chemical Dependency." *Financial World* (July 26, 1988): 11.

Blair, John M. *The Control of Oil.* New York: Pantheon Books, 1976.

Brand, David, and Pearlstine, Norman. "Petroleum Hunting Set to Spur Activity As Prices of Crude Oil Are Being Lifted." *Wall Street Journal* (March 5, 1969): 34.

Bruck, Connie. *The Preditor's Ball: The Junk Bond Raiders and the Men Who Staked Them.* New York: American Lawyer, Simon and Schuster, 1988.

Buckman, David. "Egypt: Western Desert Leads Oil Search." *Petroleum Economist* (December 1987): 443–45.

Business Week. "After the Merger DuPont Still Likes Conoco" (May 30, 1983): 73.

———. "How the Saudi's Are Fueling Big Oil Mergers (Arabian American Oil)" (March 26, 1984): 32.

———. "Nixon Orders More Oil" (December 12, 1970): 16.

———. "NuCorp Energy: Caught in Deep Debt When the Oil-Drilling Boom Collapsed" (August 23, 1982): 116.

———. "Texas International: Cutting Debt Again—This Time to Snag Oil Bargains" (June 13, 1983): 78.

Cambridge Planning and Analytics. Datadisk Database. Cambridge, MA.

Choucri, Nazli; Heye, Christopher; and Lynch, Michael. "Analyzing Oil Production in Developing Countries: A Case Study of Egypt (using dynamic computer simulation, Egyptian Petroleum Model)." *Energy Journal* (July 1990): 91–115.

Conoco 10-K reports, 1969–1980.

Cowan, Alison Leigh. "Ringside Seat on Corporate Disaster." *New York Times* (January 16, 1992): D1.

Cowan, Dan, and Hagar, Rick. "Independent Operators Struggle to Survive Tough Times." *Oil & Gas Journal* (April 4, 1983): 43.

Crow, Patrick R., and Petzet, G. Alan. "Limited Partnerships Hit by U.S. Tax Reform, Weak Oil & Gas Prices." *Oil & Gas Journal* (September 26, 1988): 21–23.

The Dun & Bradstreet Corporation. *Business Failure Record, 1985–1988.* New York.

Dun's Business Month. "Global Marine Bankruptcy a Major Blow" (March 1986): 8.

DuPont 10-K reports.

Dyer, James C. "The Cost of Reserves by Discovery vs. Acquisition—Is It Cheaper to Buy Oil Than Find It." *Oil & Gas Journal* (December 19, 1983): 96–104.

Eberhart, Allan C. "Chapter 11—Surprisingly Good for Shareholders." *Wall Street Journal* (March 26, 1992).

Economist. "Black Gold." October 19, 1991, p.101.

———. "DuPont Cuts Conoco Down to Size." August 28, 1982, p. P–49.

Ella, Charles J. "Major Oil Stocks Seen Losing Sheen Yielding Only Average Market Gains Over Next 2 Years." Wall Street Journal (June 20, 1980): 47.

Faltermayer, Edmund. "The Energy Joyride Is Over." *Fortune* (September 1972): 99.

Franks, Julian R., and Torous, Walter N. "An Empirical Investigation of U.S. Firms in Reorganization." *Journal of Finance* 44, no. 3 (July 1989): 737–69.

Fuchs, Walter M. *When the Oil Wells Run Dry.* Dover, NH: Industrial Research Service, 1946.

Gertner, Robert, and Scharfstein, David. "A Theory of Workouts and the Effects of Reorganization Law." *Journal of Finance* 46 (September 1991): 1189–1223.

Greenhouse, Steven. "An Unsettling Shift in Big Oil." New York Times (March 11, 1984), p. C-3.

Haft, Robert J., and Fass, Peter M. *1984 Tax Sheltered Investment Handbook.* New York: Clark Boardman, 1984.

Hagar, Rick, and Parker, Marcia A. "Handful of U.S. Producers Emerges from Bankruptcy." *Oil & Gas Journal* (March 26, 1984): 41.

Hermalin, Benjamin E. "The Negative Effects of Lender Liability." *FRBSF Weekly Letter*, no. 91–32 (September 20, 1991).

Institutional Investor. "Texas International Co. +411.1%" (March 1986): 60.

International Petroleum Encyclopedia. Tulsa, OK: Pennwell Publishing, 1974–1989.

Jones, William A. "Exploration vs. Acquisition, Relative Comparison (relationship between exploration and acquisition)." *Oil & Gas Journal* (November 24, 1986): 91–94.

Koenig, Peter. "The Big Oil Field Sell-Off." *Institutional Investor* (July 1982): 217.

Lowenstein, Roger. "Close Watchers of DuPont Prefer a Spinoff of Disappointing Conoco to Selling Its Assets." *Wall Street Journal* (March 28, 1989): C–2.

———. "Texas International Sells Issue with Tie to Future Cost of Oil." *Wall Street Journal* (September 19, 1983): 45.

Luek, Thomas J. "Oil Industry Push to Merge." *New York Times* (February 9, 1984): D1.

Maurice, Charles, and Smithson, Charles W. *The Doomsday Myth: 10,000 Years of Economic Crises.* Palo Alto, CA: Hoover Institution Press, 1984.

McCoy, Charles F. "Texas International Tempers Prospects on Egypt Oil Well." *Wall Street Journal* (February 12, 1985): 24.

Metz, Tim. "The Conoco Chase: How DuPont Won with the Aid of Doubt About by Big Mobil Offer." *Wall Street Journal* (August 6, 1981): 1.

Monthly Energy Review, U.S. Department of Energy, Washington, D.C., 1990.

Mupson, Steve. "Conoco Rejects a Foreign Offer, Mulls U.S. Union." *Wall Street Journal* (June 22, 1981): 3.

———. "Conoco's Vulnerability Is Main Reason That It Is Being Courted So Ardently." *Wall Street Journal* (July 16, 1981).

Mupson, Steve, and Paul, Bill. "Cities Service, Conoco Merger Might Be Near." *Wall Street Journal* (June 25 1981): 3.

Mupson, Steve, and Zehr, Leonard. "How Dome's Offer to Buy Conoco Shares Could Provide Big Benefits of Both Firms." *Wall Street Journal* (May 7, 1981): 29.

New York Times. "New Economics of Oil Stocks" (March 11, 1980): D1.

Oil & Gas Journal. "Conoco, Partners to Probe Acreage in Northwest Egypt" (March 28, 1988): 77.

———. "Egypt Shoves Oil Production Steadily Higher" (October 10, 1983): 85–86.

———. "Egypt's Western Desert Stays Accessible to Foreign Operators" (June 20, 1988): 38.

———."Fields in Egypt's Western Desert Getting Oil Line" (January 27, 1986): 50.

———. "Prices for Reserve Purchases on the Upswing" (February 16, 1987): 46.

———. "Texas International Tests Western Desert Strike" (February 11, 1985): 42.

Parker, Marcia A. "Independent Producers Tapping New Sources of Capital." *Oil & Gas Journal* (January 7, 1985): 43–48.

———. "Nicandros: Industry's Changes Spawn Need for New Approach." *Oil & Gas Journal* (January 16, 1984): P–140.

Petzet, G. Alan, and Drake, Elizabeth. "Reduced Prices Spark Purchases of Oil and Gas Reserves in U.S." *Oil & Gas Journal* (October 14, 1985): 43–46.

The Phoenix Resource Companies, Inc., 10-K reports. Oklahoma City, OK.

Platt, Harlan, and Platt, Marjorie. "Bankruptcy Discrimination with Real Variables." *Journal of Business Finance and Accounting*, forthcoming, 1994.

Platt, Harlan. "Underwriter Effects on High Yield Bond Default Rates." *Journal of Applied Corporate Finance*, forthcoming, 1993.

Platt's Oilgram News. "Conoco Offers its Egyptian Asset for Sale." March 29, 1990, p. 1.

———. "Repsol Agrees to Purchase Conoco's Egyptian Properties." June 25, 1990, p. 1.

Pringle, David F. *Petroleum Politics and the Texas Railroad Commission.* Austin, Texas: University of Texas Press, 1981.

Raw, Charles. *Do You Sincerely Want to Be Rich? The Full Story of Bernard Cornfeld and IOS.* New York: Viking, 1971.

Robinson, William R.; Winters, Jay; and Bays, Waco D. "Mature Louisiana Oil Field Gets New Life." *Oil & Gas Journal* (November 19, 1984): 75–78.

Rogers, Leslie C. "Independents Jump on the Drilling 'Fund' Bandwagon." *Oil & Gas Journal* (March 31, 1969): 31–33.

Sandler, Linda. "Revco Case Tests Junkholders' Edge Over Stockholders." *Wall Street Journal* (September 27, 1989): C1–C2.

Schifrin, Mathew. "Seller Beware." *Forbes* (January 21, 1991): 36–38.

Schmitt, Richard B. "Oil Industry Gets Lesson in Bankruptcy." *Wall Street Journal* (September 2, 1982): 19.

———. "Texas International Prospects Uncertain Following Drop in Reserves, Big 1983 Loss." *Wall Street Journal* (January 30, 1984).

Seagram 10-K reports.

S. J. Doshi—Meyerson & Co. "Underwriting Progress Report on Texas International Petroleum Corporation." San Francisco, CA.

Standard & Poors. *Industry Survey, 1970–1980,* New York, NY.

———. *Oil and Gas Industry,* New York, NY. 1974.

Stein, Sol. *A Feast for Lawyers.* New York: M. Evans and Company, 1989.

"Summary and Analysis of the Hearing Record and Investigation on Multinational Oil Corporations and American Foreign Policy." Prepared for the Subcommittee on Multinational Corporations (chaired by Senator Frank Church) of the Senate Committee on Foreign Relations, Washington, D.C., 1974.

Summers, Mark S. *Bankruptcy Explained: A Guide for Businesses*. New York: John Wiley, 1989.

Tanner, James C. "Investing in Oil, Drilling Funds Multiply but Draw Fire for Bid to Lure Less Affluent." *Wall Street Journal* (October 28, 1969): 1, 33.

———. "Small Investors Lured Into Oil Drilling Funds Often Miss the Breaks." *Wall Street Journal* (February 18, 1972): 1, 20.

———. "DuPont's Conoco Discovers Oil, Gas off of Indonesia." *Wall Street Journal* (January 16, 1990): A–13.

TEI annual reports, 1969–1989.

TEI, *Getting the Past Out of Our Future*. January 1984, Texas International, OK.

TEI July 1989 Reorganization Plan

TEI's Offer to Purchase and Solicitation of Consents, February 1992.

TEI Prospectus for 1986 Exchange Offer.

TEI Prospectus for 1987 Exchange Offer.

TEI 10-K reports, 1979–1988.

Tracy, Eleanor Johnson. "Oil Patch Hybrids (master limited partnerships)." *Fortune* (September 30, 1985): 109.

Vielvoye, Roger. "Egypt Showing Progress." *Oil & Gas Journal* (December 24, 1990): 73.

———. "Egypt's Gas Campaign (to stimulate gas development)." *Oil & Gas Journal* (December 24, 1984): 23.

———. "New Pipelines in Egypt's Western Desert Spur Exploration Activity in That Area." *Oil & Gas Journal* (August 24, 1987): 33–35.

———. "The Search in Egypt." *Oil & Gas Journal* (May 23, 1983): 39.

Wall Street Journal. "Conoco Sues Seagram in Bid to Block Offer; Damages of $1 bil. Sought" (July 1, 1981): 81.

———. "DuPont Agrees to Buy Conoco, Inc. for Cash, Stock Totaling $6.9 bil" (July 7, 1981): 2.

———. "IRS Pulled the Rug from Under Many Investors in Leveraged Oil and Gas Funds" (March 8, 1972): 1.

———. "A New Twist in Oil and Gas Drilling Ventures is Stirring Controversy" (September 1, 1971): 1.

———. "Texas International Co.'s Swap Offer is Extended" (August 26, 1985).

———. "Texas International Ex-Head, 12 Others are Cited in SEC Insider Trading Suit" (February 2, 1983): 7.

———. "Texas International Ex-Head, Son Settled Insider Case, SEC Says" (February 22, 1984): 50.

———. "Texas International Extends Expiration of Debt-Swap Offer" (July 8, 1985): 21.

———. "Texas International Extends Offer to Swap $205.6 Million of Debt" (August 6, 1985): 47.

———. "Texas International Extends Response Time of Holders" (August 9, 1985): 23.

———. "Texas International Extends Swap Offer" (August 13, 1985): 45.

———. "Texas International Extends Swap-Offer" (August 20, 1985): 48.

———. "Texas International is Extending Deadline of Swap Offer for Debt" (August 26, 1985): 28.

———. "Texas International Offer" (August 5, 1985): 30.

———. "Texas International Petroleum Corp. Reached Agreement with a New Division of AAA Enterprises Inc. for Development of Mobile-Home Parks in Five Cities" (October 14, 1969): 33.

———. "Texas International Petroleum Corp. Received Favorable Ruling in U.S. District Court in New Orleans in Litigation with Three New York Investors, Involving 60 Offshore Wells on 12,000 Acres of Land" (February 18, 1970): 14.

————."Texas International Petroleum Corp Requested Suspension of Trading in Its Common Stock, Warrants Pending Evaluation of a Decision on Litigation" (February 17, 1970): 14.

————. "Texas International Proposed to Sell All Land and Improvements Owned by Its Unit, West Aspen Co., to City of Aspen, Colorado, for $3.7 million" (December 16, 1970): 27.

————. "Texas International Sweetens and Extends Debt-Exchange Offer" (August 1, 1985): 27.

————. "Texas International Co. is Target of 8 Lawsuits" (April 17, 1984): 14.

Wall Street Transcript (November 10, 9169): 18-545, 18-547–18-548.

West, Jim. "New Drilling-Money Spout Opening for Independent?" *Oil & Gas Journal* (September 2, 1974): 15–19.

Williams, Bob. "Nahama: Megamergers Mean Opportunity for Independents." *Oil & Gas Journal* (April 1, 1985): 161.

Yergin, Daniel. *The Prize: The Epic Quest for Oil, Money, and Power*. New York: Simon & Schuster, 1991.

Index

About the Author

Harlan Platt is a professor of finance in the College of Business Administration at Northeastern University. He has published extensively on three areas related to bankruptcy and workouts: the development of early warning bankruptcy prediction models, the relationship between the economy and bankruptcy, and the yield and resilience of high-yield bonds. He is a member of the board of directors of the Prospect St. High Income Portfolio, which is on the New York Stock Exchange. In addition, he is the faculty dean for the Turnaround Management Association.